THE DIVERSITY BONUS

OUR COMPELLING INTERESTS

AN INITIATIVE OF
THE ANDREW W. MELLON FOUNDATION

EARL LEWIS AND NANCY CANTOR, SERIES EDITORS

Other books in this series:

Earl Lewis and Nancy Cantor, editors, *Our Compelling Interests: The Value of Diversity for Democracy and a Prosperous Society*

THE
DIVERSITY
BONUS

HOW GREAT TEAMS
PAY OFF IN THE
KNOWLEDGE
ECONOMY

SCOTT E. **PAGE**

PRINCETON UNIVERSITY PRESS   PRINCETON & OXFORD

Requests for permission to reproduce material from this work
should be sent to Permissions, Princeton University Press

Published by Princeton University Press,
41 William Street, Princeton, New Jersey 08540

In the United Kingdom: Princeton University Press,
6 Oxford Street, Woodstock, Oxfordshire OX20 1TR

press.princeton.edu

Jacket image courtesy of iStock. Jacket design by Faceout Studio, Tim Green

ISBN 978-0-691-17688-8

Library of Congress Control Number: 2017938361

British Library Cataloging-in-Publication Data is available

This book has been composed in Sabon and Trade Gothic

Printed on acid-free paper. ∞

Printed in the United States of America

10 9 8 7 6 5 4 3 2 1

To Pat Gurin, for helping so many of us think in deeper, more complex ways.

Great ideas push the world forward. And they can come from anywhere. At Apple, we rely on our employees' diverse backgrounds and perspectives to spark innovation. So we're hiring more inclusively, choosing partners who make diversity a priority, and creating opportunities for the next generation.

APPLE

We should understand that diversity and inclusion are not "something nice" to do in addition to our "real work," but are central to mission success.

CHARLES F. BOLDEN JR., NASA ADMINISTRATOR

Encouraging a broad range of opinions, ideas and perspectives helps us drive creativity and innovation across the company.

THE WALT DISNEY COMPANY

The issues we face demand sustained effort and insight from a broad array of people, who bring a variety of perspectives, backgrounds, knowledge, and experiences to the challenge.

ROBERT WOOD JOHNSON FOUNDATION

Our diversity makes us a better company, a stronger company, by bringing in fresh ideas, perspectives, experiences, and life responsibilities, and by fostering a truly collaborative workplace.

FORD MOTOR COMPANY

At Dartmouth, differences are embraced and ideas are challenged. Our diverse community of students, faculty, and staff come together to share perspectives, learn, and grow.

DARTMOUTH COLLEGE

The FDIC recognizes that its strength comes from the dedication, experience, talents, and perspectives of every employee.

FEDERAL DEPOSIT INSURANCE CORPORATION

CONTENTS

INTRODUCTION
EARL LEWIS AND NANCY CANTOR

RECENTLY AUDIENCES FLOCKED IN RECORD NUMBERS TO WATCH *Hidden Figures*, which told the uplifting story of three brilliant African American women who played indispensable but largely unknown roles at NASA in the iconic American success story of John Glenn's launch into orbit and the Apollo missions that followed. These women, products of the segregated South, made lasting contributions to the nation's space program in spite of social strictures that initially limited their inclusion. Their achievements improved the work of NASA's teams of scientists, enriched the space program as a whole, and helped accomplish the national goal of putting a man on the moon. For the team tackling a complex problem, their cognitive skills, grit, determination, and drive proved a plus.

Hollywood's dramatization of a moment of exclusion that begrudgingly transitioned to a moment of inclusion is set against the backdrop of unfolding social and political practices. Recall that segregation was birthed in the late nineteenth century, matured into a hardened system through the middle of the twentieth century, and ended formally in the latter quarter of that century. It didn't end voluntarily, naturally, or completely on its own. It ended because women, men, and children organized, agitated, and fought to end it. The women profiled in the film were agents in the forging of change.

DIVERSITY AND INCLUSION: CONTESTED OR VALUED?

As we prepare this introduction, diversity and inclusion remain highly contested. Americans of all faiths, hues, and histories take to the streets and the airports to protest a hastily configured immigration ban that seems to target Muslims and deny access to the refuge and the opportunities that have defined this country's core values for centuries. In London, a global city if ever there was one, marchers remind Prime Minister Theresa May that while a majority might have voted for Brexit, they won't tolerate sending their neighbors out of Britain or blocking others' entrance into it. Back in the United States, Native Americans rightfully question the normalization of one version of history: "Let me get this straight: You're afraid of refugees coming to America, killing you, and taking your property?"

At the same time, those who oppose the more restrictive rhetoric cannot ignore the fact that scores of others, in the United States, Great Britain, and across Europe, celebrate the "us" versus "them" viewpoint. Online, at family gatherings, and in the press, they fashion a worldview according to which it is better to exclude than to be victimized by those who are included. They are not all nationalists or on the political fringe; some simply question institutions they deem elite and out of touch with their realities. They seek to preserve advantages and look for ways to pass those advantages on to their children and relatives.

In the first volume in the Our Compelling Interests series, we informed readers that diversity and inclusion would not come easily, but a better understanding of what is to be derived from a fuller embrace would redound to the benefit of the broader society. Invariably the question turned to how. How would we make such a decision? How do we know that diversity and inclusion would benefit the common good? How do we imagine this working in the future? Sometimes the past provides a window into the future. During the height of the Cold War, we imagined that people of integrity and substance, once vetted, could and would enrich the United States. Then as now, we selectively let them enter the country and, once admitted, most became loving, devoted citizens. Along the way, their diverse backgrounds, intellectual powers, and honed skills helped us advance as a nation and people.

Emblematic is the story *New York Times* columnist Nicholas Kristof shares about his father, Wladislaw Krysztofowicz: "A refugee who had repeatedly faced death in the Old Country for not belonging . . . now somehow counted as American even before he had set foot on American soil, even before he had learned English. It was an inclusiveness that dazzled him, that kindled a love for America that he passed on to his son. . . . The church sponsored Krzysztofowicz even though he wasn't Presbyterian, even though he was Eastern European at a time when the Communist bloc posed an existential threat to America. He could have been a spy or a terrorist."[1] But he wasn't, and, in fact, in 1952 the Oregon farming town that embraced him as one of theirs was bettered for welcoming new talent and new diversity to its community; in time it got to claim the "favorite son" that he fathered.

What stands at the core of the argument in this book series, Our Compelling Interests, is the proposition that diversity is to be valued; that welcoming, inclusive communities are strong communities. This is true even at a time when this country (and many others) looks more insular, xenophobic, and divided than it has in some time. This is true even when the dreams of so many different groups seem similarly at risk and the "recovery" from the Great Recession fails to reach evenly across America, evoking a cry for recognition in a "hillbilly elegy,"[2] offering a stark reminder that black lives matter, and producing a searing look of insecurity on the faces of our student DREAMers. Alas, it is even true when the rise of nationalist movements around the globe, equating Islam with terrorism, scarily evoke Nazism and feed the extremism of the very groups we fear, Al Qaeda and ISIS.

Even now, or perhaps especially now, we have a responsibility to turn to first principles: remembering the inclusive assurance of civil rights in the Bill of Rights, even as it remains unrealized;[3] working neighbor to neighbor on the social connectedness ascribed to E pluribus unum, even as strong bonds of similarity remain a precondition for secure bridges across difference;[4] and according due weight to the contributions to economic prosperity from full participation in a flat world,[5] even as we continue to leave on the sidelines of educational opportunity too much of our fastest-growing talent pool[6] in the midst of a diversity explosion.[7] Diversity has tremendous value for democracy and a prosperous nation, and we all need to take a step back from the necessary struggles of actualizing it to unpack its dimensions.

A DIVERSITY BONUS

In this volume, Scott Page starts that unpacking process right at the core of our knowledge economy, examining the diversity bonus as manifest in complex, nonroutine, cognitive tasks, precisely the group problem-solving contexts that virtually define the opportunities for growth and prosperity going forward. The Silicon Valley CEOs knew this well when they all committed to diversifying the high-technology industry.[8] Such group diversity also defined the life and work of the three hidden figures at NASA who helped turn around the space race.[9] It was what educational leaders defended when they asserted, in the affirmative action cases at the University of Michigan, that diversity produces educational benefits for all students.[10] And, in those cases, it was central to the arguments put forward in the amicus brief filed by military generals who stressed the national security risk of not having a cadre of leaders as diverse as the teams under them in taxing conditions of uncertainty.[11]

There is a bonus to be reaped in bottom-line performance when diverse groups function effectively together as teams in the highly charged, competitive, fast-changing work settings we face increasingly in today's world—be it in business or in scientific discovery, in classrooms or on the battlefield. The relevant ability of an individual may not suffice—especially if those in the room share almost the same knowledge and set of approaches to problems that require the flow of all kinds of insights and the application of varied tools. Success may depend on the cognitive diversity that makes for intelligent teams, as Page demonstrates in this volume. What we want today are high-ability people who think in different ways and can function together, playing off each other and maximizing the emergent properties of diverse, inclusive, well-functioning teams.

In everyday parlance, the diversity of a team will likely be described as a function of the social identities, complex and intersectional as they surely are (arrayed along dimensions such as race, heritage, sexual orientation, class, and so on), of its members. Yet in Page's analysis, it is the cognitive diversity of a team—measured by the lack of overlap in its members' repertoires—that produces a *diversity bonus*. It is cognitive diversity that needs to be leveraged for increased profits in business, innovative solutions in science, efficiency in policy making, and deeper discussion in our classrooms. Nevertheless, identity diversity can produce cognitive diversity, both directly, by engaging unique repertoires derived from particular experiences, and indirectly, as individuals with particular identities elicit novel ideas from others in a team.

In fact, identity diversity is most likely to matter for the diversity bonus in precisely those service sectors (for example, education, finance, entertainment, and health care) in which the most postrecession jobs have been added.[12] Therefore, as Page argues, we should always err on the side of more diversity in not only training and experience but identity too. And while we fill our workplaces and our classrooms and the halls of justice and government with as identity diverse a collection of well-trained participants as we can, we can never forget the hard work it takes for a diverse team to gel, for an inclusive group to thrive, bringing out the best in everyone at the table, as Katherine Phillips's extensive demonstrations remind us in the commentary chapter.

In this regard, it is instructive to think about one arena, science and engineering, where leaders in industry, academia, and government have all agreed for quite some time that broadening participation is vital to the very excellence and health of the enterprise, making precisely the arguments that Page calls the business case for diversity and inclusion. Consider, for example, the following statement from a broad global consortium gathered to write a road map for action at the Third International Gender Innovation Summit North America, organized by the National Science Foundation (and many partners) in Washington in 2013: "A diverse STEM workforce, drawing on the ideas and talents of all members of society, is critical for expanding our pool of knowledge in STEM through boosting creativity in research and innovation. . . . Inclusion of all members of society in the scientific research enterprise is necessary not only for equity but because it widens the pool of talent, increases innovation and group performance, and increases business performance."[13]

This is precisely the three-pronged argument in Page's volume—beyond equity, diversity in science and engineering provides access to more talent, better solutions to challenging problems, and therefore better science, business, and society. Moreover, as hard as it has turned out to be to move the dial on STEM diversity, those organizations and institutions that have succeeded did it by creating more inclusive organizational cultures in which team members are better listeners and more open to more people's ideas. In turn, they have experienced a diversity bonus, not only in productivity but also in the attractiveness of their workplace to the fresh talent pool of the next generation—a continuously reinforcing cycle that affirms the value of diversity to organizations, as well as to the work itself.

There are, in reality, multiple other motivations beyond the diversity bonus in our knowledge economy for erring on the side of diversity. Some rationales draw on our founding principles as a nation (even as we have yet to come near fulfillment, as recent events confirm); others point to the value of redressing past wrongs and reducing current disparities to affirm the legitimacy of avenues of access to leadership in our institutions (as Justice Sandra Day O'Connor opined in her Supreme Court decision in *Grutter v. Bollinger*).[14] Side by side with these compelling interests for a fair and well-functioning democracy, the pragmatics of the arguments in this volume may surprise some, especially as we think of the moral force of arguments for inclusion written in the faces of the families of refugees around the globe and children striving to be educated against all odds here at home.

Yet, as we argued in the first volume of this series, *Our Compelling Interest: The Value of Diversity for Democracy and a Prosperous Society*, there is a profound synergy to be leveraged in the contributions of diverse groups of experts and citizens alike. The dynamics of identity and cognitively diverse groups produce the innovation that bolsters our knowledge economy. It also can reinforce the trust that comes when we build a "community of communities," as Danielle Allen named it,[15] teaching Americans (and our neighbors) how to operate across boundaries of difference in an inclusive society. In that light, Page ends his book by asserting that we have a compelling interest to embrace and engage our differences, and the rhetoric and reality that surrounds us all in these times adds an urgency to this clarion call to action.

THE DIVERSITY BONUS

PROLOGUE

THE CONTRARY ASSUMPTION

We have been wrong. We must change our lives, so that it will be possible to live by the contrary assumption that what is good for the world will be good for us.

—WENDELL BERRY, *The Art of the Commonplace:
The Agrarian Essays*

THE VENUE VARIES. I MIGHT BE STANDING IN NORTH DAKOTA STATE University's Memorial Union; the Great Hall of the US Department of Justice; Roper High School's gymnasium in Birmingham, Michigan; or Bloomberg's gleaming auditorium on Lexington Avenue in New York City. The composition of the audience differs even more. I might be speaking to college deans, high school students, NASA engineers, Justice Department lawyers, Wall Street titans, or Silicon Valley disrupters.[1]

The event will have been advertised as a talk on diversity. I am cast in the role of expert based on *The Difference*, a book I wrote a decade ago. The introductions run the gamut. A college administrator might read verbatim from my bio, a Fortune 500 CEO might all but ignore a prepared script and sing the praises of the University of Michigan, or a high school junior might nervously tick off bullet points from a notecard held in her trembling hand.

The next thirty seconds always play out the same. Polite applause (who is this guy again?). I walk on a stage. I shake a hand or accept a hug. I face the audience. All is quiet. I pause, smile, and begin, knowing that the conversation about to take place will not be what anyone expects.

I communicate five points before anyone can take a breath. One: I will focus on the pragmatic, bottom-line benefits of diversity in a knowledge economy. Two: I will not present an ideological argument, that is, base the case for diversity and inclusion on equity and social justice. Three: by *diversity*, I will mean cognitive diversity, differences in how we interpret, reason, and solve. My primary focus will be on differences in how we think. Identity diversity will contribute to cognitive diversity, but will not be the only cause. Four: as a mathematical social scientist, I will use models and formulae to structure arguments. At this point, if talking with students, I might ask security to lock the doors to prevent people from running for the exits. Five, I expect the interaction to be fun.

All five points—pragmatic benefits; not about social justice; cognitive diversity; mathematics; and a fun time—run counter to expectations for a diversity and inclusion presentation. They lay the groundwork for equally unexpected conclusions. I do not conclude that diversity always improves performance. Instead, I demonstrate the value of cognitive diversity on high-dimensional, complex tasks like engaging in scientific research, developing marketing plans, formulating technical trading strategies, and building a robust supply chain. I make no claim that diversity always helps. In fact, on simpler tasks like packing boxes or serving coffee, it likely has no effect.

The central takeaway is that *diversity can produce bonuses*. By *bonuses*, I mean the literal dictionary definition: something extra. I mean one plus a different one making three. These bonuses do not arise by magic. They come about when people with diverse cognitive repertoires work inclusively on complex tasks.

Though most often people frame diversity and inclusion efforts as the right thing to do, I am putting forth a contrary assumption that creating inclusive, diverse teams and workforces is the sensible and innovative thing to do—that on complex tasks, we need diversity.

That diversity cannot be arbitrary. The space of possible diversities is enormous. We cannot convene a random collection of diverse people and expect diversity bonuses. We need theoretical understandings of whether and how diversity can produce benefit on particular tasks. We need to make reasoned judgments about what type of diversity might be germane to the task at hand.

Education, life experiences, and identity—for example, race, gender, age, physical capabilities, and sexual orientation—can all contribute relevant cognitive diversity. How much each of these matters depends on the task. Diverse educational training may be more valuable on a team designing a new rocket-propulsion technology, diverse life experiences may matter most for a team rewriting a health care plan, and identity diversity may be crucial for a company launching a new product. To navigate the space of possible combinations, we need a science of diversity. And we need to gather and marshal evidence to guide our actions. As W. Edwards Deming once said, "In God we trust. All others must bring data."

I have spent the last decade talking with people from businesses, government, and education about how to put together successful diverse teams. What I offer in this book are theory and frameworks for how to realize diversity bonuses. The theory provides a road map and structures our thinking.

The first step will be classifying the type of task: are you solving a problem, making a prediction, seeking creative ideas, or trying to discern the truth? The second step will be identifying task-relevant cognitive diversity. Not all diversity will be beneficial. You cannot expect bonuses from a random group of people.

The third step involves having a culture that enables successful interactions. Team members must get along, trust one another, share a common mission, and be committed for the long haul.[2] Most organizations I have visited recognize that hiring people who look different or have different training is not sufficient to produce good outcomes. Hence, management consultants and human resource professionals speak not just of diversity, but of diversity and inclusion.

Just as the theory suggests that not any type of diversity will do, it also provides insights into how inclusion varies by task. Different tasks—creative, predictive, and so on—require different levels of engagement. On a creative task, diverse ideas can be compared. On a predictive task, diverse predictions can be averaged. Other tasks, like discerning the truth, will require deep engagement and interrogation of models, and hence, greater levels of trust.

On any task, achieving bonuses requires the right people and the right practices. Organizations that add diversity indiscriminately to reach targets and benchmarks will be disappointed. Team performance will suffer and people will come to see diversity efforts as counter to the organization's core mission.

The sophisticated diversity practitioner recognizes that diversity bonuses require thoughtful hiring practices, and the creation of a culture that enables meaningful, organic interactions between people with different life experiences, educational backgrounds, and identities. This book provides a framework for achieving those bonuses.

When presenting to an audience, I try to gather information beforehand on how to partition the audience across three groups. The first consists of true believers, the diversity advocates. They want their organization and society writ large to be more inclusive for normative reasons—to redress past wrongs or because it is the right thing to do. The second group consists of the deniers. They believe that diversity and inclusion initiatives hinder performance. Some see these initiatives as affirmative action in disguise. The third group enters the room thinking that they would rather be almost anywhere else. They suffer from what the *Economist* in 2016 called diversity fatigue.[3]

I need all three groups to change how they think. The believers must pull back from the unrealistic, magical thinking that holds that identity-diverse groups perform best on all problems. Wanting something to be true or not true does not make it so. The deniers, many of whom attribute their own success to individual abilities, must open their minds to possible benefits. They must see the shortcomings of hiring people who look just like themselves or come from the same five schools. Those suffering from diversity fatigue must see diversity and inclusion as something other than a waste of time thrust upon them by a compliance officer.

I can only accomplish so much in sixty or ninety minutes. I ask that people set aside their political and normative positions and entertain the contrary assumption that diversity and inclusion can produce bonuses. I ask that they listen with open, skeptical minds. I ask that they challenge the logic and evidence. And challenges do come—whether delivered by a precocious seventh grader wondering how gender could influence the way a person approaches a scientific problem, by a skeptical mid-level executive buying into the logic but questioning the magnitude of diversity bonuses, or by the chairman of the Joint Chiefs of Staff asking how an organization whose members must follow orders can also be innovative.

Those answers will follow, as will a summary of what I learned on a decade-long tour that has included stops in Houghton, Michigan; Monroe, Louisiana; Frankfort, Kentucky; Redmond, Washington; and Princeton, New Jersey. I learned that rewriting a company or university's diversity and inclusion statement matters far less than changing what people believe and how they behave toward one another. The right culture cannot be imposed from above by a bureaucracy or through elaborate diversity and inclusion strategic plans.

As Wes Pratt, the Chief Diversity Officer at Missouri State, remarked to me, we must be the process. The behaviors that produce diversity bonuses must emerge from the bottom up, organically. Each person who belongs to a diverse team brings a history and set of beliefs shaped by their identity. Those histories and beliefs must be validated and appreciated.

Achieving an organic, bottom-up inclusion requires that people believe in the value of interacting across differences and thus seek diversity bonuses. They must be all in. This more organic form of inclusion will be more likely in teams and organizations with a shared mission or goal. This more bottom-up inclusion will be bolstered by a shared understanding of diversity bonuses because people will see different ideas as worthy of deeper investigation.

In the best cases, people begin to appreciate the resonance between our identities and how we contribute. They see how identity differences add more than pragmatic contributions (more accurate predictions, better policies, more innovative solutions, and so on); they also add beauty, grandeur, and meaning to what is produced.

In my travels, I have been amazed by the depth and breadth of knowledge, skills, and passions people bring to their professions—be it building rockets, designing farm equipment, maintaining quality control in computer cable production, or managing financial portfolios. I have been awed by the kindness and generosity of people and of their dedication to creating more inclusive workplaces, schools, and societies. And yet, I often hear these same people lament the failures of their diversity groups.

It has been my goal to help people build more productive diverse teams. In each interaction, I could see the large gulf between precise blackboard truths and the messy reality of the world of people. Nevertheless, my experiences reinforced rather than attenuated my belief in the necessity of formal logic and models. I witnessed the power of mathematical rigor to cut through ideologically clouded thinking to reveal truths and guide action. Metaphors and stories can spur emotions and rally the team, but they cannot produce deep understandings or reveal the conditions necessary for bonuses to exist. Those conditions guide proper action, and enable us to take claims to data. That data can then be used to test and improve the theory.

As I look out through the glass walls of Mighty Good Coffee in Ann Arbor, I think of the words of T. S. Eliot: I have ended my exploring by arriving back where I started. The logic holds: cognitive and identity differences can produce bonuses. Achieving them in the real world takes practice. We need to learn the behaviors that make the theoretical bonuses real. I am not talking about just being nice. When making predictions, we have to include less accurate, diverse predictions—because we will do better. When hiring people, we have to see value in difference.

The logic I present, revealing the pragmatic benefits of diversity, intersects with and complements arguments for diversity and inclusion based on social justice. Many people, including colleagues and close friends, have said that though they accept the logic and agree that substantial evidence supports bonuses, they believe that pragmatic logics carry less weight than normative arguments. They question how I can place improvements in economic forecasts, marketing plans, and product offerings on equal standing with considerations of social justice and equity.

I do not dispute that point. One cannot equate a 1 percent increase in a portfolio's return or a 4 percent reduction in shipping costs to the value of creating a world free of discrimination. We should care more about creating a world in which each person has an opportunity to succeed regardless of his or her identity more than we care about the IRS creating a tax form that is 6 percent more readable.

That said, I do not see the social justice frame and the diversity bonus frame as in competition with one another. We need not choose between applying our differences to improve our lot and creating an equitable and just world.[4] On the contrary, I view embracing diversity bonuses as crucial to advancing social justice.

Moreover, if we ignore the pragmatic logic and emphasize only equity and social justice, we all but rule out achieving diversity bonuses. Bureaucratic rules that impose arbitrary diversity without any understanding of how to produce diversity bonuses will result in teams that do not make scientific breakthroughs, develop better health care plans, or write captivating screenplays. An occasional group may get lucky, but most diverse groups will not perform well.[5] As a result, people will see diversity as costly and see a tradeoff in their pursuit of the normative ideal. Those who want a more inclusive society will find themselves climbing uphill barefoot on streets of broken glass. If, on the other hand, we learn the logic of diversity bonuses and learn how to form teams and interact with one another so as to produce diversity bonuses, we align the normative ideal with our self-interest. We skateboard downhill on smooth pavement.

The same logic can be applied to diversity efforts based on compliance with the law and changing demographics—the idea that America will soon be a nation with no majority group, so we must be inclusive. Though each promotes inclusive workforces, each positions inclusion, at least in the short term, as a sacrifice. The diversity-bonus logic does not. It shows that diversity can improve performance.

A KNOWLEDGE ECONOMY PHENOMENON

Historically, diversity bonuses have not been a central reason for promoting diverse interactions. That should be expected. The theory will show that diversity bonuses occur most often within teams of cognitive workers engaged in nonroutine tasks. As we transition to a knowledge economy and as more people work in teams on complex tasks, diversity bonuses become more relevant. We can find diversity bonuses in scientific research, on investment teams, in groups of neonatal surgeons and script doctors, and among groups of programmers and policy makers

Diversity bonuses were less prominent in the past when most workers were engaged in routine tasks. The logic is straightforward for why routine physical tasks cannot produce large diversity bonuses. Think of a group of Domino's employees folding pizza boxes. The number they fold as a team equals the sum of the boxes folded by the individuals. No bonus exists. Similar logic holds for the number of packages delivered by the fleet of UPS drivers. The total equals the sum. No diversity bonuses arise. However, diversity does exist among the teams of engineers and mathematicians who devise the complex algorithms that route those trucks.

When diversity bonuses exist, the best group will not, as a rule, consist of the best individual performers according to some criterion. Instead, it will be diverse. I am not saying that an organization should hire less talented people. The claim is that talent is multi-dimensional. An organization should hire people with different talents and skills, an insight that I make formal by introducing the concept of a cognitive repertoire.

Similarly, selecting an optimal group requires consideration of the cognitive diversity each person adds. To be clear, a person cannot be diverse, but a person can add diversity. The diversity a person contributes will be relative to an extant group and with respect to a given task. The same person may add relevant diversity to one group on one task and not add diversity to a different group on a different task.

From a diversity-bonus standpoint, choices about whom to hire do not involve a tradeoff between excellence and diversity. If selecting a person to add to a research team or design group, the best choice will be the person who can add the most new ideas or apply the most novel tools. That may not be the person who would perform the best on her own, or who has the highest test scores. The diversity that a person adds to the group will matter as well.

The same logic applies when selecting a cohort. Each year, the University of California–Los Angeles receives over one hundred thousand applications for admission. Leading Wall Street and consulting firms receive similar numbers of resumes from job seekers. Google receives over three million applicants for employment. To cope with these numbers, organizations develop rubrics to predict the future success of applicants. These organizations do not blindly admit and hire those individuals who score highest by those rubrics. They embrace the contrary assumption and also seek diversity. UCLA wants students from multiple communities with diverse interests. They want students from Encino, Nipoma, and Brentwood. They also want philosophers, physicists, and French majors. Google wants people who learned programming from different books and professors. They want history, psychology, and ergonomics majors in addition to engineers and mathematicians.

Choosing only those people who ranked highest by the rubric would bias admits and hires and result in too many people who grew up in similar communities, attended the same small set of schools, and have had common life experiences and interests. Thus, the cohort of the best individuals will not be the best cohort. The best cohort will be diverse. It will consist of people who possess relevant knowledge bases, analytic tools, mental models, perspectives, and information. The group will include diverse, talented individuals.

Making intelligent choices of whom to hire and admit involves contemplating the bonuses that might arise from the abundance of combinations of skills. It is not a matter of deciding between the excellent candidate and the diverse one. People who find themselves torn between the highest-ranked candidate by traditional criteria and a diverse candidate often need only think harder. The diverse candidate may add more to the group or she may not.

Identifying what types of diversity may be germane requires careful thought. Relevant cognitive diversity can stem from our life and work experiences, our educational paths, and our identities. When identity diversity correlates with or causes germane cognitive diversity—and it often will—diversity bonuses underpin arguments for identity-based inclusion in the business world, the academy, and the nonprofit sector. It will not be true that identity-diverse teams always outperform homogenous teams, only that they can and do on a range of tasks. When identity diversity produces bonuses, inclusion involves no sacrifice. We do not confront a tradeoff between excellence and diversity. Excellence demands diversity.

The relevance of diversity bonuses depends in large part on the complexity of the modern world. On simple, separable tasks, we do not need diversity. We can hand them to smart, capable people. Thus, to appreciate the logic of diversity bonuses, we must first take stock of how we produce value in the modern economy, how we produce innovations, how we create art, and how we create successful policies. The short answer: we use teams. And those teams are diverse.

Work was not always this way. I grew up in the 1960s in Yankee Springs, Michigan, about thirty miles north of Kalamazoo, a place that Carl Sandburg reduces to a "spot on the map where the trains hesitate" in "The Sins of Kalamazoo." Sandburg's Kalamazoo is a place where children carve their initials on the ballyard fence, with a five-and-ten-cent store and hound dogs barking on the public square, where young people run off to see the world and, upon returning, remark that it is "all like Kalamazoo." That characterization was an accurate picture of my childhood.

Today, Kalamazoo and the rest of America differ markedly from Sandburg's caricature. Our economy no longer runs on people who perform routine jobs: cooper, farmer, blacksmith, merchant, and baker. Experts describe the modern economy with adjectives— *weightless, flat, connected, information based,* and *cognitive*—that would have made little sense in Sandburg's time.

In Chicago, a more famous subject of Sandburg's prose, people no longer butcher hogs or stack wheat. Chicagoans work in financial technology, e-commerce, plastics, medical technology, and biotechnology. The people Sandburg called "players with railroads" have been supplanted by transportation logistic engineers. The children of the hog butchers now work in biotech.

Sandburg's Kalamazoo and Chicago have been replaced by a new world that presents an array of complex challenges and opportunities: managing elaborate supply chains, developing molecules to cure diseases, understanding the brain, preventing market crashes, and confronting climate change, to name just a few. The people who work in those jobs perform nonroutine cognitive tasks. Those tasks outstrip the capabilities of any one person, so organizations rely on teams. The best of those teams are diverse. They include people with diverse training, experiences, and identities.

The teams that excel achieve diversity bonuses, and that often requires behavioral changes. Those behavioral changes require practice guided by theory. If we understand the logic of diversity bonuses—that is, if we understand the logic and read the evidence—we are better able to identify actions that produce bonuses. Believing that they are there also helps. If we see inclusive actions as in our self-interest, we are more likely to act inclusively, engage diverse ideas, and produce bonuses.[6]

THE MIDDLE OF TOWN

To explain diversity bonuses, I present frameworks, construct models, evaluate empirical evidence, and explore illustrative cases. Together, these enable me to trace the boundaries of the domains in which diversity produces bonuses and those in which it does not.

I first describe the core logic for how diversity creates bonuses. I then unpack that logic by describing cognitive repertoires and linking those directly to better outcomes. Loosely defined, a person's *cognitive repertoire* consists of the different ways in which that person thinks. Having established the logic, I take up the connections between cognitive and identity diversity by presenting three frameworks: icebergs, the timber-framed house, and the cloud.

That discussion lays the groundwork for interpreting empirical studies on diversity and team performance. The evidence of the benefits of cognitive diversity proves strong, bordering on overwhelming.[7] Studies of identity diversity and performance also align with the theoretical models, though not as strongly. I hasten to add that in interpreting those studies, we must keep in mind that the data tell us what we currently achieve. The logic shows how much we could achieve in ideal circumstances. I conclude by embedding the diversity bonus logic within the larger business and societal cases for diversity and inclusion, offering thoughts on how we might better achieve bonuses and highlighting the need for practice and bottom-up integration.

As a preview of the type of claims that follow, one result will be that when a group of people make numerical predictions, the error of their collective prediction cannot be larger than the average of their individual errors. In other words, diverse predictive groups must be more accurate than their average member. Everyone (by that I mean the collective) is above average. Always.

Furthermore, the amount by which the group outperforms its average member depends on diversity: holding the average size of an error constant and making the predictions more diverse makes the group smarter. One analysis of forty thousand predictions by economists found that averaging two predictions reduced the expected error by 8 percent.[8] That error reduction represents a diversity bonus— a significant, quantifiable improvement due to differences in how people think.

I have witnessed, read about, and heard accounts of hundreds of diversity bonuses. I believe that we can build organizations, and even a society, where we achieve them as a matter of course. Doing so requires that we understand how the bonuses occur and that we practice inclusive, productive behaviors. That is why I wrote this book—to help us generate diversity bonuses. If we can, we will improve society and expand opportunities.

My approach brackets social justice and equity-based arguments. That separation has been difficult. Over the past decade, I have met many talented people who have suffered from implicit and outright discrimination. I have met many others who have benefitted from a finger on a scale at key moments. As much as I would like to do so, I do not tell those personal stories. I omit them, not because the normative case lacks merit, but because creating diverse teams based on normative principles alone will produce few bonuses.

People will embrace the move toward a more integrated, inclusive society if they see benefits from doing so. To reach a place where each of us can contribute our unique skills, knowledge, and insights, we need to act with forethought. We need to apply logic, data, and experience in order to build effective, diverse teams capable of achieving bonuses. That type of scientific approach to diversity and inclusion veers neither left nor right. Like Main Street in Sandburg's Kalamazoo, it runs straight through the middle of the town.

CHAPTER ONE

DIVERSITY BONUSES: THE IDEA

The power of a theory is exactly proportional to the diversity of situations it can explain.

—ELINOR OSTROM, *Governing the Commons: The Evolution of Institutions for Collective Action*

ON APRIL 8, 1865, ONE WEEK BEFORE HIS ASSASSINATION AT Washington's Ford's Theatre, Abraham Lincoln visited a field hospital near Petersburg, Virginia. To raise morale among the wounded troops, Lincoln picked up an ax and began chopping wood. As a youth, he had split thousands of fence rails to earn money or goods in kind—he was once paid in dyed brown cloth sufficient to make him a pair of trousers. On the day of his visit to the field hospital, he demonstrated to all assembled that the famed "Rail Splitter" could still "make the chips fly."[1]

Suppose that you had to hire a team of people to split rails. You would look for strong, tall people like Lincoln who are best at splitting rails. The logic borders on the tautological: the best team of rail splitters consists of the best individuals.

That logic makes sense because splitting rails is a separable task. The number of rails split by the team equals the sum of the rails split by each person. That logic does not apply for teams of people who work on the complex tasks we confront in our modern, information-rich society. In those settings, a team's performance depends on the diversity as well as the ability of its members. As a result, a policy of hiring the best does not make sense on high-dimensional tasks. The best team will not consist of the "best" individuals. It consists of diverse thinkers.

The idea that diverse ways of thinking can lead to deeper insights is not new. It can be found in the writings of Aristotle. Lincoln himself applied a logic of diversity when appointing his cabinet. He did not create an echo chamber of like-minded people. He chose a diverse cabinet, the famed team of rivals.[2] He opted for diversity partly to build political consensus but primarily because he faced complex problems. As he wrote in his December 1862 message to Congress, "The occasion is piled high with difficulty, and we must rise with the occasion. As our case is new, so we must think anew and act anew. We must disenthrall ourselves."

We too must disenthrall ourselves. We now operate and interact in a complex world in which we work with our minds, not our backs. We must therefore also think anew. We must abandon the narrow and demonstrably false belief that we should admit, hire, and promote those who perform best according to a common standard. As I show later in this book, those who score highest will tend to be similar. Hiring "the best" will reduce the diversity of our scientific teams, our planning commissions, and our boards of directors, and with it their collective potential.

On the complex tasks we now carry out in laboratories, clean rooms, boardrooms, courtrooms, and classrooms, we need people who think in different ways. And not in arbitrarily diverse ways. Effective diverse teams are built with forethought. Not all teams of rivals will succeed. Not all multitudes possess wisdom. To realize the benefits of diversity, we need logic and theory to identify the types of diversity that improve outcomes and to understand the conditions under which they do so. And then we need practice.

Getting the logic correct takes precedence. Otherwise, we cannot compose the best possible teams, and we limit what we can achieve even with practice. That is the main reason for this book: to help us get the logic right. To get us to embrace the contrary assumption and to make our world better.

In this chapter, I sketch the core logic for how diversity produces bonuses. That logic relies on linking *cognitive diversity*, which I define as differences in information, knowledge, representations, mental models, and heuristic, to better outcomes on specific tasks such as problem solving, predicting, and innovating. Cognitive diversity differs from *identity diversity*—differences in race, gender, age, physical capabilities, and sexual orientation. That said, identity diversity, along with education and work and life experience, will be a contributor to those differences. For the moment, we will keep them separate.

DIVERSITY BONUSES ON COMPLEX TASKS

To sketch the core logic, I borrow a stripped-down model that I developed with Jon Bendor. This model reduces cognitive repertoires to collections of *tools*.[3] Think of these tools as analytic analogues of a carpenter's tools. A carpenter has a chainsaw; a mathematician knows the chain rule. A carpenter attaches boards with a nail gun; a plant biologist inserts DNA with a gene gun.

I use that model to show the logic of how diversity bonuses arise. I then connect assumptions about the diversity of tools that people possess to the complexity of the challenge or opportunity at hand. That second step includes two purposefully incomprehensible graphs.

In the tool-based model, I assign a unique letter to each tool. Figure 1.1 shows three people and their cognitive tools. Define ability of a person to equal the number of tools she knows. Ann possesses five tools, so she has an ability of five. Barry, in the center, has ability four, and Cam has ability three. Ann is the best.

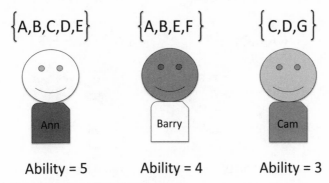

Figure 1.1 Three People and Their Cognitive Tools

Similarly, define the diversity of the team to equal the number of unique tools collectively known. If two team members know the same tool, that counts as a single tool. Next, define the diversity of a team as the percentage of the team's tools known by a single person.[4] Two people with no tool overlap have 100 percent diversity. Two people with the same tools have 0 percent diversity.

This simple model produces two types of diversity bonuses. First, a diversity bonus occurs if someone adds a unique tool. When this happens, we can add someone of less ability to a group and make the group smarter. That's a bonus. In addition, if teams can apply combinations of tools, then adding a person with a new tool produces new combinations, a second bonus.

Working through the example clarifies how bonuses arise. Figure 1.2 shows two possible teams and the union of their cognitive tools. The first team consists of the two highest-ability people, Ann and Barry. Ann has an ability of five. Adding Barry to the team adds one more tool, giving the team an ability of six. That's a bonus of one. The second team consists of Barry and Cam. Barry has an ability of four. The team of Barry and Cam has an ability of seven. Thus, when paired with Barry, Cam produces a diversity bonus of size three. If Cam were paired with Ann, he would only produce a bonus of size one. Thus, the bonus someone produces depends on the team.

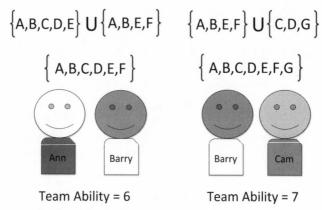

Figure 1.2 Two Teams and Their Cognitive Tools

As suggested, counting the number of tools understates the potential diversity bonuses if tools can be applied in combination. We will start with the team of Ann and Barry. Ann knows five tools, so she could apply up to ten unique pairs of tools. She and Barry know six tools, creating fifteen unique pairs. By adding Barry, she gets one new tool and five new pairs of tools.

Barry, on the other hand, knows four tools and therefore six unique pairs of tools. When Cam is added to Barry's team, Cam adds three tools, as well as three pairs of tools: $\{CD, CG, DG\}$. When combined with Barry's four tools, his three tools create twelve new pairs of tools.[5] Thus, Cam adds fifteen potential pairs of tools. That is what is meant by a diversity bonus.

Note also that Barry and Cam are the best team of size two. That team jointly possesses the most tools and therefore has the most ability. In this example, as in many others that will follow, the best team does not consist of the two highest-ability people.

Complexity and Bonuses

This example would seem to create diversity bonuses without any reliance on complexity; that is, on the task being part of a context that is difficult to predict, explain, or design. That is not true. The assumptions that I made on the tools that the people possess imply multiple relevant knowledge bases and types of approaches to solving the problem. To see why requires a second example and then some assumptions on the structure of tools.

The second example consists of three people with the tool sets shown in figure 1.3. Notice that no diversity bonuses can arise in this example. The best person knows every tool of the second-best person, who in turn knows every tool of the third person. The best team will be any team that includes that best person.

A comparison of the tool sets in figures 1.1 and 1.3 reveals the key insight. The cognitive tools that people possess in the first example are idiosyncratic. The cognitive tool sets in the second example would come about only if people accumulate tools in the same order, that is, if a person had to learn tool A before tool B and tool B before tool C.

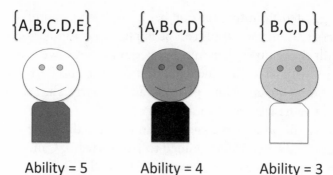

Figure 1.3 Three People Who Produce No Diversity Bonus

As an analogy, think of people riding on a train from Chicago to Los Angeles. At each stop along the way, the conductor tells the history of the station. If one person stays on the train longer than another, that first person learns about more stations than the second. She necessarily knows about every station that the second person knows about.

The cognitive tools shown in figure 1.1 do not satisfy that condition. Here, the person with the fewest tools knows tools the most talented person does not. For this configuration to occur, it must be that tools need not be acquired in a single order. Instead of a train trip, a trip to the zoo would be a more appropriate analogy. One person might spend a full day at the zoo and visit five exhibits (<u>A</u>lligators, <u>B</u>ears, <u>C</u>amels, <u>D</u>ucks, and <u>E</u>lephants). A second person might leave midafternoon after taking in only three exhibits (<u>C</u>amels, <u>D</u>ucks, and <u>G</u>orillas). The second person learns less, but she gains knowledge of gorillas that the first person does not have. The first person does not know everything the second person knows.

Figure 1.4 represents these two possibilities in network form. Assume that a person must first learn a tool on the left edge and then can follow any path. The upper path corresponds to the train ride. Diversity doesn't matter. The best team consists of the best person. Ability rules.

The lower path represents the trip to the zoo. As shown in figure 1.5, the tool sets in the first example can be constructed within this network. Ann can follow a path that leads to A, B, C, D, and E. Barry can learn A, B, E, and F, and Cam can learn tools C, D, and G.

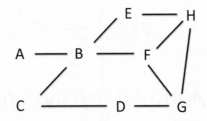

Linear Order

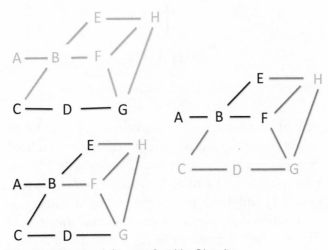

Network Arrangement

Figure 1.4 Linear and Network Arrangements of Cognitive Tools

Figure 1.5 How Tool Structure Influences Cognitive Diversity

The fact that a person can know fewer but different tools means that someone can have less measured ability than the people already in a group but still contribute.

The remaining step in the logic connects the value of diversity to complexity. The intuition will be straightforward: Our accumulation of knowledge, representations, techniques, and models produces elaborate networks of what I am calling tools. This allows people to construct distinct tool sets. That need not be the case for less developed bodies of knowledge, which often create linear orders.

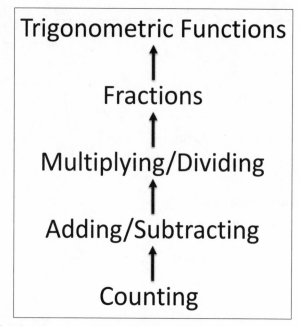

Figure 1.6 Relationships among Topics in Elementary School Mathematics

As an example, consider topics in mathematics. Figure 1.6 shows the relationships between the topics covered in elementary school mathematics. The topics build on one another in a linear fashion. You need to be able to count in order to add, to add in order to multiply and divide, to multiply and divide in order to understand fractions, and to understand fractions in order to define the trigonometric functions sine and cosine. These topics can be represented in a linear order.

In contrast, the advanced mathematical topics in figure 1.7 connect in multiple ways. This is the first incomprehensible graph. To approach a network of this complexity, ignore the technical terms and focus on the many boxes and arrows. Notice that there exist multiple paths a student could pursue. Parts of the network can be understood by anyone. For instance, in the middle of the figure, the integers (1, 2, 3, and so on) point to the rational numbers $\left(\frac{1}{2},\frac{1}{3},\cdots\right)$, which in turn point to the real numbers ($\pi = 3.1415\ldots$). To know the real numbers, a person must first understand integers and fractions. That portion of the network looks like the linear elementary school network.

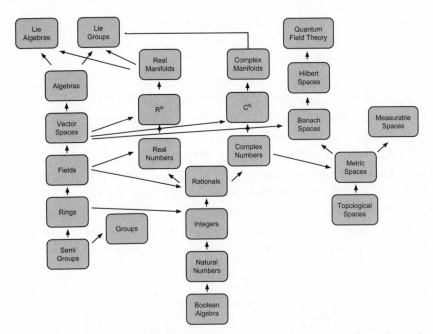

Figure 1.7 Relationships among Topics in Graduate Mathematics (courtesy Tegmark, "Ultimate Ensemble Theory?")

Making sense of other parts of the network requires deeper technical knowledge. The graph implies that a person could master Lie groups (in the upper left) without knowing Hilbert spaces, distributions, or quantum field theory (in the upper right). The implication is that the tool sets of professional mathematicians would look like those in our first example. And each mathematician would add diversity to the group.

Making breakthroughs in mathematics often involves combining different tools. A report by the National Academy of Sciences describes "an increasing need for research to tap into two or more fields of the mathematical sciences."[6] Tapping into two fields implies a diversity bonus. Something that could not be proved using either field alone can be solved with tools from two fields.

That same report notes the growing connections between mathematics and other fields including defense, entertainment, physics, economics, computer science, linguistics, manufacturing, finance, and biology. These connections reflect a broader trend toward multi-disciplinary inquiries. That can be explained by the complexity of modern challenges and opportunities.

Consider the rise of obesity. Some call it an epidemic. Fifty years ago, we might have placed the challenge of reducing obesity within the domain of nutritional sciences. We now understand that it has myriad causes that cross disciplines.

Figure 1.8 characterizes one attempt to explain the obesity epidemic with arrows denoting causal forces from the Foresight Group in the UK.[7] It is meant to be overwhelming. (Yes, this is the second incomprehensible graph.) The disciplinary knowledge embedded in the graph crosses economics, nutrition, physiology, sociology, biology, media studies, advertising, transportation and infrastructure, and genetics.

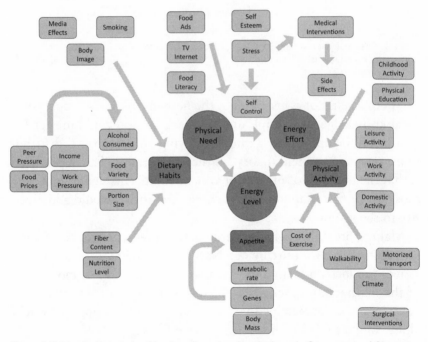

Figure 1.8 Obesity Knowledge Structure (based on Vandenbroeck, Goossens, and Clemens, *Foresight Tackling Obesities: Future Choices—Building the Obesity System Map*. Government Office for Science, UK Government's Foresight Programme, 2007, http:www.foresight.gov .ukObesity12.pdf. Accessed June 16, 2009)

No one person can understand all of the boxes and arrows in the full diagram, and no one person will find a cure for obesity. At best, the combined wisdom of a multitude of diverse people can march us toward less obesity through a constellation of interventions. The types of diversity necessary to find ways to reduce obesity differ from the types needed to advance mathematical knowledge. Though in each case, the fact that diversity in the background knowledge one acquires through education will be of central importance hardly needs explaining.

Aside: John Milton and TMI & TMK

The explosion of available information and knowledge creates a second reason we need diversity on complex tasks. On a simple task like building a tool shed, a single person might have sufficient knowledge, but that is not true for complex tasks like reducing obesity, calculating a supply chain, managing and investing a portfolio, or advancing the field of mathematics. In those domains, no single person can master all relevant knowledge. There exists too much information (TMI) and too much knowledge (TMK).

TMI and TMK imply the necessity of diversity. When Euclid was writing his axioms, a person could learn all of mathematics. That is not true today. Think back to the diagram of mathematical knowledge. There's too much to know.

The polymath John Milton might well be the pivotal person in the transition from all-knowing experts to a world of intelligent people with diverse repositories of information and knowledge. Born in 1608 in Cheapside in the city of London, England, Milton introduced more than six hundred words into the English language. He traveled the world, discussing ideas with luminaries from Galileo to Isaac Newton.

In 1640, at the peak of Milton's career, the British Library contained fewer than forty thousand books. A voracious reader in a dozen languages, Milton learned a substantial percentage of what was knowable. Reading two books a day, he could have read fifteen thousand books by age thirty and, by age fifty, could have made his way through the bulk of the British Library.

With nearly one and a half million books now published each year, a modern Milton could not make it through a week's production of knowledge. To finish the quarter million books published by traditional book publishers each year would involve reading fifteen books a day for fifty years, leaving little time to digest the more than one and a half million academic papers published annually.

A modern Milton can only know a thin slice of what's knowable. That observation holds true within academic disciplines, professions, and industry. The information and knowledge produced within organic chemistry, oncology, or economic sociology overwhelms the capacity of any one person. Hence, we need teams. And we need teams that include people with diverse information and knowledge.

IDENTITY AND COGNITIVE DIVERSITY

The Milton problem demonstrates the necessity of working with people who explore different parts of the library and the web. Many of our complex challenges involve understanding the actions, preferences, and capabilities of diverse people. Thus, identity diversity also contributes relevant cognitive diversity.

The aforementioned efforts to reduce obesity require understanding economic, social, and psychological influences on behavior, as well as the impact of media. Our understandings of those dimensions will benefit from identity-diverse teams. The analysis of the effects of infrastructure will benefit from people from different geographic regions and from urban and rural locations. Overall, identity diversity may weigh in with similar magnitude as disciplinary diversity. To not include any men, or any women, on a team formulating an obesity-reduction program would be as shortsighted as not including a geneticist or a psychologist.

The connections between identity diversity and relevant cognitive diversity in mathematics are less obvious. Could gender, race, ethnicity, or physical capabilities influence the representations and analytic tools a mathematician applies? Sure. In mathematical research, identity is less germane than academic training, though it is possible that a person's identity could influence how she represents a mathematics problem as well as the problems she chooses to tackle. That's truer for the frontiers of math, where mathematicians often rely on analogies and knowledge from other experiences.

The lack of an obvious logic linking identity diversity to germane cognitive diversity in fields like math or physics does not mean that those fields do not need to be inclusive. On the contrary, because mathematics community confronts hard problems, it needs cognitive diversity.

Permit me a slight digression to make a larger point linking inclusion to cognitive diversity. Define the capacity of a mathematician as the number of tools she can acquire. We can think of her career as traversing a path in figure 1.7. A great mathematician might learn about twenty topics, a good one only fifteen. Excluding some identity groups from being mathematicians or making the field less attractive to some groups results in a cohort of mathematicians with lower overall capacity. If a woman with a capacity of twenty opts out of mathematics, and a man with capacity sixteen replaces her, then mathematics suffers. The profession loses talent because she has more capacity, and it loses diversity because of her larger capacity.

Fifty years ago, people chalked up the low representation of women and some racial groups in mathematics, and science generally, to a lack of interest—"Women do not want to become physicists." As recently as twelve years ago, some attributed the low numbers in these professions (offensively, I might add) to a lack of cognitive ability. Current thinking points to the effects of limited opportunities and exposure, the lack of role models, and the effects of noninclusive behaviors and discrimination.

Personal accounts of women who entered school with the interest and ability to excel at mathematics and science but pursued other paths reveal the accumulated dampening of interest produced by repeated acts of discrimination. Some actions were overt and direct. Others were subtler. Combined, they made science an unwelcoming place.

As an undergrad, I took a two-year math sequence listed as Honors Track II that students referred to as "math for gods." Lacking any training in calculus, I struggled during the first two courses. Recently, I looked up three students who had excelled in those classes.

All three have enjoyed successful careers. One works as the chief actuary and risk officer at a large insurance company. A second serves as a chaired professor of law at the University of Chicago. The third, the only woman of the three, began her career in engineering, rose to become a senior software engineer, and now works as a life coach, facilitator, and counselor.

Personal accounts of women who tried to pursue scientific careers reveal any number of obstacles, both direct and indirect.[8] The fact that the two men remain in technical fields and the one woman opted out is not surprising, but it is disheartening. We lose talent and diversity when environments are not inclusive.

Data gathered by the National Science Foundation reveal low representation of women and minorities in many technical fields, and we cannot but infer lost diversity bonuses. In 2013–2014, 1,200 US citizens earned PhDs in mathematics. Of these scholars, 12 were African American men and just 6 were African American women. From 1973 to 2012, over 22,000 white men earned PhDs in physics, as compared to only 66 African American women and 106 Latinas. Those numbers translate into over 550 white men and fewer than 2 black women earning PhDs each year. Over that same time period, about 15 Asian American women earned physics PhDs each year.[9]

In addition, recall how mathematics connects to other disciplines and how those connections can produce bonuses. A person may apply his mathematical tools to a problem that leverages identity-based knowledge or interests.

Thus, even if we see no obvious direct links between identity and relevant cognitive diversity within a technical field, diversity and inclusion produce bonuses by increasing the pool of talent and the range of problems studied. Think back first to the complicated graph of mathematical knowledge. People with greater capacity can trace out longer paths in that graph. Their talent adds diversity. In addition, on cross-disciplinarity complex tasks like the obesity epidemic or rising opioid use, identity-based knowledge or perspectives become germane, and identity brings relevant cognitive diversity.

LESSONS FROM THE TOOLBOX MODEL

The toolbox model reveals how complexity, whether within a field like mathematics or in the context of a problem like obesity, creates the potential for diversity bonuses. If the domains were not complex and tools were arranged linearly, the smartest person would know everything that everyone else knows. When tools can be acquired in any number of orders and there exist a large number of relevant tools—that is, when the domain is complex—the potential for diversity bonuses exists.

Complexity and Diversity Bonuses

If cognitive tools must be accumulated in a particular order, like the stations on a train trip, then the best team consists of the highest-ability person and no diversity bonuses exist. If cognitive tools can be accumulated along multiple paths, that is, if the field (mathematics) or the challenge (reducing obesity) is complex, then diversity bonuses can exist because different people master different relevant tools.

The toolbox model represents people as possessing a collection of tricks or techniques to solve problems. If a person possesses different tools, then she produces bonuses. The same logic described with respect to these tools can be applied to the various parts of a person's repertoire: her information, knowledge, models, representations, or heuristics. When there exist only a few tools that must be acquired in a specific order, then we should not expect bonuses. A single person could master all the tools necessary. We need not build teams or seek diversity bonuses. When repertoires can be accumulated along multiple paths and when there exist an abundance of relevant ways of thinking for some task, then diversity bonuses will exist.

Like any model, this tool model oversimplifies. It assumes that everyone trusts and understands one another, that people can recognize improvements, and that no communication costs (or other costs, for that matter) arise when enlarging the team. Without any costs to scaling, the model implies that we should make teams as large as possible. Larger teams would possess more tools and be more likely to excel at a task. In real situations, communication and coordination costs rise with team size, so even though more people would mean more cognitive tools, larger teams need not perform better.

THE (INAPT) PORTFOLIO ANALOGY

I have found that the most common explanation that people give for the benefits of identity diversity rests on a *portfolio analogy* from finance. That analogy is inapt and unfortunate. Diversity bonuses are not at all the same as portfolio effects. Not only does portfolio thinking offer little guidance for how to hire employees or assemble teams, it also systematically understates diversity's contribution.

The portfolio analogy can be stated as follows: Fund managers invest in a variety of diverse stocks to earn robust returns. By analogy, organizations should create identity-diverse and cognitively diverse teams. For the analogy to be useful, the benefits fund managers receive from diverse investments must be analogous to the benefits organizations receive from diverse people. That is not true.

Fund managers select diverse investments to reduce variation in returns—to lessen risk. Organizations want diverse employees for different reasons. Why they want diversity and the type of diversity they want depends on the task. For example, organizations want diverse problem-solving teams because those teams come up with more ideas that they can recombine to produce bonuses. They want diverse forecasting teams because those teams make more accurate predictions. In both cases, diversity produces bonuses. It does not reduce risk.

A more detailed comparison of investment portfolios and teams of people reveals that the mechanisms through which diversity operates also differ. When building an investment portfolio, a fund manager wants high return and low risk. As a rule, higher-return investments come with higher risk. That follows from economic logic: if high-return, low-risk investments were available, they would attract many investors. This would raise the price of those investments and lower their returns.

A fund manager therefore must accept risk to earn high returns. A manager can earn (relatively) high returns with low risk by investing in negatively correlated stocks, that is, a diverse portfolio. Figure 1.9 shows a portfolio containing four stocks: a technology stock that returned 4 percent, an oil stock that returned 9 percent, an airline stock that lost 4 percent, and an automobile stock that earned 3 percent.

When the fund manager made these investments, she did not know what their returns would be. The returns depend on what financial analysts call the *state of the world*. No one can know the state of the world a year ahead of time. The idea is to select a portfolio of stocks that pays well regardless of what happens in the economy.

In our example, perhaps the airline stock lost money because of high energy prices. Airline stocks suffer under those conditions. Luckily, in that same state of the world, oil stocks perform well. Had

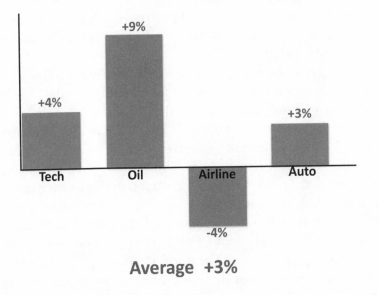

Average +3%

Figure 1.9 A Diverse Portfolio and Risk Reduction

a different state of the world arisen, the airline stock might have done well while the oil stock fell in price. This balancing, called negative correlation, explains why a fund that includes airline and oil stocks has less risk.

The mathematics is not complicated. The fund manager's return on the entire portfolio equals the *average* return from each investment. Diversification brings value by reducing the variation in that average return.

A team of diverse people solving a problem does not operate at all like a collection of stocks. The analogy that people have different payoffs depending on the state of the world is strained at best. Furthermore, the problem-solving team's performance does not equal the average of its members. Instead, the team could ignore everything except the best solution. The analogue would be that after the state of the world was realized, the fund manager could drop every investment except for the oil stock and earn a 9 percent return. Of course, she cannot. She's stuck with the average of her pool of investments.

Note the difference: the portfolio performs like the average. The problem-solving team performs like the best. Actually, the team can perform even better if team members share ideas. If they can improve on the best idea or combine it with another idea, they can do better than the best (see figure 1.10).

The relative importance of diversity in the two settings should be clear. If the return on a stock portfolio could exceed its best single investment, fund managers would construct much more diverse portfolios than they do at present. They would not care if an investment had a high probability of a large loss, provided it had some chance of generating a huge return. Thus, when applied to problem-solving teams, the portfolio analogy misstates the reasons for diversity and understates its value.

On predictive tasks, the analogy also fails. Later, I show that the average of a diverse collection of predictions must be more accurate than the average prediction. The portfolio analogy therefore understates the contribution of diversity. Groups again do better than average. The portfolio analogue also undervalues the contribution of

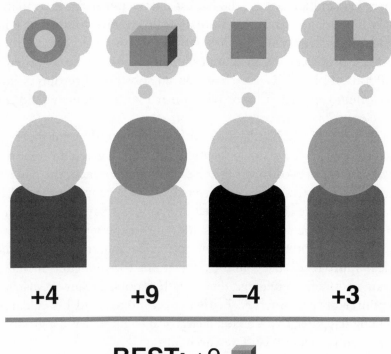

BEST: +9 ■
COMBINED: +16 ○■L

Figure 1.10 Diverse Problem-Solving Teams Can Outperform Their Best Member

diversity for generating ideas, verifying truth, evaluating projects, and innovating. Nor will the analogy apply to situations in which diverse repertoires originate something new. In each case, diversity does more than reduce risk. It produces bonuses.

THE NETFLIX PRIZE

On October 6, 2006, Reed Hastings, the CEO of Netflix, announced an open competition to predict customers' movie ratings. On that date, Netflix released data consisting of one hundred million movie ratings of one to five stars for seventeen thousand movies from their nearly half million users—the largest data set ever made available to the public. Contest rules were as follows: any contestant who could predict consumer ratings 10 percent more accurately than Netflix's proprietary Cinematch algorithm would be awarded a $1,000,000 prize.[10] Netflix had poured substantial resources into developing Cinematch. Improving on it by 10 percent would not prove easy.

The story of the Netflix Prize differs from traditional diversity narratives in which a single talented individual, given an opportunity, creates a breakthrough because of some idiosynchratic piece of information. Instead, teams of diverse, brilliant people competed to attain a goal. The contest attracted thousands of participants with a variety of technical backgrounds and work experiences. The teams applied an algorithmic zoo of conceptual, computational, and analytical approaches. Early in the contest, the top ten teams included a team of American undergraduate math majors, a team of Austrian computer programmers, a British psychologist and his calculus-wielding daughter, two Canadian electrical engineers, and a group of data scientists from AT&T research labs.

In the end, the participants discovered that their collective differences contributed as much as or more than their individual talents. By sharing perspectives, knowledge, information, and techniques, the contestants produced a sequence of quantifiable diversity bonuses.

Winning the Netflix Prize required the inference of patterns from an enormous data set. That data set covered a diverse population of people. Some liked horror films. Others preferred romantic comedies. Some liked documentaries. The modelers would attempt to account for this heterogeneity by creating categories of movies and of people.

To understand the nature of the task, imagine a giant spreadsheet with a row for each person and a column for each movie. If each user rated every movie, that spreadsheet would contain over 8.5 billion ratings. The data consisted of a mere 100 million ratings. Though an enormous amount of data, it fills in fewer than 1.2 percent of the cells. If you opened the spreadsheet in Excel, you would see mostly blanks. Computer scientists refer to this as *sparse data*.

The contestants had to predict the blanks, or, to be more precise, predict the values for the blanks that consumers would fill in next. Inferring patterns from existing data, what data scientists call *collaborative filtering*, requires the creation of similarity measures between people and between movies. Similar people should rank the same movie similarly. And each person should rank similar movies similarly.

A team knows it has constructed effective similarity measures if the patterns identified in the existing data hold for the blanks. Characterizing similarity between people or movies involves difficult choices: Is Mel Brooks's spoof *Spaceballs* closer to the *Airplane!* comedies or to *Star Wars*, the movie that *Spaceballs* parodied?

Early in the competition, contestants' similarity measures of movies emphasized attributes such as genre (comedy, drama, action), box office receipts, and external rankings. Some models included the presence of specific actors (was Morgan Freeman or Will Smith in the movie?) or types of events, such as gruesome deaths, car chases, or sexual intimacy. Later models added data on the number of days between the movie's release to video and the person's day of rental.

One might think that including more features would lead to more accurate predictions. That need not hold. Models with too many variables can overfit the data. To guard against overfitting, computer scientists divide their data into two sets: a *training set* and a *testing set*. They fit their model to the first set, then check to see if it also works on the second set.[11] In the Netflix Prize competition, the size of the data set and the costs of computation limited the number of variables that could be included in any one model. The winner would therefore not be the person or team that could think up the most features. It would be the team capable of identifying the most informative and tractable set of features.

Given a feature set, each team also needed an algorithm to make predictions. Dinosaur Planet, a team of three mathematics undergraduates that briefly led the competition in 2007, tried multiple approaches, including clustering (partitioning movies into sets based on similar characteristics), neural networks (algorithms that take features as inputs and learn patterns), and nearest-neighbor methods (algorithms that assign numerical scores to each feature for each movie and compute a distance based on vectors of features).

At the end of the first year, a team from AT&T research labs, known as BellKor, led the competition. Their best single model relied on fifty variables per movie and improved on Cinematch by 6.58 percent. That was just one of their models. By combining their fifty models in an ensemble, they could improve on Cinematch by 8.43 percent.

A year and a half into the competition, BellKor knew they could outperform the other teams, but also that they could not reach the 10 percent threshold. Rather than give up, BellKor opted to call in reinforcements. In 2008, they merged with the Austrian computer scientists, Big Chaos, a team that had developed sophisticated algorithms for combining models. BellKor had the best predictive models. Big Chaos knew better ways to combine them. By combining these repertoires, they produced a diversity bonus. However, that bonus was not sufficient to push them above the 10 percent threshold.

In 2009, the team again went looking for a new partner. This time, they added a Canadian team, Pragmatic Theory. Pragmatic Theory lacked BellKor's ability to identify features or Big Chaos's skills at aggregating models. Pragmatic Theory's added value came in the form of new insights into human behavior.

They had developed novel methods for categorizing distinct users on the same account. They could separate one person into two identities: Eric alone and Eric with a date. These two Erics might rank the same movie differently. Pragmatic Theory also identified patterns in rankings based on the day of the week—some people rated movies higher on Sundays. They found that for some movies, rankings depended on whether people rated the movie immediately or after having time for reflection. As the credits roll, the hilarity of *Snakes on a Plane* or *Anchorman* results in high rankings. With time for reflection, most people no longer consider a flaming flute or a burrito in the face to be hallmarks of quality films and assign fewer stars.[12]

The combined team, now called BellKor's Pragmatic Chaos, had thought up a jaw-dropping eight hundred predictive features.[13] More diversity meant more ideas. Recall that the goal was not to come up with the most features. Not all the features would improve accuracy. The team had to select from among them to create powerful combinations. Eventually, the team developed a single model that improved on Cinematch by 8.4 percent. They now had a single model as good as BellKor's entire ensemble of models. When BellKor's Pragmatic Chaos combined that and other models, they produced even more accurate predictions.

The combined team's composite models proved up to the task. On June 26, 2009, nearly three years after the contest began, BellKor's Pragmatic Chaos surpassed the 10 percent threshold. Game over. BellKor's Pragmatic Chaos won the $1,000,000 in prize money.

Although, not yet. They had to wait. To safeguard against the possibility that 10 percent would prove too easy, the organizers wrote the rules so that the contest would end thirty days after a team passed the threshold. Had the threshold been 5 percent, a level that was bested a mere six days into the contest, this decision would have been prescient. As events unfolded, this delay seemed unnecessary.

It was not. The fun had only begun. As if drawn from the script of *Jurassic Park*, the dinosaurs came roaring back. And they brought reinforcements. More than thirty teams, including top performers Grand Prize Team, Opera Solutions, and Vandelay Industries, joined forces with the Dinosaur Planet team to form the Ensemble. Within a few weeks, the Ensemble blended forty-eight models using a sophisticated weighting scheme and took the slightest of leads.

The ultimate winner would be decided by determining which model performed best on the testing data—the data held back by Netflix. The result was a tie. Each had improved on Cinematch by an identical 10.06 percent. The winner was determined by order of submission. By turning in their code twenty-two minutes before the Ensemble, BellKor's Pragmatic Chaos won.

Winning the contest required knowledge of the features of movies that matter most, awareness of available information on movies, methods for representing properties of movies in languages accessible to computers, good mental models of how people rank movies, the ability to develop algorithms to predict ratings, and expertise at combining diverse models into an ensemble. What had begun as a contest to determine the best data scientist became a demonstration of diversity bonuses.

Some parts of those repertoires—algorithm development and model aggregation procedures—required deep technical knowledge and skills that might be learned in graduate school. Other parts—the ability to identify significant features and to construct models of how people rate movies—leveraged personal experience and social knowledge. The winning formula required deep knowledge of spectral analysis and appreciation of the superficial humor of Will Ferrell.

Passing the 10 percent threshold required a team with both diverse technical training and deep intuitions and knowledge about how a diverse consumer base rated movies. It required cognitive diversity. BellKor's diversity had its roots in education, experience, and identity. The BellKor team consisted of Robert Bell, an African American statistician who spent two decades at Rand Corporation on the West Coast engaged in public policy research; Chris Volinsky, a European American data-mining expert from upstate New York who specialized in fraud detection and social networks; and Yehuda Koren, an Israeli expert in data mining and data visualization.

Despite their brilliance and diversity, BellKor could not exceed the threshold. They needed help. They turned to people demonstrably less capable than themselves. This approach runs counter to what we do on physical tasks. If incapable of unscrewing the lid from a jar of mayo, you do not seek out someone *weaker* than you are. You look for someone stronger. Bell and his team had no one smarter to call. They were the smartest. They therefore sought diversity bonuses, and they found them.

Ironically, diversity bonuses also almost cost them the prize. The runners-up who formed the Ensemble generated enough bonuses to forge a tie. None of these teams had models as accurate as the best models of BellKor's Pragmatic Chaos. The Ensemble had less ability. Their strength lay in their diversity. The forty-eight models they combined relied on diverse features, embedded different knowledge, and applied diverse insights about how people rank movies. The Ensemble also made breakthroughs in combining those models using sophisticated weighting algorithms. Given more time, the Ensemble might well have won.

In the end, being smart was not enough. That was the key lesson. Exceeding the 10 percent threshold required different ways of thinking, seeing, solving, and coding. Eliot Van Buskirk (see box) noted the quantifiable diversity bonuses. The bonuses are not metaphorical musings. They are a measurable fact.

"The secret sauce for both BellKor's Pragmatic Chaos and The Ensemble was collaboration between diverse ideas, and not in some touchy-feely, unquantifiable, 'when people work together things are better' sort of way. The top two teams beat the challenge by combining teams and their algorithms into more complex algorithms incorporating everybody's work. In combination, the teams could get better and better and better."

—Van Buskirk, "How the Netflix Prize Was Won"

The Netflix Prize story reveals diversity bonuses threefold. The diverse repertoires within the AT&T team produced bonuses, the diverse representations and tools brought to the team by Big Chaos and Pragmatic Theory produced bonuses, and so did the diverse models of the teams in the Ensemble.

Similar bonuses arise in any crowdsourced prediction contest. Kaggle, a platform launched in 2010, allows anyone to organize similar contests. Companies or nonprofits post data and a prize. Scientists, data miners, and computer scientists then compete to predict everything from brain seizures to home prices in Ames, Iowa. In Kaggle, participants construct code using *scripts* that anyone can access. Discussion boards reveal interchanges of ideas and diversity bonuses. A new version of the Netflix Prize story could be written each week, revealing more bonuses upon bonuses.

THE CONDITIONS FOR DIVERSITY BONUSES

The Netflix Prize story and Kaggle provide measurable evidence of diversity bonuses. To understand how and why diversity bonuses occur, we need a theory and models. That theory will help us move away from belief-based reasoning toward scientific understanding. Holding the conflicting ideological positions that "diverse teams perform better" and that "we should hire by ability" does not move us forward. We need to understand the conditions for bonuses to occur.

As an analogy, consider the claim that markets work, that is, that they allocate goods efficiently, and the alternative claim that markets fail. Each claim is one part ideological thinking and one part bad economics. The claims lack conditionality. An economics textbook will include neither claim. Instead, it will list conditions that must hold for each claim to hold.

For a market to work, the environment must not include negative externalities: unpriced consequences that lower the well-being of people not involved in a transaction. A person smoking a cigar in an elevator imposes a negative externality on other passengers. Markets without externalities, such as the markets for luggage, socks, and tablecloths, work rather well. No one cares much about the color of your socks.

In contrast, the real estate market includes any number of potential negative externalities. A person wishing to buy an empty lot in a residential neighborhood with the hope of building a five-story, yellow-stucco home to which he plans to affix enormous exterior audio speakers so that he can enjoy his collection of vintage Whitesnake albums would infuriate his neighbors if his vision became reality. The market, in this case, would not produce an optimal outcome.

To prevent negative externalities of this sort, communities enact zoning laws. They limit building height and preclude the playing of loud music. What constitutes a negative externality varies by location. Santa Fe, New Mexico, requires that a home's exterior resemble that of a traditional adobe structure. Vinyl-sided McMansions would destroy Santa Fe's charm, so the law forbids them. Holland, Michigan, caps the number of dogs at two. Ann Arbor, Michigan, allows chickens but no roosters. These regulations lead to quieter neighborhoods than would an unfettered market.

In sum, sometimes markets work, and sometimes they fail. Logic, models, evidence, and experiments help us to learn the conditions in which they work and to design better markets. People who believe markets always work ignore logic and evidence. They predict poorly.[14] The same criticism applies to people who believe diversity bonuses always exist. That is also not true. Diversity exists only for some problems. We must think through the logic and determine when they do.

To organize our thinking, we can place each task in one of two boxes, as shown in figure 1.11: tasks for which no bonuses exist and in which ability dominates, and tasks for which bonuses exist and in which both ability and diversity matter. The Netflix Prize obviously belongs in the box on the right.

To determine how to allocate tasks to these boxes, I rely on a categorization from economics that distinguishes between physical and cognitive work and between routine and nonroutine work.[15] We perform physical work with our hands and bodies. Cognitive work is done with our minds. Routine tasks can be handled by a program or machine. Nonroutine tasks differ from day to day or moment to moment.

Routine tasks need not be easy. Before the development of computers, people worked as calculators, summing up columns of numbers to keep track of inventories, revenues, and costs. Those jobs required mathematical expertise.

Those two distinctions create four categories of jobs, shown in figure 1.12: *manual routine, manual nonroutine, cognitive routine,* and *cognitive nonroutine.* Manual routine jobs include assembly-line worker, truck driver, and warehouse worker. Manual nonroutine jobs include those of many health care workers, hotel and restaurant employees, and fitness center employees. Routine cognitive jobs include positions in data entry, sales, and insurance.

Cognitive nonroutine jobs include those of medical researchers, doctors, lawyers, scientists, financial analysts, management, and policy makers. This category includes workers who solve technical problems and people who manage organizations. It can be further subdivided into analytic and interpersonal cognitive workers.

Significant diversity bonuses exist primarily for cognitive nonroutine tasks. As shown in figure 1.13, that category contains the largest proportion of workers. Those workers also earn the highest incomes, implying a significant potential impact of diversity bonuses.

The predominance of nonroutine cognitive workers is a recent phenomenon. A century ago, at the peak of Thomas Edison's career,

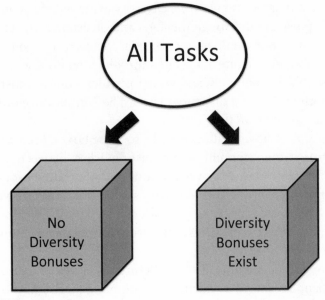

Figure 1.11 Classifying Tasks

fewer than 5 percent of people worked in professional and technical jobs. Farmers and farm laborers constituted over a third of the workforce. Those people who did not farm worked mostly in routine manual jobs, often in mines, factories, or forests. Most people did not work in jobs that could produce meaningful diversity bonuses. That remained true through the middle of the twentieth century during the postwar growth period as workers shifted from farm to factory. The passage of the GI Bill, which enabled millions of (mostly white) soldiers to attend college, bootstrapped the trend toward more cognitive nonroutine work.[16]

By the mid-1980s, cognitive routine workers composed the largest share of the workforce. Since that time, most job growth has been in that category as well. In 1983, the US workforce consisted of one hundred million people. The number of workers with nonroutine cognitive jobs, twenty-eight million, equaled the number working in manual labor. There were twenty-seven million workers engaged in routine cognitive work, and fifteen million in nonroutine manual labor.

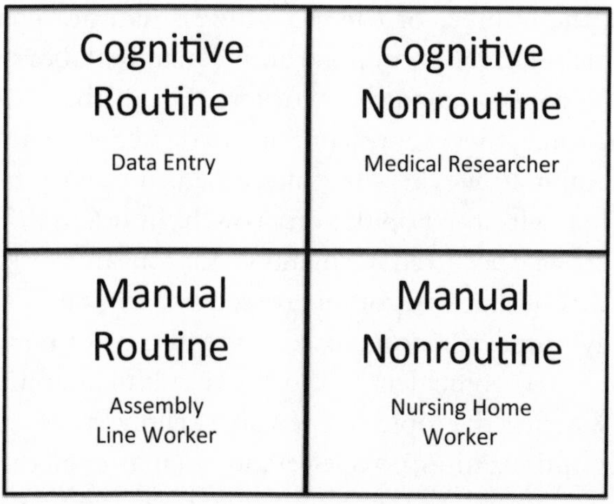

Cognitive Routine Data Entry	Cognitive Nonroutine Medical Researcher
Manual Routine Assembly Line Worker	Manual Nonroutine Nursing Home Worker

Figure 1.12 Categories of Workers (Autor, Levy, and Murnane, "Skill Content of Recent Technological Change")

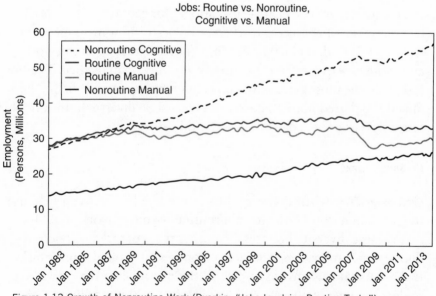

Figure 1.13 Growth of Nonroutine Work (Dvorkin, "Jobs Involving Routine Tasks")

By 2016, the number of routine workers had not changed. The workforce included thirty million routine manual labors and thirty-three million routine cognitive workers. Given the growth in the overall workforce, these represent relative decreases. The number of nonroutine manual workers had increased to twenty-five million, roughly in line with the population growth. In other words, almost all real job growth occurred in cognitive nonroutine work. The number of workers in that category increased to sixty million.

As already noted, a vast increase in the corpus of human knowledge has occurred coincident with the growth in cognitive nonroutine work. Whether the topic is renewable energy, diabetes, fuel cells, or nonlinear optimization, no one person can master all that is known and relevant. In building that knowledge base, the tens of millions of cognitive workers also develop new analytic tools, create new perspectives and categories, and make new models of how the world works. No one person can keep up. Hence the rise in teams. By definition, those teams must be diverse.

The multistep logic bears elaboration: Our economy consists of a large number of cognitive workers who perform nonroutine tasks; within any task domain, they produce knowledge, tools, frameworks, and models. Any one person can master only a small slice. Therefore, even the most accomplished person relies on outside help. That outside help need not be smarter, but it must be diverse. It must possess different knowledge or skills to add value.

No Bonus Tasks

Understanding when diversity does not create bonuses can help us to see when it does. Only for nonroutine cognitive work should we expect large diversity bonuses. The other types of tasks will not produce significant bonuses. The lack of bonuses on manual routine tasks is the most straightforward. Recall the example of the pizza box folders. Assume that each employee can fold 800 boxes in an eight-hour shift. Together, the two should be able to fold 1,600 boxes. They produce no diversity bonus.

Organizational scholars refer to such tasks as *additive* because the contribution of the group equals the sum of the contributions of the group's members. Selecting runners for a four-by-four-hundred-meter relay represents the canonical additive task. The best relay team consists of the four fastest runners. Measured ability, a runner's time in the four hundred meters, correlates perfectly with her contribution to a relay team.

The same logic applies to any other additive task so diversity bonuses cannot be large. For teams who fell trees, shovel driveways, or sort clothing, we should not expect significant diversity bonuses because these tasks do not depend on deep thinking. These tasks offer few openings for diverse ideas. To expect a diversity bonus, to think that two people capable of felling eighty trees each per eight-hour shift could somehow fell two hundred trees together, is to engage in magical thinking (see figure 1.14).

The additive logic also applies to routine cognitive work: filling out claims forms, processing expense reports, working as a bank teller, or processing driver's licenses at the secretary of state's office. If one person can process ten forms, then two people can process twenty. We should not expect these tasks to produce significant diversity bonuses.

Nor should we expect bonuses for the manual, nonroutine tasks carried out by sales agents, janitors, security guards, tour guides, waiters, and nursing-home workers. While the situations people confront in these jobs vary from day to day, those tasks do not offer an opportunity for significant bonuses from diversity because of a lack of transferability. A waiter who identifies a better route to and from the kitchen acquires idiosyncratic knowledge, as does a health care worker who learns how to better motivate a patient to exercise. Neither gains knowledge that applies broadly.

Before closing the door on the possibility of diversity bonuses within these three categories of tasks, I need to address a few complications. First, semiroutine tasks that require expertise, such as painting houses, performing electrical work, or cooking, can produce modest diversity bonuses. Consider the process of making a meringue

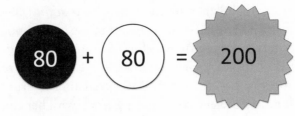

Figure 1.14 Magical Thinking for Additive Tasks

topping for a pie. A meringue consists of egg whites and sugar. The two combine to form protein chains that unfold and then reform around air bubbles. The sugar also performs a second function by stabilizing the protein-encased bubbles.

A cook learning to make a meringue acquires the following knowledge: The sugar cannot be too coarse or too fine—the finer the sugar, the faster it dissolves. A successful meringue also depends on properly aged eggs. As eggs age, they become more alkaline, loosening their protein bonds. Weaker bonds make for fluffier and less stable peaks. The strength of the bonds also varies with the eggs' temperature. Colder eggs create stronger bonds. The temperature and the age of the eggs therefore interact. Older eggs should be cooler; fresher eggs should be warmer.

The cook also learns that if the egg whites touch fat, the meringue will not form. Even the slightest amount of fat-laden yolk contaminates the meringue, as will any fat residue lingering on the sides of the mixing bowl. Chefs therefore clean their bowls with lemon juice or vinegar before adding the egg whites. The technique for combining also matters. Beating the egg whites too vigorously breaks the protein chains and loses fluffiness. The proper mixing technique begins slowly and increases in speed.

All these details drive home the point that making a meringue requires mastery of a craft. Success depends on subtle interactions between ingredients, the absence of fat, and proper blending techniques. Similar types of knowledge and skill would be required in learning to paint a ceiling, build picnic tables, or make whiskey.

With experience, a person can improve at each of these tasks. We can capture those improvements on a *learning curve* showing quality improvements with repetition. Studies of manufacturing find that people improve at predictable rates.[17] Broader inquires show that people improve in their abilities to apply any new technology.[18] A portion of that improvement comes from repetition and refinement. Improvements also come from watching others and mimicking their behaviors. Only improvements that result from the latter can be considered diversity bonuses. So while bonuses can exist on these tasks, they are just not very large.

Second, many complicated tasks can be decomposed into specialized, additive tasks: an example would be building a table, which consists of sawing, gluing, sanding, and staining. These gains from specialization do not constitute a diversity bonus as defined here. The best table-building team will consist of specialists on each task. We could think of that as a gain from diversity, and it is. However, if we define each task separately, then those gains are not diversity bonuses. On each specific task, we should hire based on ability. Following a similar logic, we should not rush to assign diversity bonuses to basketball teams who rely on centers, guards, and forwards or to the workers at a hair and nail salon.

Third, some routine tasks require sophisticated coordination. On these tasks, homogeneity can be beneficial if it correlates with shared understandings. Diversity, rather than producing bonuses, can impose costs. Doubles tennis provides a near-ideal example of a task that involves elaborate coordination. Players must communicate nonverbally and be able to anticipate the actions of their partners. Sibling doubles teams dominate more than would occur by chance. The Williams sisters have dominated women's doubles for more than a decade. In men's tennis, identical twins Bob and Mike Bryan have held the number one ranking for more than eight years and won a record number of Grand Slam tournaments and championships. A similar logic might apply for event planners, real estate agents, or coaches. The benefits of familiarity and trust advantage homogenous teams.

These complications aside, my previous summary still holds: routine cognitive and noncognitive tasks tend to be additive. We should not expect diversity bonuses. On manual nonroutine tasks, improvements tend to be idiosyncratic and do not scale or transfer. When hiring people to perform any of these three types of tasks, organizations should focus on ability. The best team likely consists of the best individuals.

Tasks with Diversity Bonuses

Diversity bonuses, when they exist, do so on complex, high-dimensional tasks: solving a problem, predicting an outcome, designing a policy, evaluating a proposed merger, or undertaking research. Bonuses arise when these cognitive nonroutine tasks prove too complex for any one individual. No one person can possess sufficient knowledge, tools, or understandings to handle this type of task alone.

These tasks must also be difficult to separate into simpler components. When a task has these two attributes—high dimensionality and indecomposability—diversity bonuses become likely.

If that logic is correct, then we should see actors in industries that employ cognitive workers on nonroutine tasks to enact policies and procedures that attract, maintain, and develop diverse thinkers. And we do. Wall Street firms hire physicists, computer scientists, and psychologists in addition to financial analysts. Leading consulting companies hire PhDs in fields as diverse as chemistry, art history, and philosophy. The academy and think tanks all but trip over themselves in advocating that their researchers leave their academic silos and engage in interdisciplinary projects.

Designing an airplane provides an illustrative example that demonstrates why they seek diverse thinkers. Airplanes are large, complex objects. A Boeing 787 Dreamliner contains 2.3 million distinct parts and costs over $150 million. A 747–8 has 6 million parts and costs over $350 million. Over five thousand suppliers employing nearly a half million people produce parts for a 747–8, and they manufacture each part to exact specifications.

These many parts interact. Navigational and entertainment systems draw from a common electrical power source. Wing, tail, and engine designs affect aerodynamics in combination. Seat, lighting, and overhead storage designs all influence ergonomics. Every part adds to the weight and affects the fuel efficiency of the plane, so the people designing the interior of the plane must coordinate with the engineers designing the propulsion system.

Thus, unlike building a table, making an airplane cannot be decomposed into separate tasks performed in isolation. This indecomposability is desirable. It creates the possibility for diversity bonuses. On indecomposable tasks, people must share ideas and information to achieve a good outcome.[19] To reduce the weight of the airplane, Boeing made the daring decision to build the 787 Dreamliner from composite materials, that is, plastic, rather than aluminum. That decision interacted with other decisions. Design teams tasked with creating a better flying experience long knew that people prefer more humidity inside the plane. In aluminum and steel planes, humidity levels were kept low to avoid corrosion. A composite plane cannot corrode, so the interior can be more humid. Of course, the plane must then carry more water to produce that humidity.

Algebra makes clear the potential magnitude of diversity bonuses on large-scale problems like building an airplane. Boeing's total revenue in 2015 was approximately $100 billion. Revenues from the approximately fifty Dreamliners they sell each year constitute about 8 percent of that total. Boeing's profit margin averages around 10 percent. Those Dreamliners cost around $7 billion to build. If the team designing the Dreamliner had a diversity bonus that reduced that cost by 1 percent, Boeing's profits would increase by $70 million, or about $500 per employee.

A similar algebra of scale can be applied to Amazon, which ships upwards of four hundred boxes every second of every day. Amazon tasks teams of engineers, economists, packaging experts, ergonomists, and trend analysts with determining the sizes and shapes of those boxes. Amazon's shipping costs exceed $10 billion per year. A diversity bonus resulting in a mere 3 percent improvement in shipping costs would correspond to over $300 million in savings.

Boeing's and Amazon's potential bonuses pale in comparison to the savings possible through improvements in energy usage and transmission. The United States produces about four trillion kilowatt hours of electricity each year, producing revenue of $400 billion. Between 5 and 6 percent of that energy, or between $20 billion and

$25 billion, is lost in transmission and distribution. Reducing the loss to 4 percent would save billions.

DAILY BONUSES

Just as marginal improvements in building airplanes, organizing warehouses, or managing the electric power grid can translate into large economic effects, so too can the accumulation of smaller diversity bonuses produced by the tens of millions of cognitive workers engaged in nonroutine tasks.

To think that at every moment of every day, every team of cognitive nonroutine workers produces a diversity bonus overstates the likelihood of such bonuses. To quantify their impact, we must think in terms of tasks, not jobs. Any job consists of tasks with bonuses and tasks without them.

An emergency room doctor (a cognitive nonroutine worker) will not seek bonuses on every single task. During a workday, a doctor may gather information and decide on tests. She may make diagnoses and formulate treatment protocols. She may perform surgery.

Some of these tasks involve prediction; others involve problem solving. Some of her work consists of cognitive routine tasks (diagnosing strep throat). Other parts involve routine manual tasks (taping a sprained ankle). The doctor should only seek out diversity bonuses on the most challenging of the tasks. She should not bother seeking out diverse opinions on a routine ankle injury, but she should seek advice when treating an admitted patient presenting nontraditional or contradictory symptoms.

Alternative diagnoses can create diversity bonuses if another doctor possesses a different knowledge base or different insights and can offer a more effective protocol. In medicine, the tasks with diversity bonuses are often the most consequential. A poorly taped ankle is a misfortune; a misdiagnosis of bubonic plague is a tragedy.

Medical practice benefits from diversity bonuses within and across specialties. The Vermont Oxford Network serves as an illustrative example. Founded in 1989 as a consortium of thirty-four neonatal intensive care units (NICUs), the network now includes over one thousand NICUs. The network assists in the formation of interdisciplinary teams to improve outcomes. Those teams share best practices and quality improvements through intensive training and online collaborations. The network also organizes randomized controlled trials across hospitals to compare treatments. A trial might cover a topic such as respiratory distress or temperature regulation.

The members of the Vermont Oxford Network share a common goal to lower the neonatal mortality rate. As was the case with the Netflix Prize, their success comes not in the form of a singular brilliant answer but in the accumulation of many small improvements discovered by diverse people.

The network enables large-scale testing of promising ideas. Not all proposed ideas work. Occlusion wraps (encasing a baby's body from the neck down in a plastic bubble) were thought to be a potential way to regulate temperature in newborns. Coordinated empirical tests revealed they did not produce significant effects.[20] Other ideas have worked. The sustained efforts of the Vermont Oxford Network have saved lives. Over the past twenty-five years, the neonatal mortality rate has fallen from 5 percent to less than 3 percent in England and from over 6 percent to around 4 percent in the United States.

In medicine, diversity bonuses come in the form of better solutions to problems and more accurate predictions. In other domains, the bonuses may be in the form of improved designs, technologies, or models. The logic will not be one size fits all.

The diversity bonuses described so far apply to an existing challenge or opportunity. A person who notices or emphasizes a novel dimension or attribute might also create something entirely new. In these cases, rather than a diverse repertoire improving performance on an existing task, it *originates* a new product, technology, and even an entire market—later, I will describe cases of entrepreneurs who saw opportunities that others missed because of their experiences and identities. I refer to these as *originating diversity bonuses*. Where people see opportunity will be a function of what they see and where they look.

DIVERSITY IS THE WORD

The Netflix Prize competition showed how people with diverse cognitive tools, understandings, and experiences could better predict
movie preferences. The Vermont Oxford Network tapped into diverse
knowledge and tested diverse ideas to save the lives of newborns.
Within the field of collective intelligence, one can find thousands of
other examples of teams who produced bonuses.[21] These include
the scientists at England's Bletchley Park who cracked the Germans'
Enigma machine, the contributors in Edison's laboratory, and the
teams of scientists, composed of men and women of all races, who got
us to the moon.

We must keep in mind that the evidence we have of diversity bonuses understates the potential contribution of diversity because the
evidence comes from the world as it is, not the world as it could be.
A more inclusive society would produce larger bonuses.

Some of the most compelling evidence comes from the growth of
teams in scientific research, a domain teeming with hard problems.
A half century ago, single-author papers outnumbered papers by teams
of four or more by a ratio greater than four to one. Today, that ratio
has reversed.[22] This trend can be explained by the fact that team-
written papers land in better journals and have more influence. Deeper
statistical studies attribute these papers' successes to a mixture of
depth and diversity.[23]

Organizations show a similar trend toward team-based work.[24]
In the 1990s individuals managed over two-thirds of equity funds.
By 2016, more than three-fourths were run by teams of two to five
managers. As with the scientists, the investment teams performed
better. And, as with the Netflix Prize, their advantage could be quantified. In this case, the accounting was done in dollars.[25]

In the Netflix Prize competition, diverse algorithms, representations, and models created bonuses. The weighting algorithms and
models were not chosen randomly from the World Wide Web. Their
choices of what to try were based on evidence and guided by theory.
Later, I present some of that theory expressed in mathematics. One
of those mathematical equations implies that the average of two

equally accurate diverse predictive models must be more accurate than either one. The result is not that most of the time the average will be more accurate, but that it *will always* be more accurate.

Knowing that mathematical fact, the members of the Ensemble averaged their model's final predictions with those of BellKor's Pragmatic Chaos. Keep in mind that each model had improved on Cinematch by the same 10.06 percent. In the competition's final days, either team would have been thrilled to identify a 0.005 percent improvement. When the Ensemble averaged the two models, accuracy increased by thirty times that amount.

In *Invisible Man*, Ralph Ellison wrote, "Whence all this passion towards conformity anyway? Diversity is the word."[26] His words ring even truer in today's complex world, where we apply our brains more than our shoulders. Diversity *is* the word.

CHAPTER TWO

COGNITIVE REPERTOIRES

People throw around the word "diversity" like it's a tip at a restaurant. But really, having people who have different mental perspectives is what's important. If you want to explore things you haven't explored, having people who look just like you and think just like you is not the best way.

—ASTRO TELLER

THE FIRST STEP IN UNPACKING THE LOGIC THAT EXPLAINS DIVERSITY bonuses involves making formal definitions. Specifically, I need to define what I mean by diversity before I can derive logical claims that sketch out the boundaries for when diversity produces bonuses and when it does not. The focus of this chapter, therefore, will be to define what I call *cognitive repertoires*. Repertoires consist of five components: *information, knowledge, heuristics or tools, representations*, and *mental models and frameworks*. In the next chapter, I link these repertoires to better outcomes.

My use of repertoires is not traditional. I rely on repertoires and not dimensional evaluations like IQ scores because IQ scores lack sufficient granularity to reveal how diversity bonuses arise. This limitation becomes apparent when trying to determine the ability of a team. Suppose that one person has an IQ of 120 and another has an IQ of 110. Any composite IQ for the team of both people will be idiosyncratic. The team's IQ will not equal the sum of their individual IQs. It will not be 230. Nor will the team's IQ equal the maximum of their IQs. That would make the pair only as smart as the smarter member—an equally implausible assumption. We could rely on some ad hoc rule—the average of the maximum ability and the sum of the abilities, or the square root of the sum of the IQs. If we did so, we would bake in whatever results we derived.

Put in mathematical terms, we lack an algebra of IQs. The algebra problem remains even if we decompose intelligence into multiple dimensions, such as Howard Gardner's nine dimensions: *linguistic, mathematical, musical, spatial, interpersonal, existential, intrapersonal, naturalist,* and *bodily.*[1] While nine dimensions can embed more information than one, they do not overcome the algebra problem. If anything, they exacerbate it. We now need a method for adding vectors of abilities. Instead of one ad hoc rule, we need nine.

In contrast, using repertoires makes aggregation straightforward. The repertoire of a group of people equals the union of their individual repertoires. If one person knows double-entry accounting and a second knows linear regression, the group knows both. In this way, a group resembles a person with a large repertoire. High-ability teams, like high-ability people, will have large collective repertoires. One way for a team to have a large repertoire is if the members of that team possess different repertoires. That straightforward logic underpins many of the results that follow.

The use of repertoires also allows for intuitive measures of both diversity and ability. A team's diversity can be measured by the lack of overlap in members' repertoires. A person's ability on a task can be measured by how well a person's repertoire performs on that task, not on a general intelligence test. Given these measures, increasing the diversity of a team or the ability of a member will add tools to the team's repertoire and improve the team.

This formulation also allows for a person to be intelligent on some problems and less so on others. Someone with a PhD in mathematics may have a large repertoire, but it may not be well suited for formulating a health care policy, developing a marketing plan, or designing a fall fashion line.

I constructed my characterization of repertoires as consisting of *information, knowledge, heuristics or tools, representations,* and *mental models and frameworks* with an eye toward elaborating the conditions in which diversity does and does not produce bonuses. In this chapter, I develop the components of that categorization at length. Before I dig into the details, I should note that this is not the only possible categorization of cognitive diversity. One alternative categorization of diversity distinguishes between *acquired* and *inherent diversity*.[2] Acquired diversity consists of experiences, along with learned behaviors and traits. We choose some acquired differences. Others we obtain by chance. Inherent diversity consists of immutable attributes: race, age, physical qualities, gender, ethnicity, and sexual orientation.

Another framework distinguishes between social category diversity, informational diversity, and value diversity.[3] *Social category* or *identity diversity* refers to differences in age, race, gender, ethnicity, physical qualities, sexual orientation, and religion. This differs from inherent diversity in that some types of social diversity, notably religion, can be acquired. *Informational diversity* refers to differences in knowledge and perspectives—two of the components of my repertoires. Value diversity corresponds to differences in principles and standards.

Other scholars add personality and behavioral diversity. Both of these have been shown to affect team performance. Teams with a mix of introverts and extroverts may reach better solutions to problems than teams of all introverts or all extroverts.[4] Behavioral diversity also matters for team success. Differences in norms and expectations can be detrimental to team performance.

When compared to these other categorizations, my cognitive repertoire approach stands out as the one most naturally suited to analyzing diversity bonuses. Modeling how a person applies knowledge to a problem, a model to a predictive task, or information to an evaluation will be straightforward. It is less clear how someone could apply her identity, her integrity, or her goals to a prediction or to a problem-solving task. However, as I discuss, a person's identity can shape her repertoire, and, thus, have an effect.

The cognitive repertoire framework is not without shortcomings. It fails to capture the full range of human cognitive differences, as people differ in their short- and long-term memory, in their visual and auditory abilities, and in their reaction speeds. It also muddles distinctions between fluid and crystallized intelligence and between slow and fast thinking.[5]

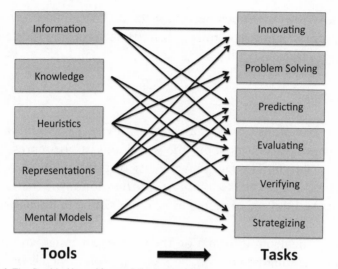

Figure 2.1 The Double Unpacking and the Logical Links

Some foreshadowing will be helpful in interpreting the influence of various parts of cognitive repertoires. In the next chapter, I link those parts to diversity bonuses on six types of tasks: *innovating, problem solving, predicting, evaluating, verifying,* and *strategizing.* What constitutes a better outcome, and a bonus, depends on the task. Better predictions are more accurate. Better solutions to problems have higher values.

That process of mapping repertoires to outcomes requires a double unpacking of the type shown in figure 2.1. The drawing is meant to be illustrative only. Each line represents a connection between a component of a repertoire and a task. As drawn, not every component applies to each task. Diverse heuristics apply to problem solving and not to verifying truth. Diverse representations improve performance on creative tasks, prediction, and problem solving. In practice, which parts of a person's repertoire matter for a given type of task may vary.

I make no claim that this is a complete characterization of how cognitive diversity can produce bonuses. The connections implied by the omitted lines may also exist and be of greater significance and magnitude than those drawn. The figure drives home the point that to identify the conditions necessary for diversity bonuses to exist, one must first define repertoires, then define tasks, and then connect repertoires to tasks.

INFORMATION

The first component of cognitive repertoires is *information*. Information consists of facts about the world and can be represented as pieces or objects. The fact that the city of Dayton, Ohio, occupies fifty-six square miles is a piece of information, as is the fact that Susan B. Anthony was arrested in 1872 for voting in Rochester, New York.

Using tools from information theory, we can assign an information content to any raw data, be it a collection of pixels on a computer screen or numbers on a spreadsheet. Those data need have no meaning to a human observer. When those pixels combine to form the letter C, they take on meaning and become what I call information. The same goes for numbers on a business spreadsheet. They become information when we know that they describe sales figures and inventories.

Information: *Interpretable, meaningful data.*

Throughout our lives, we accumulate information. We learn it in school, acquire it at work, and absorb it at the knees of our parents and grandparents. No two people possess the same information. Our educations, experiences, and identities all influence the information we possess, as do our interests, motivations, and capacities. People who study anthropology know different information from people who study English literature. Accountants know different information from event planners. Given that people who belong to different identity groups read different books, watch different movies, and confront a different set of challenges and opportunities, then identity diversity will also correlate with information diversity.

With the Internet, we can pull up incomprehensible amounts of information in an instant. If we do not know the primary causes of ulcers, we can go to the World Wide Web, and it provides the answer: the bacterium *Helicobacter pylori* and overuse of anti-inflammatories. We might then think that technology renders informational diversity of little value. That is not true. Even though we have a world of information at our fingertips, having relevant information front of mind remains of value. A chemist would never mix ammonia and bleach to create a cleaning solution. A college student majoring in philosophy might. He would then have to contend with a noxious array of toxic chemicals and gasses.

KNOWLEDGE

Knowledge of a subject or domain of inquiry consists of a working or practical understanding. A person who knows German can speak, write, and understand the German language. A person with knowledge of biology can define the terms in the glossary of an introductory textbook and explain the main concepts. A person who knows accounting can read a balance sheet and perform double-entry accounting.

Knowledge: *Theoretical, empirical, or practical understanding of patterns, literatures, or domains of inquiry.*

Knowledge differs from information. Information consists of facts that can be represented in bits and pieces and can be thought of like the items in a junk drawer. It includes the capital of Oregon (Salem), the name of the tallest person who ever lived (Robert Pershing Wadlow), and the middle name of Venus Williams (Ebony Starr). It also includes the preamble to the United States Constitution: *We the people, in order to form* . . .

Knowledge structures information. Recall the diagram of mathematical knowledge from the previous chapter and how different bodies of knowledge depended on other bodies of knowledge. Knowledge also assumes coherence. Knowledge of the Constitution consists of more than memorizing the preamble and the twenty-seven amendments. Knowledge requires an understanding of how the

Constitution defines the branches of government, delineates and separates their powers, and describes amendment procedures.

HEURISTICS OR TOOLS

Heuristics are methods or techniques for generating new ideas. That new idea could be a solution to a problem, a strategy, or a psychological experiment to test a theory. This definition encompasses formal heuristics such as mathematical techniques and rules of thumb for making it through the day. It includes scientific techniques such as the ability to isolate chemical compounds. It includes opening moves in a chess match.

Heuristics: *Methods for finding solutions or generating new ideas.*

Heuristics include rules learned in math class like Newton's method to find roots and Euler's method to solve differential equations. They include the trick to solve an easier related problem. Heuristics also include the rule of thumb to save ten times your annual income for retirement and tricks for solving Sudoku puzzles. A glimpse of the vast array of informal heuristics can be seen by typing "rules of thumb for ____ " into a search engine.

> *Home Decorating:* Your rug should be no closer than eighteen inches to the wall.
> *Negotiating:* Ask for more than you need initially.
> *Grilling Steaks:* Rule of threes: three minutes direct heat on each side, followed by three minutes indirect heat on each side.
> *Meeting People:* Never make a joke about someone's name at a first meeting.

We learn heuristics from textbooks (Newton's method), from novels (E. M. Forster's "only connect"), and through interactions with friends, family, and coworkers (measure twice, cut once). Any one person's collection of heuristics will be an idiosyncratic mixture of purposefully acquired techniques—a computer scientist, architect, or tax accountant will learn hundreds of domain-specific heuristics—and a smattering of tricks encountered and absorbed by chance. That small collection will come from a vast set.

Three features of heuristics make them a likely source of diversity bonuses. First, any given heuristic fails on a large set of problems. All human problem-solving heuristics have blind spots and biases. Even a sophisticated mathematical heuristic can be misled by a deceptive problem. A second heuristic, even a less effective one, may be misled on a different set of problems. If so, it produces a diversity bonus— not by being better but by being different.

Second, in well-developed fields, we need not learn heuristics in a specific order. This creates diversity bonuses. For example, heuristics for the traveling salesperson problem, a canonical optimization problem, try to improve on a route connecting a collection of cities by reducing total travel time. These heuristics fall into categories, like the exhibits at a zoo. One class of heuristics chooses a city at random and adds cities. In a second class, the heuristics improve on a randomly chosen initial route by switching pairs of cities or inserting others. In a third class, the heuristics create and winnow a population of possible routes. A person could learn the heuristics within these classes in any order.

Third, heuristics can traverse domains. Physician and author Atul Gawande describes how hospitals adopted a checklist heuristic used by airline pilots to reduce medical errors.[6] The transferability of heuristics, particularly rules of thumb, can also produce bonuses. Those might be called cross-disciplinary bonuses.

REPRESENTATIONS: PERSPECTIVES AND CATEGORIZATIONS

Representations, or perspectives, are the most often mentioned and vaguely defined component of cognitive repertoires. Many businesses, universities, nonprofit organizations, and government agencies sing the praises of diverse perspectives on their web pages, in their recruiting documents, and in their mission statements. They use *perspective* to mean "a way of thinking or representing." This use of *perspective* differs from both dictionary definitions, in which *perspective* means "a point of view," and formal definitions in art, in which the term *perspective* refers to the representation of three-dimensional objects in two dimensions.

Here, I distinguish between two types of representations: *perspectives* and *categorizations*. Perspectives assign a unique name to each object. Categorizations do not. They group the possibilities into disjoint sets. Identifying each element by an atomic number creates a perspective. Partitioning the elements based on their state at room temperature—gas, liquid, or solid—creates a categorization.

Perspective: *A representation that assigns a unique identifier to each member of a set of possibilities or alternatives.*

Mathematicians and engineers represent points in physical space using numerical perspectives. In two dimensions, the Cartesian coordinate system represents points by their horizontal and vertical displacements from the origin. A second perspective, the polar coordinate system, represents those same points by a radius (a distance from the origin) and an angle. Figure 2.2 shows a point on a plane represented within the Cartesian perspective as $x = 3$ and $y = 4$ and in the polar perspective as an angle of 53.1 degrees and a radius of 5.

The choice between these two geometric perspectives influences the points that we think of as near an existing point. Imagine that

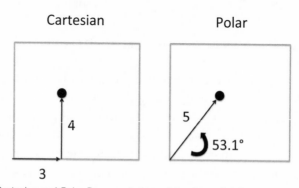

Figure 2.2 Cartesian and Polar Representations of the Same Point

Cartesian   Polar

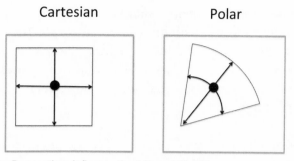

Figure 2.3 How Perspectives Influence the Adjacent Possible

figure 2.3 represents the possible location of a windmill on a large field. Two engineers might be seeking a location that maximizes the power the windmill generates.

If one engineer searches for locations using the Cartesian perspective, she will vary the horizontal and vertical positions of the windmill. The neighboring locations consist of a square. Complexity scholar Stuart Kauffman refers to these points as the *adjacent possible*.[7] If the other engineer applies a polar perspective, the points in the adjacent possible lie within a given angle and radius. The polar perspective creates a wedge on the field.

The two perspectives create distinct adjacent possibles. Engineers who use polar coordinates will think of different solutions from engineers who use Cartesian coordinates. These different sets of possible answers create a potential diversity bonus.

Perspectives need not be geometric. Each of the following creates a perspective on the one hundred largest cities in the United States: rank by population size, rank by area in square miles, longitude and latitude of city center, alphabetical order, and order by date of founding. Each arranges the cities differently and creates a different adjacent possible. If I say "Detroit," a person using an alphabetical perspective might think of Des Moines. A person thinking of population size might think of Seattle. As with the earlier example of Cartesian and polar coordinates, here diverse perspectives create distinct adjacent possibles that can result in diversity bonuses.

Perspectives uniquely identify alternatives. Often, we choose to be less precise and lump possibilities into categories. We say, "I saw Tonya at a coffee shop. She just bought a new pickup that is the same color of red as her sunglasses." The lumpy categories—car, red, and coffee shop—suffice. We need not add more detail to communicate the main ideas.

Categorization: *A partition of the possibilities or alternatives into disjoint sets.*

Categories enable us to navigate, predict, and understand our world. We use categorizations to make statements and inferences. Rada writes poetry. Maia excels at wrestling. Cooking in a broiler leads to undercooked centers.

To make precise inferences requires fine categorizations. This is why experts use more categories than nonexperts. A master gardener might classify daffodils according to their growing zone, color, and time of bloom.[8] A weekend gardener wandering in the nursery might classify all the varietals, including the delicate Canaliculatus, into a single category called "daffodils." A teenager might place them all in an even lumpier category called "flowers" or "plants."

Crude categorizations by novices offer fewer prospects of diversity bonuses. For a categorization to produce a diversity bonus, one of the categories must refine or only partly intersect with existing categories. The new category must organize the world differently.

Distinct categorizations also create different adjacent possibles. Figure 2.4 shows a categorization of ten cities by an American undergraduate. She places the four foreign cities in one pile, the three cities on the East Coast in a second pile, and the three western cities in a third pile.

Figure 2.5 shows a possible categorization of the cities by a European. She classifies New York, London, and Paris as cosmopolitan cities; Los Angeles, Sydney, and Barcelona as beach cities; and the other four cities as regional, American cities.

If a conference organizer had planned a meeting in New York but a lack of hotel space forces her to consider other locations, the American student might recommend Philadelphia or Boston. These are her

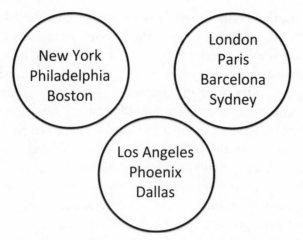

Figure 2.4 An American Categorization: East Coast, Western, and Foreign Cities

Figure 2.5 A European Categorization: Cosmopolitan, Beach, and US Regional Cities

adjacent possibles. An adviser with the European categorization might suggest London or Paris instead. The distinct categorizations create different adjacent possibles and, perhaps, a diversity bonus.

MENTAL MODELS AND FRAMEWORKS

Models are simplifications that identify key features. Models take many forms. Some models consist of a set of assumptions. Given those assumptions, the modeler then derives results. Other models are built to resemble the real world. Still other models fit data to functional forms. All models simplify. They leave out variables, lump distinct objects into different categories, and omit causal relationships.

Models also differ in their complexity. Laypeople apply intuitive mental models to make predictions and draw inferences. Economists construct sophisticated mathematical models that often rely on only a small number of variables. Climate scientists build elaborate models with thousands of variables that they calibrate to data.

Models have become ubiquitous. Organizational consultants, intelligence analysts, domestic policy advisers, and academics all use formal models to predict, design, explain, act, and explore. They also use models to get the logic right.[9] The rise of models is not a mystery. Model thinking outperforms thinking without models. In head-to-head predictive contests, models outperform human experts.[10]

As we will be applying models to tasks, I define them in relation to some domain, such as investing in stocks, writing a health care plan, or investing in infrastructure.

Model: *A systematic, simplified description that shares or captures relevant features of a domain.*

We often rely on folk models that describe relationships between categories: red sky at night, sailors' delight; defense wins championships; and so on. These models vary in their accuracy. When asked to make a prediction, we construct models. These models create a causal or correlative framework that connects what we know to what we expect to happen (see box).

Mental Models

Mental models are critical to allowing individuals to process what otherwise would be an incomprehensible volume of information. Yet they can cause analysts to overlook, reject, or forget important incoming or missing information that is not in accord with their assumptions and expectations.

—US Government, Tradecraft Primer

The most accurate mental models satisfy the laws of probability and are logically consistent. They do not ignore disconfirming facts, and they respond to new information.[11]

Models, along with categorizations, play a central role in prediction. Models relate information about the current situation to potential outcomes. People who are better at making predictions and forecasts employ many models.[12] Imagine an ensemble of models in a person's head, each one competing for attention. Good predictors search among them and combine insights from the best models. The person comes to resemble a diverse team.

To be accurate, models need information. Formal models embed information within equations. Models that forecast the weather include barometric pressure, wind speed, temperature, and humidity and then map these into distributions over outcomes.

Mental models and frameworks tend not to be as sophisticated and rely on categorical information. The aforementioned phrase, "Red sky at night, sailors' delight. Red sky at morning, sailors take warning," categorizes morning and evening skies as red or not red and makes predictions. That model, though not as accurate as modern meteorological models, rests on scientific foundations. High barometric pressure holds particulates lower in the atmosphere. These particulates scatter the longer red light waves, producing red skies. A red sky at night, that is, to the west, correlates with high pressure and good weather coming the sailors' way.

While model diversity can result from different categorizations, it can also arise from different causal structures applied to the same categories. Think of the categories as the nouns and causal structures as the verbs. One person's model might be that the richest one-fifth vote Republican because they want lower taxes. Another person's model might be that wealthy people vote Democratic because their financial security allows them to be empathetic to others. Though the two models use the same category (the richest one-fifth), they make different predictions.

These two mental models could be brought to data. The data would corroborate that the richest one-fifth have more often voted Republican in the past. If so, the empirical evidence would not be definitive. The data could be biased, or the future could differ from the past. Those caveats aside, data adjudicate between mental models. Useful mental models align with facts.

Different models can align with distinct facts. A realist model of international relations sees nation-states as self-interested actors and assumes that power dictates relations between states; a liberal model assumes larger, transnational interests. Realism assumes states in conflict; liberalism assumes coalitions with common purposes. These two models both compete and complement. Individually they might advocate different actions. Collectively, they lead to deeper understandings.

Neither model is right or wrong. One can find evidence for both models. Realists point to the failure of the League of Nations. Liberals respond with data on the rarity of wars between democracies.

THE GROUP AS THE UNION OF REPERTOIRES

In the best-case scenario, a group will have access to every component of its members' repertoires. If so, the group could apply any heuristic, mental model, or categorization known by a member. It could access any piece of information or knowledge of a phenomenon. It could act as a single individual with an enormous repertoire.

The challenges of coordination and cooperation mean that a group is not the same as a person with a large repertoire. Furthermore, an individual's repertoire may exhibit a coherence, a gestalt that a group's lacks. A person gathers information and knowledge that plugs into her mental models. A person develops representations and heuristics in tandem. Pieces fit together.

When we combine the repertoires of two people, no gestalt need emerge. One person may possess deep knowledge of international human rights treaties. A second person may know advanced techniques for translating text into categories. When they combine repertoires, they may find that the first person's categorization of treaties cannot be applied to the existing categories. The whole, in this case, may be less than the union of the parts. Had the person who categorized the treaties known how to apply translation techniques, she would have developed a tractable categorization.

Though a group may not apply its full repertoire ideally or may lack coherence in its repertoire, the fact remains that groups possess larger repertoires than the people who compose them. That largeness enables groups to produce diversity bonuses. The logic underpinning those bonuses is the focus of the next chapter.

DIVERSITY BONUSES: THE LOGIC

He who loves practice without theory is like the sailor who boards a ship without a rudder and compass and never knows where he may cast.

—LEONARDO DA VINCI

I NOW TURN TO MY PRIMARY AIM: TO EXPLAIN THE LOGIC OF DIVERSity bonuses. I do so by applying the formal characterization of cognitive repertoires to predicting, creating and innovating, problem solving, integrating knowledge, and strategic decision making. I first analyze the contributions of diversity to each activity separately and then describe how many decisions and actions require a combination of these activities. A team in charge of building a new airport terminal must predict demand, evaluate designs, and choose among locations. Each task will benefit from different types of diversity.

My central finding will be that diversity bonuses become more likely and more significant on complex tasks. Complexity increases in a problem's dimensionality and interdependencies. On complex tasks, no single person's repertoire will be sufficient, so teams will be needed, and those teams must be diverse.

The claim that we need teams is noncontroversial and backed up by mountains of data. However, the necessity of teams alone need not imply a diversity bonus. The best team could consist of the best individuals. To show the contribution of diversity in those teams, I rely on a collection of models. The models reveal mechanistic logic. In some cases, the models produce testable hypotheses. When data align with those hypotheses, we do not prove the models to be true so much as we demonstrate a resonance of the logic of the models with the real world.[1]

The models also provide guidance about whom to hire, admit, or include. Should Hollywood include more Muslims? Should colleges allocate spots to Native Americans? Do we make sure every academic conference panel includes one woman? To address those questions we must understand the causal mechanisms that can make two (different) heads better than one.

The field of chemistry provides an apt analogy. Diverse elements combine to form useful compounds like water, salt, sugar, baking soda, and bleach. These compounds exhibit properties distinct from those of their constituent elements. Biochemists attempting to create new compounds, whether for use in household cleaning solutions or as lifesaving molecules, do not randomly drop chemicals in a tube, stir, and hope for a miracle. They select chemical components based on understandings of their properties. Theory tells them where to look and to avoid wasting time on trying to turn base metals into gold. Theory provides rudder and compass.

To explain how diversity bonuses arise requires connecting cognitive repertoires to outcomes on specific tasks and then examining whether repertoire diversity improves outcomes. For any task or activity, the relevant parts of the repertoire differ. In predicting, a person's information, categorizations of that information, and models determine her individual accuracy. In innovating, diverse knowledge, representations, and heuristics result in more ideas. In problem solving, people also apply representations and heuristics. In knowledge integration, people leverage their knowledge sets. And in strategic play, people apply representations and heuristics, along with models of how competitors will respond.

For each of these tasks, how and why diversity bonuses arise varies. In prediction, diversity produces bonuses through negative correlation. In problem solving, heuristics build off one another. Where one person gets stuck, another person can find an improvement. On creative tasks, diverse representations create more possibilities. In knowledge integration, diverse understandings reduce the set of possible truths. In strategic play, diversity means less correlation in mistakes and better choices.

PREDICTIVE TASKS

In prediction, a group estimates a numerical value or range of possible values. These might be a future event (next year's unemployment rate), the result of an intervention (the effect of a regimen of low-dosage anti-inflammatories on a patient's heart rate), or a backcast of a historical event (the height of the ash plume from the Mount Vesuvius eruption in AD 79[2]). Inferring hidden values—such as the relative proportions of luck and skill in soccer and tennis—is also a form of prediction.[3]

Governments, nonprofits, and businesses devote billions of dollars to making predictions. NASA scientists and the International Panel on Climate Change predict the climatic effects of greenhouse gasses using environmental data. The Federal Open Market Committee predicts future inflation, growth, and unemployment rates using economic data. The Ford Motor Company predicts vehicle sales based on attributes of its fleet and those of its competitors. Google predicts the number of click-throughs based on the size of banner ads. These predictions inform actions. They assist NASA in setting thresholds for particulates, the Federal Open Market Committee in deciding on interest rates, Ford in determining production targets for cars, and Google in configuring ads.

People make predictions in a variety of ways. Some predictions derive from sophisticated causal models. Einstein's general theory of relativity predicted that light would bend in a gravitational field. During the 1919 solar eclipse, Arthur Eddington and Frank Watson Dyson showed that prediction to hold true by measuring light diffraction at two distant spots on the earth.

Scientific models like Einstein's *predict and explain*. Such models represent an ideal. More often, we lack rich theories and make predictions that extrapolate from past patterns. Machine learning algorithms make predictions in this way. They identify patterns based on training data and test those patterns on other data.

These algorithms bin the data into multiple categories and identify patterns. The internal logic of the predictive models is impenetrable to the human mind. We cannot know why the algorithms predict what they do. We may not care. When we wake in the morning and see a 90 percent chance of rain in the afternoon, we do not care about the details of the meteorological model. We care about the forecast's accuracy. We want to know whether to pack an umbrella.[4]

Similar thinking applies to predictions of surgical interventions. If a machine learning algorithm applied to tens of thousands of cases finds that older women who receive titanium hip replacements who perform mild exercise at least three times daily exhibit fewer long-term complications than those who do not, you should tell your aunt Deloris to exercise. And she should listen to you, even though the algorithm provides no reason.

All else equal, we would prefer to have an explanation and an understanding of a phenomenon. If doctors knew the determinants of hip replacement success, perhaps increased tendon flexibility, they could develop better rehabilitation protocols. Nevertheless, the millions of people receiving hip implants, including your aunt Deloris, benefit now from the accurate prediction. They need not wait for an understanding of why exercise improves outcomes. The same pragmatism applies to predictions of the recidivism of criminals, the success of a new sales hire, or the length of an economic recession. We can take useful actions with accurate predictions even if we lack a causal understanding.[5]

Machine learning techniques require lots of data. When we have less data, we use people and simple models. For easier predictions, a single person or model may suffice. We do not need a diverse team to predict tomorrow's sunrise in Anchorage, Alaska. Diversity begins to matter and becomes significant on difficult predictions, where no one model will be correct. In those cases, predictions based on different information, categories, and models will make different errors. These less correlated errors produce a more accurate collective prediction. In the ideal case, to borrow Richard Levins's phrasing, the truth will lie "at the intersection of our independent lies."

That said, a diverse group offers no guarantee of perfect accuracy. However, as I show next, diversity does improve accuracy.

The Diversity Prediction Theorem

Diversity bonuses in prediction can be quantified with a mathematical identity: the diversity prediction theorem.[6] That identity reveals that ability (measured by accuracy) and diversity contribute equally to collective accuracy. Thus, the best predictive groups will include both accurate and diverse predictors.

The formal statement of the diversity prediction theorem requires four statistics calculated from the predictions of a group of people or models.[7]

Prediction Error: *The square of the difference between a prediction and the true value.*
Average Error: *The average of the group members' prediction errors.*
Collective Error: *The prediction error of the average of the group members' predictions.*
Predictive Diversity: *The variance of the group members' predictions.*

A low prediction error corresponds to high ability. A group with a lower average error has higher average ability. Collective error corresponds to the ability of the group. Finally, predictive diversity corresponds to the variation in the predictions.

The diversity prediction theorem states that collective error equals average error minus predictive diversity (see box). In other words, the accuracy of the group depends equally on the average accuracy of its members and their collective diversity. No tradeoff between diversity and ability exists. Accurate collective predictions depend on both.

The diversity prediction theorem describes a mathematical identity. It holds true for any collection of predictions. Those could be guesses of the number of jelly beans in a jar by third graders at Angell Elementary School or predictions of interest rates by economists working for the United States Federal Reserve.[8]

Diversity Prediction Theorem

Collective Error = Average Error − Predictive Diversity

(Group Ability = Average Ability + Diversity)

Numbers from a real case make the logic clearer. I once asked sixty students to guess the number of ridges on a US quarter. The correct answer is 120. The average of the predictions was a little over 137. Some guessed fewer than 50 ridges. Others guessed more than 250. Plugging their predictions into the diversity prediction theorem produced the following equation:

US Quarter Predictions

Collective Error (296) = Average Error (6726) − Predictive Diversity (6430)

In interpreting these numbers, recall that we measure errors as squares of differences. The group missed the mark by a little more than 17. The average error exceeded 80. The average error far exceeds their collective error because the predictions were diverse. Some students predicted above 120, while other students predicted below 120. The high and low guesses cancel out.

The same students predicted the length in miles of the London Tube. In this case, the collective prediction (249 miles) was within one of the true value (250 miles) even though, on average, most students made wildly inaccurate predictions, as shown in the equation below:

London Tube Predictions

Collective Error (1) = Average Error (63,698) − Predictive Diversity (63,697)

In this case, most students guessed fewer than 200 miles, while two people guessed over 750 miles. Each of those two people produced squared errors in excess of 250,000. These two students knew that the Tube covered most of London and overestimated. Most of the other students had not been to London and assumed limited public transportation systems.

From these two examples, it might appear that the diversity prediction theorem guarantees a diversity bonus. That is not true. Adding an inaccurate prediction can increase average error by more than it increases predictive diversity. If so, the net accuracy falls.[9]

To see how adding wildly inaccurate predictions can make the group less accurate, consider the extreme case of an easy prediction in which each person makes an accurate prediction. Collective error, average error, and diversity all equal zero. Adding an inaccurate, and, by definition, diverse prediction, makes the collective prediction incorrect. Though the bad prediction increases diversity, it increases average error even more.[10]

The diversity prediction theorem has three corollaries that bear keeping in mind. The first corollary states that crowd error cannot be larger than average error. This holds because diversity cannot be negative. In the students' predictions of the length of the London Tube, the crowd error was substantially less than average error. A group that lacks diversity will not be much more accurate than any one predictor. Large predictive error will therefore be more likely among groups that think alike. To the same extent that the *wisdom of crowds* depends on diversity, the *madness of crowds* depends on a lack of it. A price bubble depends on inaccurate price estimates that all err in the same direction.

Three Features of Predictive Groups

(i). A diverse group will always be more accurate than the average of its members.

(ii). A group's accuracy depends in equal parts on the average accuracy of its members and their diversity.

(iii). Adding a more accurate predictor or a more diverse predictor can make a group more accurate.

The idea behind the second corollary—that the collective will be more accurate because of diversity—is not a new idea. It goes back to at least Aristotle and was echoed and emended by Friedrich A. Hayek in the context of the economy.[11] The fact that they contribute equally we obtain through algebra. The equal weighting of accuracy and diversity leads to counterintuitive insights.

Imagine that we had to select three students out of a class of twenty to make a group prediction. Assume that we know the accuracy of each student on past predictions and we know the diversity for all groups of three students.

Our first intuition might be to select the three most accurate students. That group would have the lowest average error. Recall though that the group's error depends in equal measure on their diversity. By choosing the group with the smallest average error, we ignore diversity. We ignore half of the equation. If the three most accurate people all think the same way, then we have no diversity. Selecting the group of three people with the largest diversity makes even less sense. To have high diversity, the group must have an even higher average error. The best approach is to search among all 570 possible groups for the one whose diversity is closest to its accuracy.

The final corollary reveals two routes to creating a more accurate group prediction: we can add someone more accurate or someone diverse who is not horribly inaccurate. In the Netflix Prize competition, BellKor was the most accurate, so they had no one better to add. Here again, we see why problem difficulty correlates with diversity bonuses. On difficult predictions, developing a different predictive model is often easier than developing a more accurate one.

The same logic that applies to groups applies to individuals. Individuals who excel at predicting keep many models in their head. They mimic a diverse crowd. Individuals who employ a single model or way of thinking are less accurate than many model thinkers. In fact, a single-model thinker will be less accurate than random selection in predicting whether a trend will increase, decrease, or stay the same.[12]

Information, Categories, and Mental Models

Within a single person or a group, diverse predictions have similar causes. People make predictions, whether formal or informal, using their cognitive repertoires. They apply models to categories of information. Different information, different categorizations of that information, or different models will produce diverse predictions. These causes of diversity apply individually or in any combination.

Suppose, for example, that two people possess different information but categorize the world similarly and use similar models. Those two people will make different predictions even if they use the same category and the same model.

That different information could come from different life experiences. Two students trying to determine the number of miles in the London Tube might both use the same category, *major international city public transportation systems*, and the same model, *public transportation systems have similar numbers of miles of track per resident*. The students would make different predictions if they based them on different information. One student may have been to Paris and Amsterdam. Paris has a population of 2.2 million residents. The Paris Metro has 113 miles of track, or 1 mile of track per 20,000 residents. Amsterdam has a population of 750,000 residents and 25 miles of track in their metro system, an average of 1 mile per 30,000 residents. Taking the average of the two cities gives a predictive model of 1 mile of track per 25,000 residents. Using that estimate, the student would predict 350 miles of track for London's 8.75 million residents.

The second student could apply the same model but use information from Rome and Vienna. Rome's metro has 37 miles of track and Vienna's U-Bahn has 49 miles of track. Given Rome's 2.7 million residents and Vienna's 1.7 million, she calculates that Rome has 1 mile per 70,000 residents and Vienna 1 mile per every 35,000 residents. If the student estimates 1 mile per 50,000 residents, she then predicts that the London Tube will have 175 miles of track.[13]

The two students make different predictions because they have visited different cities. Those experiences could connect to identity diversity: One student may have visited Paris because of her French ancestry. The other might have visited Rome because of her Italian mother. Or, the experiences could have come about for some other reason. What is relevant is that their different experiences caused them to rely on different information when making a prediction.

Category diversity can also produce diverse predictions. Functional categorizations group items with relevant features. To predict the quality of restaurants in Chicago, categorizing restaurants by their first three letters would not capture relevant features. That categorization would lump Chicago's Tre Kronor, an upscale Swedish restaurant; Tres Amigos, a low-priced Mexican restaurant; and Tre Soldi, a trattoria and pizzeria, into the same category: restaurants beginning with *Tre*.

A more useful categorization would classify restaurants by their distance from the Loop (the city center). This would be a relevant categorization provided that restaurants nearer the Loop have higher quality. A second useful categorization would distinguish between restaurants in posh hotels and restaurants not in those hotels. The corresponding model would be that hotel restaurants have higher quality. A third categorization could distinguish restaurants by their longevity. The associated model would predict that Chicago's Berghoff restaurant, which has been in continuous operation since 1898, would be of high quality.

Each of the models based on these categorizations produces better-than-random predictions. Each also makes mistakes. Chicago's Billy Goat Tavern, famous for its cheeseburgers, has been in operation since 1934. Contrary to the longevity model, it is not of high quality. The model based on hotels will classify the Billy Goat correctly, thought it does err on the Berghoff. The other two models classify the Berghoff correctly. In addition to being around for more than one hundred years, it is also near the city center.

People who rely on diverse categorizations will make distinct predictions and, therefore, by the diversity prediction theorem will be more accurate as a group than they are on average. The potential for diverse categorizations increases in the dimensionality of the data or experiences. Restaurants can be categorized in dozens if not hundreds of relevant ways. Each of those categorizations can create a diverse model. Thus, we see a link between dimensionality and the potential for diversity bonuses.

The linkage between diverse categorizations and diverse models also reveals why more data implies more potential for diversity bonuses. A group of analysts fed only a small amount of data cannot construct many different models. Analysts with access to rich data sources can construct any number of plausible models. Those diverse models can combine to make a more accurate prediction, and they can offer up more accurate worst- and best-case scenarios.

Diverse models provide a third source of diverse predictions, even if people can have access to the same data and rely on similar if not identical categories. On difficult predictions, that is, in contexts in which the relationship between the data and outcomes is more complicated, models will be more likely to differ. The same holds for models with more variables. If two people fit the model $y = mx + b$, and have the same data for x and y, they will arrive at the same values of m and b. Two climatologists building complex climate change models with thousands of variables will not choose the same functional forms and therefore will not arrive at the same coefficient. Each model will make different predictions. And we know that a combination of those models will be more accurate than the average model. For this reason, the International Panel on Climate Change combines twenty-three distinct atmosphere-ocean general circulation models to make its predictions.

We should interpret this diversity of models as a method for handling the complexity of the predictive task and not as a lack of understanding. Climate change is far too complex to predict exactly. However, if the different models based on the same data are approximately equal in their accuracy, then collectively they will be more accurate than *any* of the models.

We already saw how that occurred in the Netflix Prize competition. The two final models had equal accuracy and differed. Therefore, their average had to be more accurate. Figure 3.1 shows the same phenomenon occurring in models of genotype identification. The graph measures *discordance*, so lower lines correspond to more accurate models. The top line represents the Eli Broad Institute at MIT, and the next two interwoven lines represent the Sanger Institute at Harvard and Goncola Abecasis's lab at the University of

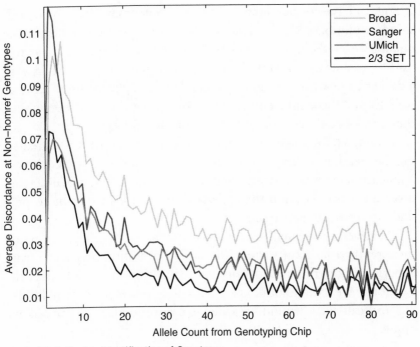

Figure 3.1 Collective Identification of Genotypes

Michigan. To make these identifications, the biostatisticians rely on DNA, so they necessarily use the same information. The diversity that arises must therefore arise from different categorizations and models.

In this example, all three models have roughly the same discordance. The bottom line in the graph represents the discordance of a collective classification based on majority voting (labeled as $\frac{2}{3}$ in the graph). The collective outperforms each model. Given that the three models differ and have approximately the same accuracy, that must be true.

These results and those of the Netflix Prize competition both show how everyone can be a winner. In each case, an ensemble of all the participants outperformed the individual winner. The Eli Broad Institute's model, though least accurate, contributes to the winning ensemble.

So far I have considered predictions of outcomes that can be measured in numbers like interest rates and rainfall. People also make qualitative predictions such as whether a foreign-policy action will lead to greater or less stability or whether painting an interior wall a darker color warms a room. A related logic applies in those cases as well. Even if those predictions cannot be averaged to a single number, they can be coalesced into a richer understanding.

In sum, whether analyzing data in a scientific laboratory, predicting the weather or climate, or estimating future downloads of a new application, diverse information, categorizations, and models create diverse predictions, and those diverse predictions combine to produce accurate collective predictions.

The diverse information, categorizations, and models that create these predictions have various sources. Information may come from experiences or training. Identity and education may well affect the categories we use and our experiences. In addition, our formal training and our background knowledge can influence the models we apply.

The weight we might place on identity varies by case. If predicting consumer demand for the Dyson Supersonic hair dryer, we would probably want gender and racial diversity. Given the product's cost ($399), we might prefer wealthier consumers; that is, not want income diversity. Nor might we seek out religious diversity.

In contrast, to gauge the appeal of a political candidate or the usefulness of a new student loan program, we would want diversity of wealth and religion, as borrowing practices vary by religion. In making predictions about the likely side effects of a drug, identity might play a small role, if any. But if predicting the ability of a diverse set of people to follow a treatment regimen that includes the drug, we would again want to cast a wide net.

As a rule, we should seek out diverse people. We should contemplate how and why identity diversity might matter. In any given case, the choice of whom to include requires careful thought. We should not blindly pursue identity diversity any more than we should necessarily take the best, that is, most accurate, people.

The diversity prediction theorem shows why and how diversity bonuses occur. It also shows why adding diversity without forethought offers no magical bonus. If we ask a random person on the street how much oceans will rise in the next fifty years or what will happen to interest rates in Greece in the next five years, we will not experience a diversity bonus. Those people will increase diversity but reduce accuracy.

Accurate groups consist of people with distinct information sets, diverse and informative categorizations, and diverse accurate models. No hard and fast rule exists for whom to add to a group. If deciding to add the opinion of another person or to add a second predictive model, data and theory support a rule of thumb called the *not half-bad rule*: the second person should be included so long as he or she is not more than 50 percent less accurate.[14]

Artificial Intelligence: Boosting Diversity

The same types of machine learning algorithms that forecast medical outcomes have revolutionized the field of artificial intelligence. Over the past three decades, the field of artificial intelligence has shifted away from single, sophisticated algorithms to ensembles of diverse predictors. For example, the state-of-the-art Google Translate software relies on ensembles of predictors that scan the web for words, phrases, and sentences and learn patterns. The program constructs translations by predicting sentences and structures based on writings it finds on the web. This results in more natural sentence structures. In the past, programs that translated French into English would contain internal French-English dictionaries and would apply built-in rules of syntax and grammar.

Computer scientists describe these individual classifiers as *weak learners*. For the ensemble as a whole to predict accurately, the classifiers within the ensemble must differ.[15] They must look at unique feature sets or assume different relationships between features. The weak learners range from relatively sophisticated neural networks to the simple if-then decision rules used in *random forest algorithms*.[16]

The diversity prediction theorem provides a logic for the accuracy of these ensembles: the average of diverse predictions must be more accurate than the average prediction. That same logic applies to groups of people. A puzzle therefore remains as to why these ensembles of algorithms outperform groups of people by such a wide margin. The theorem provides intuition for that as well.

The collective accuracy of an ensemble of people or machines depends on the accuracy of each predictor and their diversity. Ideally, we would restrict the ensemble to accurate and diverse predictors. That would make the ensemble accurate. Machine learning programs do exactly that. The aforementioned random forest algorithms begin with a collection of random decision-tree predictors.[17] Using a sample of the data to determine accuracy, the algorithm separates out the accurate decision trees. This procedure kicks out the inaccurate predictors. We cannot always do that with groups of people. We may not be able to evaluate people over past cases and boot out less accurate predictors.

Futhermore, ensemble methods train their predictors on subsets of data. This all but guarantees predictors that are accurate. We have no guarantee that people make reasonable inferences. People often apply woefully inaccurate models. Thus, the machine learning ensembles have a built-in accuracy advantage.

The algorithmic ensembles also build in diversity. They do so through *bagging* and *boosting*. Bagging trains predictors on randomly drawn subsets of examples. So the predictors learn from different experiences. This all but guarantees diversity. The analogy to the benefits of including people with different experiences holds with a small caveat. The machine learning algorithms determine the number of experiences, that is, the size of the bags, that is large enough and representative enough that the predictors will be accurate yet small enough to ensure some diversity. A person's experiences may not be representative, and that could lead to an inaccurate prediction. For a new, diverse predictor to increase accuracy, it must be relatively accurate.

The second technique, boosting, engineers diversity by adding predictors that are accurate when the ensemble makes mistakes.

Suppose that we want to train an ensemble of predictors to classify bank loans as either successes or failures and that we have one thousand cases for which we know the outcome. We can use those to train our predictors. We might first generate eighty random predictors. For each, we might choose four hundred random cases (recall that this is bagging) and only keep those predictors that classified more than 55 percent of their cases correctly. We next have those predictors collectively classify the one thousand cases. We might find that the ensemble predicts correctly on eight hundred cases. Call the other two hundred cases the *difficult cases*.

To perform boosting, we create a new random set of predictors. We train those predictors on the two hundred cases for which the previous ensemble made mistakes. We add to the ensemble those predictors that classify the two hundred cases correctly more than half the time. Given that the original ensemble classified those cases incorrectly, these new predictors must be diverse. Adding them to the ensemble increases accuracy.[18] Thus, boosting, like bagging, generates diverse predictors and helps to produce an accurate ensemble.

Prediction Markets

In light of the awe-inspiring breakthroughs of artificial intelligence that leverage the combined power of accuracy and diversity, we might ask whether we cannot achieve similar success with groups of people. We know the end goal: an ensemble of smart, diverse people. One route mimics the machine learning algorithms and applies the logic of the diversity prediction theorem. Begin with a large set of predictors, test them, and choose accurate predictors that are diverse. Evidence supports that approach. Teams of the best predictors predict with high accuracy, as do teams chosen by the diversity of their predictions.[19]

These approaches rely on a top-down organization to construct the ensemble. Prediction markets provide a novel bottom-up approach to obtain similar results. In a prediction market, individuals place bets on outcomes and receive payouts based on their success.

Prediction markets ensure a degree of accuracy through market forces. Predictors who consistently lose money will leave the market. People who make money, those who are more accurate, will remain.

Prediction markets create incentives for diversity because predictions that disagree with the majority earn higher payoffs if correct. In a winner-take-all prediction market, people may buy assets that pay one dollar if a specific outcome occurs. That outcome could be the winner of an election or a sporting event or the release of a new product by a certain date. If people do not think an event will occur, then the price of the corresponding stock will be low. A bargain, in a prediction market, is a stock corresponding to a likely event that has a low price. The large payoffs from these bargains create an incentive to identify systematic biases in prices. In theory, that incentive mimics a boosting algorithm, resulting in accurate aggregate predictions.

Though theoretically appealing, prediction markets have not been widely implemented. One obvious reason is the lack of a population of engaged accurate predictors. Unlike the classifiers included in ensemble methods, the models applied by individuals in prediction markets need not be accurate. To make accurate predictions, a prediction market needs intelligent, informed, diverse predictors. If we ran a market of fifth graders who were to predict the price of the Japanese yen against the euro in three months' time, we should not expect accuracy.

Prediction markets suffer from two other potential shortcomings. If the stakes are too small, people may not take them seriously or experiment with manipulating the market to exploit trends. Also, under some conditions the implicit probabilities produced by a prediction market do not align with the participants' beliefs of those probabilities.[20]

These potential shortcomings aside, several large companies including Ford, Google, HP, Best Buy, and General Electric have experimented with or operate internal prediction markets. Rarely are the predictions the sole reason for taking an action. Instead, their predictions are combined with or contrasted with other methods.

They become part of an ensemble of predictors. HP and Best Buy have relied on prediction markets and forecasts of experts. By having two diverse methods for predicting, they hope to obtain more accurate predictions. Corporate prediction markets also promote a culture of inclusion. They provide a mechanism for employees to give voice to their opinions, albeit in numerical form.

CREATIVE TASKS

When we predict, we apply what we know to estimate something unknown. We organize our information and experience into categories and apply models. Those models range from elaborate statistical estimates to gut intuitions. In either case, we know the form those predictions will take. The outcome of an election will be one of a handful of candidates, a mean temperature will be a number between −40 and 120 degrees, and a stock price will be a positive number. We know the arrival time of a flight to Los Angeles will not be "banana" or "Luxembourg."

When we create, we try to come up with novel idea or solution. We may lack any conception of the form a solution or idea will take. The mechanical clock was a long-shot winner in the contest to develop a method for determining a ship's longitude.[21] Sometimes, creative ideas are constructed from whole cloth. They can also derive from existing artifacts and products. Apple's iPod is a miniature personal jukebox, the television remote control is a repurposed garage-door opener, and the 1970s mood ring is thermotropic medical tape transformed into jewelry.[22]

We can think of a creative act as pulling an idea or thought from a set of possibilities. What a person imagines that set of possibilities to be depends on how she represents or categorizes the world, and on her information and knowledge. Thus, diversity in those parts of our repertoires will produce diverse, creative ideas.

New ideas also arise from recombinations of items: the combustion and steam engine combined parts sitting on the factory floor, Hormel's Spam mixed ham and pork in a perfect ratio, and the fax machine combined the copier and the telephone. Recombination produces superadditivity. One plus one equals three because each new idea contributes on its own and in combination with the others.[23]

Owing to the potential for repurposing and recombining, the value of a new idea or an innovation will not be revealed for some time. The practical applications of the laser, the combustion engine, and the wheel all rolled out over time.[24] The team that developed small, user-controlled drones probably did not anticipate their use by realtors to capture aerial shots of properties, by journalists to view political uprisings and crime scenes from above, or their long-term potential for pizza delivery.

Creativity involves a mixture of intelligence, perseverance, and serendipity. A group's creativity will also be enhanced by its cognitive diversity. We already saw how diverse perspectives of physical space produce distinct adjacent possibles. That result provides a hint as to why the most creative groups need not consist of the most creative individuals. The people must also bring diverse repertoires.

Measuring Creativity

To demonstrate the contribution of diversity to the creativity of a team requires a measure of creativity. Psychologists measure creativity by the ability to generate original, diverse, and useful ideas. One common measure equals the number of ideas. More sophisticated measures include the depth and variety of ideas.

Regardless of the measure we use, we should expect a person's creativity to correlate with her richness of experiences, and studies do find that multicultural experiences increase creativity.[25] We should also expect a person's creativity to increase with the number of perspectives or categories she can apply to a task and with the granularity or fineness of her categorizations. A furniture builder who distinguishes among hundreds of types of dressers should be able to create more new designs for a dresser than a layperson who categorizes them by the number of drawers.

Psychological tests used to measure creativity pose open-ended questions. In the *tourist problem*, subjects generate ideas for increasing tourism to the United States.[26] In the *fame problem*, subjects must conceive of a route for a person with no special talents to achieve fame.[27]

The canonical creativity test, the *Alternative Uses Task*, presents a subject with a common object, often a brick. The subject must describe as many uses of the brick as possible within a fixed time period.[28] A person's score on this brick test can be measured by the number of ideas, by the originality of those ideas, by the amount of detail elaborated, or by the number of categories of uses.

A noncreative subject might respond that a brick could be used as a boat anchor, to build a wall, to build a house, or to break a window. This list consists of four unoriginal ideas, expressed with little detail. These answers could be placed in three common categories: brick as weight, brick as construction material, and brick as weapon. None of his answers would be classified as original.

A higher-scoring subject might offer that a brick could secure a tablecloth during a windy picnic or a tarp during a roof repair, displace water in a toilet tank, represent a brick building in a model train display, hammer tent stakes, serve as a Medieval knight's coaster, level a table with uneven legs, sharpen knives, or, if broken into pieces, make arrowheads, knives, jewelry, chalk, or screwdrivers. These answers add new categories: brick as tool, brick as representation, and brick as composition.

The Alternative Uses Task maps directly to real-world situations. A chef must think of what to do with an excess of day-old halibut, a developer must think of development options for a piece of land, and a theater owner must think of events that will draw crowds on Saturday morning.

Not all creative tasks involve thinking up uses for a single object. Some tasks require the opposite: they require people to come up with multiple objects for a single use. Designing emojis is an example of an opposite task. A successful emoji will be fun, informative, and nonoffensive. In the October 2015 release of iOS 9.1, Apple added 184 new emojis, including a lion, a snowboard, a taco, a unicorn, a rolled-up newspaper, and the popular face with rolling eyes.

Diversity Bonuses on Creative Tasks

On a creative task, we can define a person's diversity relative to a group as the number of unique ideas that she adds.[29] Using this measure of diversity, it follows that the creativity of a group will depend on both the creativity of individuals and their diversity. Walking through the algebra of an example shows why. Imagine that four people take the brick test. The two most creative people each generate ten ideas. The two least creative people each generate six ideas.

The creativity of the group of the two most creative people equals twenty minus the overlap in their ideas. If they have no diversity, then their joint creativity will be no greater than their individual creativity. If they have maximal diversity, that is, if they have no overlap in their ideas, then the two of them generate twenty ideas. Similarly, the number of unique ideas from the two least creative people equals twelve minus the overlap in their ideas. Barring almost complete overlap between the two most creative people, those two will be more creative as a team than the least creative two.

There also exist two groups consisting of one creative person and one noncreative person. Each of those groups generates at most sixteen ideas. If one of these groups has little to no overlap, they could form the most creative group. The key intuition builds on the logic developed in the stylized tool model. If the creative people both think of ideas using the same line of thought, that is, if their ideas arise in the same order like in the train trip analogy, they will have complete overlap and produce no bonuses. If they generate ideas along different routes, like in the analogy of the trip to the zoo, they will produce bonuses.

We can define the problem of finding the most creative group as follows:

The Most Creative Group Problem: *Given a set of people, choose a group of a given size that has the highest creativity.*

For the reasons just mentioned, the most creative group need not consist of the most creative people. To gain insights for when it will and when it will not, we can again use the brick test. There exist thousands of possible uses for a brick. It could function as a stand for a dog bowl. It could represent a couch in a Barbie play scene. Imagine writing each possible idea on a piece of paper and placing all of those pieces of paper in a giant box.

We can then think of an individual who generates an idea as reaching into that box. Creative people reach into the box many times. Noncreative people reach in less often. If people randomly draw from the box, then any two people draw each idea with the same probability. If that were true, then the most creative group would generally consist of the most creative people.[30]

Instead of assuming that all ideas belong to the same box, we might alternatively assume two types of ideas: typical ideas and unusual ideas. Typical ideas include using bricks to build walls or fireplaces and destructive uses like breaking a window or smashing pottery. Few people think of using the brick as a couch for a Barbie.

To model these two types of ideas, we can keep the typical ideas *inside the box* and take the unusual ideas *outside the box*. Suppose there exist one hundred inside-the-box ideas and an enormous, near-infinite number of unusual, outside-the-box ideas. The latter assumption implies that no two outside-the-box ideas will match.

In this more elaborate model, a person's creativity still equals the number of ideas she generates. Her creativity score does not depend on whether an idea comes from inside or outside the box. However, if forming a large group, we care more about the number of outside-the-box ideas a person generates than her total number of ideas. To see why, suppose we are forming a group of ten people. Creative groups of nine people will generate most of the inside-the-box ideas. Adding a person with fifty inside-the-box ideas and only five outside-the-box ideas adds few new ideas. A person who thinks of twenty inside-the-box ideas and also twenty outside-the-box ideas adds more new ideas. Though she is less creative, her ideas do not duplicate those of others.

The Alphabet of the Famous

On actual creative tasks, an idea that is obvious to one person may be outside the box to another, so I drop the assumption of ideas as either inside or outside the box. Instead, I think of ideas as belonging to knowledge domains. A person's training, experiences, and identity influence her knowledge domains and therefore the types of ideas she generates. A diver thinks of using a brick as ballast. A chef thinks of cooking chicken on bricks.

The link between identity diversity and diversity bonuses on creative tasks operates through these knowledge domains. Interests vary by identity group. Men and women watch different television shows, visit different websites, and read different books. Race, religion, ethnicity, and age also correlate with these activities. Identity-diverse groups can therefore produce more ideas because they draw from different experiences, interests, and knowledge bases.

I have found that links between identity and knowledge can be revealed by the *Alphabet of the Famous Test*. This test measures ability by a person's capacity to think of famous people. To conduct the test, each subject writes the alphabet vertically on a sheet of paper. Someone chooses a sentence that contains at least twenty-six letters, such as "Keen at the start, but careless at the end," by Cornelius Tacitus. Each subject writes that sentence vertically, pairing each letter with a letter from the alphabet. Each letter pair represents a pair of initials. The subject tries to think of a famous person

A	K	Andy Kauffman (Comedian)
B	E	Barbara Ehrenreich (Writer)
C	E	
D	N	
E	A	Ethan Allen (Patriot)
F	T	
G	T	

. . . . . .

Figure 3.2 Possible Answers to the Alphabet of the Famous Test

A	K	Al Kaline (Baseball)
B	E	Billy Evans (Baseball)
C	E	
D	N	Dickie Noles (Baseball)
E	A	Elvis Araujo (Baseball)
F	T	Frank Thomas (Baseball)
G	T	

. . . . . .

Figure 3.3 Baseball Answers to Alphabet of the Famous Test

for each pair of initials, as shown in figure 3.2. The criterion for being famous must be agreed upon beforehand. It might be having a Wikipedia page with more than five hundred words.

On this test, any knowledge proves useful. People who perform well tend to be experts in domains with lots of famous people. The test therefore advantages people who follow popular music, the movies, or professional sports like football, baseball, or soccer. Each of these domains contains a large number of famous people. People with knowledge of classical music, tennis, or video games perform less well, as these domains have fewer stars. Professional tennis has fewer famous players than baseball, football, or soccer, and the movies feature hundreds of stars, while video games include few real people.

As a result, the most creative people in the Alphabet of the Famous Test, those who follow football, baseball, movies, or music, often overlap in their knowledge domains. If so, the best group on this test will not consist of the best individuals. To make that claim more explicit, consider that a baseball fanatic might come up with the names shown in figure 3.3.

If the best performers are all baseball fans, they might have similar lists. A group of the best will not score much higher than the single best person. In contrast, a group of less creative individuals consisting of someone who follows women's tennis, a person who followed 1970s television, a political junkie, and a follower of reality

A   K   Andy Kauffman (Comedian)
B   E   Barbara Eden (Actress)
C   E   Chris Evert (Tennis Player)
D   N   Deborah Norville (Former News Anchor)
E   A   Ethan Allen (Patriot)
F   T   Fred Thompson (US Senator)
G   T   Georgia Toffolo (Reality TV Star)

. . . . . .

Figure 3.4 A Diverse Group's Answers to the Alphabet of the Famous Test

television might generate a famous person for each of the first seven pairs, as shown in figure 3.4. The group's diversity, not their individual creativity, would enable them to outperform the group of the best individuals, all of whom happen to be baseball fans.

On scientific creative challenges, identity may play less of a role than background. Carol Fierke's chemistry lab at the University of Michigan investigates compounds that inhibit farnesyltransferase (FTase) as potential antitumor agents. Finding inhibitors involves searching microbial plant sources for the proper chemical structures. Only students trained in chemistry and biology (or possibly physics) possess the relevant knowledge. Knowledge of baseball, reality television, or music will not be of much use.

On this task, the relevant diversity corresponds to a person's information about various plants or her knowledge of chemical compounds. These types of diversity result from differences in training, or different laboratory experiences. To achieve those diversity bonuses, scientists populate their laboratories with postdoctoral students trained at different universities or with unique specializations. An identity diversity effect could arise if, based on her cultural background, someone knew of a particular fungus. Though such serendipity can occur, it is not a long lever on which to stand.

The Alphabet of the Famous Test and the FTase inhibitor task capture the two extremes. In the former, identity diversity correlates with variation in interests. In the latter, we would not expect identity diversity to have much of a direct effect. The scientific tasks require diversity among specialists. In between these two extremes lie an enormous number of creative tasks confronted on a regular basis by information specialists, lawyers, consultants, civic engineers, teachers, architects, administrators, project managers, and hospitality directors. The role of identity will again vary. In coming up with a provocative advertising slogan or a novel legal defense, identity diversity may matter significantly. For other creative tasks, such as coming up with an oven exhaust hood design, identity may matter less.

No hard and fast rules apply. Identity diversity probably matters more when people's preferences or interests determine an idea's value. Groups proposing restaurant designs, themes for a party, changes to an employee-compensation plan, possible recipients of honorary degrees, or designs for a public park should expect identity-driven diversity bonuses. The identity characteristics that are relevant when proposing degree recipients, likely race and gender, may differ from those relevant to designing a public park, perhaps age and physical abilities, as may the weight of identity and whether it acts alone or in combination with experiences and education.

The Medici Effect

Up to now, we have considered creative ideas in isolation. Often, ideas can be recombined. If so, this creates an additional bonus. Recombinations arise through interactions. People do not walk into a room, dump their ideas on the table, and leave. Ideas are shared, challenged, refined, and recombined.

These interactions occur on multiple scales. We share and combine ideas within small work teams, within scientific disciplines, and across cities and nations. If we look across time and place, we see many instances—Florence in the fifteenth century, Detroit at the dawn of the twentieth century, or Silicon Valley today—in which the geographic concentration of ideas enabled recombinations and refinements with wondrous consequences.[31] Italians incorporated pasta from China into their cuisine. Henry Ford brought the assembly line from meatpacking and gun assembly to the car industry.

The potential for recombination increases the value of ideas. If we count by ideas alone as we have done so far, creativity is *subadditive*. One person has ten ideas. The other person has eight ideas. Together they have at most eighteen ideas. If the two people overlap on four ideas, together they have fourteen ideas. Mathematicians describe these calculations as *subadditive* because fourteen is less than eighteen, the sum.

Counting by the number of combinations reveals the potential for *superadditivity* from sharing. A person who thinks up ten ideas can create 45 pairs of ideas. A second person who thinks up eight ideas can combine them to create 28 unique pairs, for a total of 73 pairs. Recall that the number of ideas thought up by the pair is additive at best. That is, at most they could think up eighteen ideas. More likely, they would overlap in their ideas and only create, say, fourteen total.

However, those fourteen pairs produce 91 combinations. Individually, the pair created only 73 combinations $(45 + 28 = 73)$. Recombination, in this case, is superadditive, that is, more than the sum. If the pair had no overlap of ideas, they could create 153 combinations of ideas, an even greater amount of superadditivity.[32]

These combinatoric calculations portend an explosion of possibilities. Were a high percentage of those combinations useful, creativity would be child's play. We would be overwhelmed with useful new ideas. Sadly, they are not.[33] We gain little by combining the remote control and the donut or the telephone and the blender. Idea combinations that work often come from related fields or domains.[34] This low probability of any one combination succeeding partly cancels out the benefits of the superadditive combinations.

That said, within a product category, it will often be the case that almost all combinations function just fine. The Italian fashion brand Prada allows customers to design their own shoes by choosing among nineteen styles, ninety-two leathers, five soles types, and a gold or silver monogram. Each of the more than seventeen thousand designs will function. A person could wear them. While some designs will be more fashion forward than others, nothing horrible can happen. None will be the equivalent of a Vegemite-flavored tofu ice cream sundae with blue cheese topping. And, hopefully, somewhere in that giant space of possibilities will be a jaw-dropping design or two. By crowdsourcing design, Prada taps into an enormous, diverse, talented population. If consumers copy attractive designs, Prada can mine their sales data to improve their own creativity.

No Test Exists

Notice that whether or not we allow for recombination, the most creative team need not consist of the most creative people. A similar finding held for prediction: the most accurate team needed not consist of the most accurate individuals. In fact, we can state an even stronger result: *no test can be applied to individuals so that we are guaranteed to select the most creative group.*[35]

Reread the last sentence. It says *no test*. If a similar result holds for Google hiring employees, then Google cannot develop *any* test to give to their three million plus job applicants such that the highest performers constitute their best hires. If a similar result holds for college admissions, UCLA cannot apply a formula to its 119,000 applicants and expect to get the best class.

To show this result holds for the *most-creative-group problem* requires two logical steps. First, any test applied to an individual can only measure that individual's ideas. Second, a clone of the person who scores highest on whatever test we apply necessarily adds less to the group than a second person with a single different idea. Therefore, in the most-creative-group problem, no test can exist. We cannot evaluate people individually and determine an optimal group.

No Test Exists (on Creative Tasks)

If selecting a group for a creative task, a person's contribution depends on her ability to produce ideas that differ from those of others in the group. *No test applied to individuals will be guaranteed to produce the most creative group.*

The impossibility of a test undermines the meritocratic idea that choosing according to some objective criteria results in optimal choices. Creativity is defined in isolation. A person's contribution depends on the group composition. A test cannot measure a person's diversity unless it knows the group's composition.

We must be careful not to misinterpret the *no test exists* result. It implies that blindly hiring or admitting by any fixed criterion cannot guarantee the best group. It does not imply that we should ignore ability or that less able people add more to a creative group. If we want the most creative group, we must weigh cognitive diversity as well as individual creativity. We will also want people who can work collaboratively.

PROBLEM SOLVING

In problem solving, we either seek a solution that satisfies conditions (a light bulb that produces five hundred lumens and uses fewer than five watts of electricity) or improves on the state of the art (a more aerodynamic wing design). To build the iPhone required both types of problem solving. Apple had to improve on existing technologies for screens, batteries, and memory and fit them in a small box.

The long arc of increasing economic prosperity rests on our ability to identify and frame problems, derive solutions to those problems, and communicate those solutions. Humans transitioned from small bands of hunters and gatherers to modern societies by solving problems. Innovation and problem solving fueled the Roman Empire, the Renaissance, and the Industrial Revolution, not to mention the Information Age.[36] Our capacity to pose and solve problems and to develop new technologies will also drive future growth. Evidence suggests that this will require teams of intelligent, diverse people embedded within political systems that allow innovations to take hold and spread.[37] Some economists tie epochs of economic growth to specific technologies. Breakthroughs in electricity, urban sanitation systems, the internal combustion engine, chemicals and pharmaceuticals, and communication technology drove economic growth from 1870 to 1970.[38]

Within each broad category of inventions reside hundreds if not thousands of problems solved. The October 6, 1934, *Chicago Daily*

Tribune ran the headline "Gold and Silver Extracted from Atlantic Water." The article told of Willard Dow's announcement that an electrochemical process developed to extract bromine from seawater also produced gold and silver as by-products. Dow had solved an important problem: how to extract minerals from the sea. He could even extract gold. The gold received the headlines. The bromine brought him great wealth. Its return exceeded that of the gold by a ratio of more than twenty to one.

Dow used a technical tool to solve the problem of mineral extraction. In describing the double helix structure of DNA, Francis Crick and James Watson also solved an open problem, as did the German engineers Hans Tropsch and Franz Fischer, who developed a chemical process for creating synthetic oil. These breakthrough solutions are the stuff of history books. Attempts at breakthrough solutions either succeed or fail. On these problems, we can measure the ability of a person or a group as their probability of finding a solution.

Far more often, problem-solving activities improve on a best practice. They result in a battery that charges faster, an engine that requires less fuel, or a tomato that remains firm after being picked and tastes a little less like cardboard. For these types of problems, ability corresponds to the magnitude of the improvement to the status quo.

To show how cognitive diversity can produce bonuses in both breakthroughs and small improvements requires different types of models. To analyze breakthroughs, I return to the toolbox model introduced earlier.[39] To analyze iterative improvements, I apply two models: one based on representations and heuristics and another that characterizes problem solvers as statistical distributions of solutions.[40]

All three models simplify the process of problem solving. Solving problems and finding improvements to existing solutions involves every component of our cognitive repertoires. We tap into information and knowledge for potential answers. We apply models and frameworks to identify routes to solutions. We embed abstract problems within formal representations within which we apply heuristics and analytic tools. Students who obtain engineering degrees acquire repertoires for the purpose of solving problems. MIT's Donald Sadoway suggests we might even label engineering PhDs as PSDs—problem-solving degrees.[41]

The Toolbox Model

I start with a model of breakthrough solutions. I assume that a team confronts a problem in need of a solution. This could be an open problem of great import: eradicating the Zika virus or developing fusion energy. It could be a riddle: How do we move a fox, a rabbit, and a head of cabbage safely across a river in a small boat?

I represent methods for solving the problem as a *set of tools*. A tool could be a heuristic applied to a representation. It could be the application of an analogy. Each tool has a probability of solving the problem. I refer to this as its *potential*. When a person applies a tool, she either obtains a solution—a cure for a Parkinson's disease—or not.

I also assume that each person has a *facility* with a subset of those tools. Facility equals the probability of applying the tool correctly. A person who lacks familiarity with a tool has a facility of zero. A person with experience using a tool could have a facility near one. The probability that a person solves a problem with a particular tool equals the product of the tool's potential and the person's facility with that tool.

Suppose that the problem is to chop a tree. An ax's potential would equal 100 percent. A person's facility with the ax would depend on her stamina and strength. Facilities would lie between zero and one. In this example, facility equals ability. No diversity bonus exists. Hiring should be done by ability. As already discussed, we might want a team of Abe Lincolns.

Instead of felling trees, suppose that our problem requires solving an integral. If we consider the calculus to be a single tool, then facility with calculus would again equal ability and no diversity bonuses would exist. Once again, we should hire by ability.

The single-tool assumption makes sense for the ax. It does not fit the calculus. Calculus consists of a body of knowledge, along with a collection of heuristics. To solve integration problems, a student cannot swing her dog-eared copy of Tom Apostle's *Calculus* with the hope of knocking the problem down. She applies the tools (heuristics) explained within the book. These include expanding, completing the square, performing a substitution, adding zero, multiplying by one, substituting for a trigonometric identity, performing a change of variables, and applying integration by parts.[42] On a given problem, each of these tools would have some probability of success.

A student would have facilities defined over this set of tools. One person may be adept with trigonometric identities and not proficient at integration by parts. A person's ability no longer corresponds to a single facility. Instead, it equals the probability that she solves the problem. That probability depends on her facilities across the many tools. High-ability people have facility with high-potential tools.

To see how diversity bonuses can arise, assume that calculus involves solving only integration problems and that these problems can be solved using one of four tools: *expansion, adding zero, multiplying by one*, and *substitution*. Each person can be represented as a vector of four facilities, one corresponding to each tool. One person might have 50 percent facility on each. A second person might have 60 percent facility with expansion, adding zero, and multiplying by one but might never have learned substitution. A third person might have never learned expansion or how to add zero and might have 60 percent facility with multiplying by one and substitution. Figure 3.5 represents these facilities graphically.

For the purposes of this example, I assume that each tool has a 50 percent chance of solving the problem. A few calculations show that the first person has a 68 percent probability of solving the problem. That equals her ability. The second person has an ability of 64 percent and the third an ability of 51 percent.[43]

The ability of a two-person team equals the probability that at least one solves the problem. To stack the deck against diversity

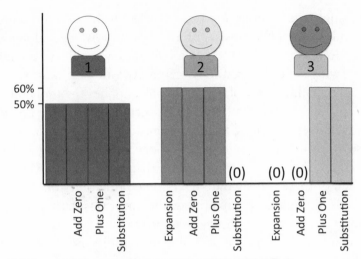

Figure 3.5 Three Individuals and Their Facilities with Integration Tools

bonuses, assume that if one person has higher facility with a tool than another, then any time the second person successfully applies the tool, the first person does as well. Given that assumption, the facility of a team with a tool equals the highest facility of any team member.

Figure 3.6 shows that the team of the two lowest-ability people has weakly higher facility on every tool than any other team. Therefore, that team has the highest ability even though it does not contain the two highest-ability problem solvers. A diversity bonus exists.

The existence of a single example of diversity bonuses does not imply that they always occur in problem solving. We can infer from this example a more general insight into the conditions necessary for them to exist. In the example, the highest-ability person can apply every tool. The two lower-ability people specialize on different sets of tools. That diverse specialization produces the bonus. That intuition applies broadly. A diversity bonus will exist when a lower-ability person has the highest facility with a tool. No diversity bonus can exist if the higher-ability people have greater facility with all tools.

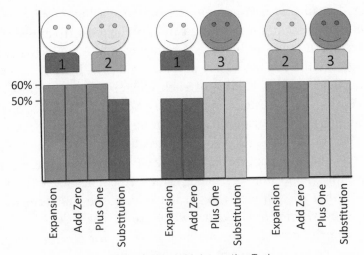

Figure 3.6 Three Teams and Their Facilities with Integration Tools

Extending this intuition, if many tools can be applied to a problem, there exist more types of specialists. And, for larger groups, these specialists may be part of the optimal group. It follows that the ratio of the number of potential tools to the group size plays a role in whether diversity bonuses matter. If the group size equals or exceeds the number of tools, then the optimal group consists of the best person on each tool, and hiring by diversity will be optimal. If the best person on each tool happens to be one of the highest-ability people, then hiring by ability will also be the best thing to do.

Once again, there exists a straightforward connection between the growing knowledge base of tools and diversity bonuses. As the number of tools increases beyond what any one person can master, diversity bonuses become more prevalent. Within the many subdisciplines in science, engineering, mathematics, and medicine, thousands of tools have been developed. In acquiring a master's degree in bioinformatics, a student learns hundreds if not thousands of tools, tricks, heuristics, methods, and techniques for evaluating and organizing data. Similarly, in chemical research, the number of possible molecular compounds that might be tested grows with each passing week.

For domains with large numbers of tools, a high-ability person can have high facility with only a subset of the tools. To explain how this results in diversity bonuses, I return to and expand the earlier analogies of the trip to the zoo and the train ride. Imagine the tools arranged in clusters. Think of each cluster as an exhibit at the zoo. Within each cluster, the tools may be acquired in a sequence, resembling the train ride of information, or they may be learned idiosyncratically like at the zoo. To extend the analogy, once we arrive at the snake exhibit, we may find we have to follow a specific path. Or, we might find that the snake exhibit resembles a zoo within a zoo and that we can visit the garden snakes, the tiny adders, and monstrous pythons in any order we desire.

We can think of the organization of tools for econometricians, surgeons, or any other specialist similarly. Econometricians use statistical tools to reveal relationships in data, to make inferences, and to state and test hypotheses. Econometrics apply Bayesian methods, non-Bayesian methods, and matching methods. Each of these methods can be thought of as a cluster containing sets of tools. Some of these tools must be acquired in a specific order. Others can be learned in any order once a baseline set of skills has been acquired.

For surgeons, clusters include intestinal surgery, hip replacements, and heart surgery, and tools include physical implements like laser knives and surgical techniques. Clusters of tools also exist for lawyers, information scientists, string theorists, mathematicians, and anesthesiologists.

Owing to the enormous number of problem-solving tools within each of these domains, even the highest-ability people possess facility in a small subset of the relevant possible clusters. An analogue of the Milton problem holds here as well. Any one person can only know a small proportion of the relevant tools.

In the toolbox model, high-ability people possess facility with high-potential tools. If the best tools reside in a single cluster, the highest-ability people will have similar facilities. Other people who have less ability may know different clusters of tools. These other people may not be necessary for easy problems. They become valuable when the standard tools fail to solve the problem.

On some problems, none of the usual tools succeed. Success may require applying tools from a related cluster. That requires people adept with those tools.[44] If no tool from a related cluster succeeds, this could lead to the search for a new tool. We might think of that as a creative task, and we have already seen how and why diversity matters there.

As an example of the value of related clusters, consider a problem faced by the International Monetary Fund (IMF). The IMF primarily employs economists. These economists possess facility with a range of analytic tools. They know development economics (D), econometrics (E), game theory (G), and political economy (P). The economists may lack knowledge of cultural anthropology (CA) and social psychology (SP).

Figure 3.7 shows hypothetical potential hires for the IMF represented by their abilities and by their tools. If the IMF hired by ability only, its staff would consist only of economists. The tools of economists perform better, on average, for the problems the IMF confronts than do the tools of cultural anthropologists and social psychologists. By the IMF's standards, people trained in these disciplines possess less ability.

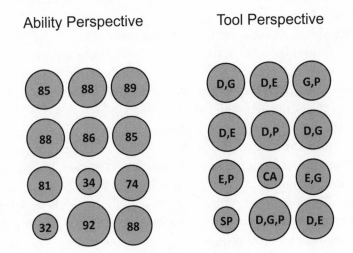

Figure 3.7 Representing People by Abilities and Tools

Nevertheless, cultural anthropologists and social psychologists can add value when the economists get stuck, that is, on difficult problems. So while the IMF wants high-ability people, they also want diversity, so they do not just hire economists. Neither does the Bank of England. Their research group includes psychologists.

Recall that in the model, a person's *ability* equals the probability that she possesses a tool that solves the problem. This means that high-ability people master multiple useful tools. The collective ability of a group equals the probability that someone in the group solves the problem. High-ability groups include people with high facility with different tools.

Note the paradox of aggregation: even though high-ability people and high-ability groups have identical characteristics—high facility with many useful tools—high-ability groups need not consist of the highest-ability people. The best group need not consist of the best parts. Once again, a *no test exists* result will apply.[45]

The logic goes as follows: Any one person has facility with only a set of the possible tools, and the tools that someone masters will be clustered. The highest-ability people will be concentrated in a few clusters—those clusters with the highest-potential tools. The clustering of high-potential tools implies a clustering of the highest-ability problem solvers.

More detail makes the logic transparent. Figure 3.8 shows a group of three people with diverse tools. Assume each has high facility with the tools represented. Given their tool diversity, this represents a high-ability group. Each person knows a different cluster. They differ in their facilities.[46]

For the sake of argument, suppose that the person on the right has the highest ability, that his four tools have a higher probability of solving the problem than the tools of the other two. If other problem solvers of high ability possess only those same tools, then groups of high-ability problem solvers will not be the best. Selecting by diversity, or even randomly among competent problem solvers, could result in a better group.[47]

Figure 3.8 A High-Ability Group with Diverse Tools

Diversity versus Ability

If the following conditions hold—(i) individuals possess sets of tools; (ii) no tool solves the problem with certainty; (iii) people master clusters from a larger set of tools; and (iv) the group will be chosen from a larger population—then the best group will generally not consist of the best problem solvers on some tasks.

The role of problem difficulty merits emphasis. High-ability people can solve moderately difficult problems. On those tasks diversity bonuses do not exist. Only when the high-ability people cannot solve the problem do diversity bonuses materialize.

Iterative Improvements

The second type of problem solving I consider consists of improvements in existing best practices such as when teams try to improve production processes, increase worker safety, lower costs, increase brand loyalty, or raise graduation rates. In these contexts, solutions can be assigned numerical values and better solutions score higher.

To model these iterative improvements, we can represent a person as being a collection of ideas. If the problem involves increasing production in a canning facility, a person may apply lean management techniques and consistently find solutions that increase production by between 5 percent and 7 percent. A second person might rethink the entire process from scratch. Half of the time, this approach fails. The other half of the time, production increases by 8 percent.

In this model, a person's ability equals the expected value of her solution. The first person would have an ability of 6 percent and the second person an ability of 4 percent. We are abstracting away from repertoires here, but if two people had the same repertoire, they would have the same distribution and, perhaps, come up with the same solution.

Once again, we can imagine a large set of problem solvers from whom we want to choose a group. We can order these problem solvers by their abilities. First assume that the ability of the group equals the expected value of the best solution found by some member of the group. Notice that high-ability people and high-ability groups differ. High-ability people, on average, produce good solutions. High-ability groups, in contrast, must include at least one person who generates a great solution.

It follows that when putting together a group, a person's ability matters less than the probability that she comes up with a great solution.[48] The expected ability of a group that consists of ten people who produce solutions with values between five and seven cannot exceed seven.[49] A group consisting of ten people who each have a 50 percent chance of producing a solution of value eight will produce a solution of value eight more than 99.9 percent of the time.

Therefore, we should seek people with the potential to generate great solutions, not people who do well on average. Ability is not the correct criterion for selecting group members. The optimal criterion evaluates people by their likelihood of finding high-value solutions.[50]

Implicit in this construction is that one person's probability of finding a high-value solution cannot be correlated with another person's. Thus, the best groups consist of people who produce high-variance solutions using diverse cognitive repertoires. If people applied the same knowledge, heuristics, and mental frameworks, their solutions would be correlated.[51]

Combining Heuristics

The toolbox model and the distribution model lack any interaction among group members. Each person applies her tool or proposes her solution, and the group's performance equals that of the best group member. That construction ignores the possibility of combining ideas. If two people generate different better ideas, both can be applied.

This accumulation of feature improvements is common. Remaining competitive, be it in smartphones, lawn mowers, or shoes, requires constant innovation. The iPhone 6 added Apple Pay, image stabilization, higher-quality video recording, more sensors, and Wi-Fi calling. The 2016 John Deere Signature Series mower added a new mower deck with lift-off spindle covers, a backlit electronic instrument panel, and a tachometer.

We could assume that improvements are *additive*: that two ideas that each improve output by 4 percent improve performance by 8 percent. We might instead assume that each improvement reduces the impact of the others. Or the improvements could be superadditive: one improvement could make the other more valuable. Improved image stabilization and higher-quality videos may be of more value together on an iPhone than separately. In this last case, the bonuses would be even larger.

The larger point is that recombination turns combinations of bonuses into more bonuses. The size of those bonuses will depend on the context. We should not expect superadditivity, nor should we rule it out.

The results from these three models show that diversity bonuses can exist and have significant magnitude in problem solving. Each model includes a set of parameters and assumptions. In the toolbox model, these are the number of tools, the probabilities that they solve the problem, the size of groups, and the number of tools a person can master. In the distribution-based model, the assumptions consider how the values are combined—whether the group's solution is the best individual answer or a nonlinear combination of those answers.

The importance of diversity in each model depends on the assumptions. It is conditional. In the toolbox model, for the best group not to consist of the best individuals, the problem must be difficult (no one solves it for sure) and the highest-ability individuals cannot know every tool that someone else knows (a diversity assumption). In the distribution model, the value of diversity increases as the function becomes nonlinear.

SCIENTIFIC RESEARCH: REPRESENTATIONS + MODELS

Scientific researchers apply multiple parts of their repertoires. They develop hypotheses based on background knowledge. They bring novel information to bear. They borrow and develop heuristics to find solutions and improvements. They apply various perspectives and categories to organize data.

As an exercise, you can select almost any academic paper or patent that has had impact and you can find evidence of diversity bonuses. I do not recommend this for those who struggle with academic jargon or prose. Reading these papers is like walking into a French movie an hour after it has started.

In preparing this book, I performed this exercise about a half a dozen times. Each time I could find support for a diversity bonus. By that I mean that I could see how a new perspective, heuristic, or model resulted in new knowledge. One such paper, written by Bell Labs scientists, contributed to the field of physical chemistry. The paper studies well-mixed chemical systems. Cream stirred into coffee is well mixed. Chocolate syrup swirled on top of the coffee is not.[52]

I knew nothing about those systems, so I did some background reading. In one background paper, the author referenced the "well known Brusselator limit cycle model." The French movie now seemed a walk in the park by comparison.[53]

I learned that at the time there existed two approaches to studying well-mixed systems. One approach models the rate of chemical change using mathematical equations. An equation might describe the change in the amount of a chemical as increasing by five units per second or decreasing at a rate equal to fourteen divided by the number of seconds. These mathematical representations reduce a complex process to a deterministic set of flows.[54] The deterministic approach models chemical systems as smooth. The levels of the various chemicals are represented by curved lines on graph paper.

The second approach, made possible by computers, simulates chemical processes as stochastic—that is, random—processes. This approach allows the modeler to include local correlations and fluctuations. Instead of a single, smooth prediction, it produces a distribution of jagged predictions. Each graph resembles a sequence of stock prices over time.

The two types of models give different insights. In this case, I had identified a bonus before getting through the paper's abstract. As I dug into the paper, I learned that computational constraints limit the precision of the simulations. That constraint led to a creative solution.[55]

The relevant sentence from the abstract reads as follows: "The motion of isolated adatoms and small clusters on a crystal surface is investigated by a novel and efficient simulation technique. The trajectory of each atom is calculated by molecular dynamics, but the exchange of kinetic energy with the crystal lattice is included through interactions with a 'ghost' atom."

Set aside academic jargon and focus on the "ghost" atom. That constitutes the main contribution. No ghost atom exists. It serves as a placeholder to represent a population of atoms on the surface. Assuming the ghost atom makes the model calculable. The authors thought of the entire crystal lattice as a single atom. That reduced an enormous number of equations to one.

How they came up with this ghost atom is a mystery. I contacted one of the authors and he could not recall, though he did say that it was a new idea at the time. That should not be surprising. When problems become intractable, we pull from our repertoires of information, knowledge, models, tools, and representations in search of a new idea. When we happen on a solution, we may have no idea of its origin or cause. Some ideas may be more salient to some identity groups than others. Other ideas may be more available to certain professions. We also reason from analogy.

I chose to write about this paper because the ghost atom idea reminded me of a novel representation known to anthropologists as well as a heuristic used by economists. The representation comes from the navigational framework of the Micronesians. They imagine themselves as fixed and think of islands as objects that float past. If they lack islands in the appropriate places, they construct *phantom islands* defined in relation to their positions with respect to the moving stars overhead. These phantom islands, like the ghost atoms, simplify calculations.[56]

The economist Leo Hurwicz taught me a similar heuristic. He called it *assume what you need*. Kenneth Boulding's more memorable *assume a can opener* version goes as follows: There is a story that has been going around about a physicist, a chemist, and an economist who were stranded on a desert island with no implements and a can of food. The physicist and the chemist each devised an ingenious mechanism for getting the can open; the economist said, "Assume we have a can opener!"[57]

Make up a ghost atom, create a phantom island, assume a can opener—these build on the same idea: *make up what you need so that the math works*. You can then go back and worry about the particulars. The point of this digression is that the process of science involves testing new ideas. Teams of people with diverse repertoires will have more ideas to test and perform better. Later we see that this will be borne out in the data.

INNOVATION: {CREATING, PROBLEM SOLVING} + PREDICTION

Innovation consists of both creative activities and problem solving. Some innovations, like the Slinky and the Internet, are out-of-the-blue ideas. Other innovations, like the near-endless improvement in chip design captured by Moore's law, result from directed, purposeful problem solving.

In evaluating innovation, we care less about the number of ideas than about the value of the best one. Thus, experts characterize innovation as consisting of two parts: generating ideas (either by creating or problem solving) and then choosing the best from among them. Innovative teams still believe that more is better—all else equal, having a larger set of ideas to choose from increases the odds of having one really good idea.

If we think of innovation as combining a *creative task* or *problem-solving task* with a *predictive task*, and if we recall how diversity bonuses exist for each task, we can therefore conclude that diversity bonuses also exist in innovation. We might even infer a potential triple diversity bonus—one for each part of the task.

A deeper reading of the literature reveals a more complicated picture, as well as richer insights into the contributions of diversity. The first subtlety arises when we realize that the parts of our repertoires that produce the diversity bonuses differ for creating, problem solving, and prediction. The bonuses in the creative and problem-solving tasks result from diverse perspectives and heuristics and from diverse knowledge. The bonuses in the predictive task result from diverse categories, information, knowledge, and predictive models.

We should therefore not expect those people who are good at predicting to be the most creative or the best problem solvers, and they are not.[58] Nor should we expect the optimal diverse team for creating ideas or solving problems to be the same as the optimal team for selecting among them. Put simply, as innovation consists of distinct tasks, the people who have ability and who add diversity on each of those tasks may differ. The criteria for putting together a diverse predictive team will differ from those used to identify diverse, creative people or problem solvers.

A second subtlety concerns what constitutes creative search. Originally, the first part of innovation was conceived of as blind search, not unlike the mutations and recombinations that occur in evolutionary systems.[59] More recent models assume intentional search in line with the cognitive repertoire model described here.[60] The literature distinguishes between deep, foundational search within a discipline or paradigm, more like problem solving, and the more creative recombination of ideas.[61]

The dichotomy between deep and narrow search and speculative broader search recombinations both begs a practical question and introduces an attributional conundrum. The practical question centers on which type of search produces more value, or the best method of finding breakthrough innovations.

Evidence shows that established firms more often generate high-value innovations through broad search.[62] While it is possible that deep knowledge and narrow search limits the potential for breakthrough ideas by limiting the set of possibilities considered, it is more likely to produce something entirely new.[63] Those new ideas become the building blocks for later recombinations. Thus, it may be unfair to give credit to the recombiners and not to those who originate the ideas being recombined.

Setting aside the credit assignment issue, evidence from patent data reveals that recombination predominates. The United States Patent and Trademark Office distinguishes among utility patents (the light bulb), design patents (the Coke bottle), and plant patents (hybrid corn). It classifies patents within 474 technology classes and over 160,000 technology codes. A study of all patents issued from 1790 to 2010 shows that in the nineteenth century more than half of patents were classified by a single technology code. That percentage has steadily decreased to around 12 percent.[64] Over the entire data set, more than three-fourths of patents combine multiple codes.[65] While the patent data do not "prove" that diversity bonuses predominate, the data reveal the value of combining diverse ideas and an unmistakable trend toward recombination as a driver of innovation.

The conundrum concerns the relative roles of ability and diversity. A first pass might assign credit for all recombinations to diversity and credit for the deep, novel innovations to ability. That attribution errs in both directions. On the one hand, many recombinations come from the mind of a single talented person. To call this an (internal) diversity bonus would stretch the diversity-bonus logic too far. On the other hand, many of the deep, narrow insights are produced by diverse teams.

KNOWLEDGE INTEGRATION

I next take up knowledge integration. When integrating knowledge, a group's objective is to determine the veracity of a claim or the wisdom of an action. Unlike in creative tasks, where diversity implies more possibilities, in knowledge integration diversity reduces the set of possibilities. A team of cardiologists considering surgical techniques to improve blood flow needs to know possible complications. Knowledge integration rules out some techniques.

Grahame Knox's group exercise Lost at Sea teaches the value of diverse knowledge.[66] I provide a partial version here so as not to spoil the exercise for others. Lost at Sea describes a scenario in which a group of people abandon a sinking ship and board a lifeboat. They must rank a set of fifteen items in terms of their value for survival. These items include a shaving mirror, rope, shark repellent, and a transistor radio. More than a trillion rankings are possible.

In the first stage of Lost at Sea, each person produces a ranking. For each item, she might think through a collection of possible scenarios and then ask which items would be most useful.[67] During a shark attack, the shark repellent or the flare gun would be more valuable than a sextant.

In the second stage of Lost at Sea, people share their knowledge, update their rankings, and come up with a collective ranking. In this stage, the group members combine their diverse knowledge. Items initially ranked as unimportant often move up in the rankings. The large clear plastic sheet earns a high rank when people realize that it could catch rainfall and provide shelter from the wind.

Lost at Sea has a best ranking determined by experts. So, it is possible to score the rankings of each individual after the first stage and to compare their scores to the collective group ranking. This exercise has been run thousands, if not tens of thousands of times. To the best of my knowledge, groups almost always outperform the average person, and typically outperform any individual.

In Lost at Sea, the integration of diverse knowledge produces deeper knowledge. This also happens in the real world. If one police investigator knows that the killer wore small gloves and another investigator knows that a particular suspect has enormous hands, then by combining their knowledge, they can rule out that suspect. Alone, neither could.

We can formalize that intuition and show the power of diverse knowledge integration using an experiment my students and I developed called the Diversity LSAT.[68] The experiment relies on a logic problem like those on the Law School Admission Test (LSAT).

Logic Problem: *Boeing, Ford, Alphabet, Molex, and Caterpillar just released annual revenues. Boeing's revenues exceeded Molex's. Alphabet did not have the highest revenue among the five firms, though its revenue did exceed Boeing's. Caterpillar has never had higher revenues than Molex.*

Which of the following **must** *be true?*
  Claim 1: Alphabet had the second-highest revenue.
  Claim 2: Ford did not have the highest revenue.
  Claim 3: Caterpillar had the lowest revenue.

Solving these problems involves identifying the set of relevant facts and then determining their implications. This particular problem includes four facts:

Fact 1: Boeing > Molex
Fact 2: Alphabet not highest
Fact 3: Alphabet > Boeing
Fact 4: Molex > Caterpillar

In the experiment, we assign each participant one fact. We then ask if anyone can answer the question. None can. The person who knows Fact 1, that Boeing earned higher revenues than Molex, cannot determine if any of the three claims must be true. We then form two groups of size two. One group knows Facts 1 and 2. The other knows Facts 3 and 4. The group that knows Facts 1 and 2 knows that Boeing earned more than Molex *and* that Alphabet did not have the highest revenues. They remain unable to determine which, if any, of the three claims must be true. Nor can the group that knows Facts 3 and 4.

We then let the first group pick a third member from the second group. If they pick the person who knows Fact 3, the group will know that Alphabet had higher revenues than Boeing, which in turn had higher revenues than Molex. They will also know that Alphabet did not have the highest revenues. They can then deduce that Alphabet ranks above Boeing and Boeing above Molex and that either Ford or Caterpillar (or both) ranks above Alphabet, but they cannot discern the true ranking.

Last, we let all four people work together. The fourth person knows that Molex is ranked above Caterpillar. The group can see that if Molex is ranked above Caterpillar, then Ford, and not Caterpillar, must be ranked above Alphabet. The order now falls into place. It must be the following:

Ford > Alphabet > Boeing > Molex > Caterpillar

Therefore, both Claim 1 and Claim 3 are true.

In problems like this, discerning the truth requires intersecting what each person knows to be possible. Each person's diverse knowledge *reduces* the possible orderings. The logic contradicts the intuition that diversity creates bonuses by increasing the number of alternatives. In this example, we assign people different facts. In a real-world setting, people would know different facts. Diverse knowledge therefore can contribute to truth verification.

To see how identity diversity might play a role in truth verification, consider a panel of judges who are determining whether a particular action violates the Constitution. Each judge takes in facts, applies knowledge, and makes a binary decision. If every judge on the panel came from the same identity group, had similar life experiences, and attended the same law school, where they were taught by the same professors, then no matter how much ability each had, they might categorize the case similarly. If the judges had diverse identities, had distinct life experiences, and learned the law at the knees of diverse faculty, we would expect a richer collective interpretation of the law.

STRATEGIC PLAY

Next, I consider strategic contexts that I model as games. In a game, a player's payoff depends on his or her own actions and on the actions of other players. Payoffs can also depend on random events. Chess is a game. Soccer is a game, as are poker, politics, and competition between firms. The field of game theory analyzes strategic behavior in games. Game theory, for the most part, assumes optimal behavior, so game theorists often restrict attention to games they can solve, that is, simple games. For the class of games in which individuals can deduce or learn optimal actions, cognitive diversity plays little role other than in games that have multiple possible outcomes.

In more complex games such as chess, Go, business competition, political elections, sports, and warfare, optimal strategies have yet to be discovered. Furthermore, each game requires a sequence of actions taken under time constraints. During a time-out, a basketball coach has at most two or three minutes to decide on an action.

These action choices appear to resemble searches in problem solving. In each case, a person makes a choice and gets a payoff. The key difference is that in a game, the payoff also depends on the actions of others. That distinction proves crucial because players not only must learn how payoffs depend on actions, they must also anticipate the actions of their opponents. To do so, a player needs a model of the other players. As with any predictive task, diversity in the models of the other players will improve accuracy.

The relative importance of predicting and problem solving will depend on the game. In some games, the set of possible actions at a given stage may be small, so accurate predictions may matter more than increasing the set of the adjacent possible. For example, a person playing checkers or chess may be deciding among five or six moves. A poker player may decide between folding or calling.

Further complicating matters, in sequential games like Go or chess, each move alters the configuration. The value of a move taken now can depend on how the game unfolds. Taking an action therefore requires a predictive model of future paths of play by the opponent. Different predictive models may advocate different actions. Having a diversity of models confers a strategic advantage.

That advantage can be seen by considering actions in the game of backgammon. Backgammon has a handful of basic strategies. One involves playing offensively, trying to get your pieces around the board and off as fast as possible. Another strategy does the opposite. It holds as many pieces back as possible in the hope of blocking the opponent from getting his pieces off the board. A third tries to form blockades that trap the opponent, and a fourth holds just a few pieces back on the opponent's home board with the goal of exploiting a later opening.

Early in a game, a roll of the dice may present four possible moves, each associated with one of the possible strategies. Think of four roads diverging in a wood: a player who knew the strategy of the other player and had a computer to simulate billions of trials of possible rolls of the dice for the continuation of the game could calculate the expected winning percentages from each action. Lacking a computer, the best she can do is to make inferences based on short sequences of possible rolls.

In making those inferences, she needs a model of the other player. She must predict whether the other player will take risks or play it safe. Strong players not only have the ability to calculate probability distributions of future rolls, but they also have accurate models of what the other player will do given a roll.

If we imagine a team of players with diverse models, they will be even better at backgammon than an individual. Consider each possible action to be a choice from a set. Assume only one of those actions is best; that is, it maximizes the probability of winning. The ability of a player corresponds to her probability of choosing the best action at each step. A great player may make the correct choice 90 percent of the time. A lesser player may only be correct 80 percent of the time.

Now, suppose two teams of five players compete against each other. One team consists of five people using a single strategy that makes the correct move 90 percent of the time. This team of five will be no better than any one of its members. The other team consists of five players who each make the correct move 80 percent of the time but who use different models. For convenience, assume that each has an independent probability of identifying the correct move. If the second team's members vote on the correct move, the majority will be correct more than 90 percent of the time (93 percent, to be exact).[69] The diversity of models makes for a better team.

The previous example might be dismissed as a straw man. I compared one team of people using identical models to a team with models so diverse one person's correctness was independent of another person's. That construction might appear to favor the diverse team. However, in contexts in which there exist many alternatives, the independence assumption may well understate the overlap of the diverse group.

Suppose that when the second five-member team votes on a move, they are selecting among tens or hundreds of possibilities. That is true in backgammon, where a roll of doubles can create more than a thousand potential moves. Given the positions of the other player's pieces, perhaps one hundred of them might be possible and not unreasonable. Thus, when the five people vote on a move, they are choosing among one hundred alternatives. In that case, the winning move need not get three votes. It might get only two votes.

If two people's models select the correct action, so long as the other votes go to different incorrect moves, the best move will win a plurality. In our example, if we assume one hundred possibilities and an 80 percent chance of finding the best move, this increases the probability that the best move gets selected to above 98 percent. Therefore, the team of five people, each of whom selects the correct action independently 80 percent of the time, now outperforms an individual who selects correctly 97 percent of the time. Evidence from simulations and real-world experiments agrees with the logic. Ensembles of diverse Go algorithms outperform ensembles of better similar algorithms.[70]

A return to the concept of the *adjacent possible* clarifies the intuition and helps make the larger point about the value of diverse ways of seeing and thinking. Suppose that the most able people make choices from a similar set of adjacent possibles. Suppose that a more diverse team consists of people with different sets of adjacent possibles. A plurality of the members of a more homogeneous, more able team may well match on the same incorrect choice. That possibility is less likely when people are choosing from different sets of possibilities.

This same logic applies to decisions by committees. In most corporations, board committees help select a company's CEO. This process consists of identifying a set of candidates and then selecting from among them. While companies hire headhunters who seek out potential candidates, they also rely on their board members to encourage people to apply. A board member's social network can influence the set of candidates considered. Greater board diversity therefore can increase the size of the set of potential candidates who arise through personal connections. These connections occur across industry—people from telecom know other people in telecom—and across identity groups. The latter are facilitated by formal organizations like the Black Board of Directors Association and several groups promoting women on boards.

When selecting from among those candidates, board diversity can lead to better choices. If board members with similar backgrounds, training, and experiences rely on similar criteria for gauging past performance and employ similar heuristics when conducting interviews, they will be more likely to prefer the same person for CEO. This board might vote 11–0–0 or 10–1–0 among three final candidates. If not diverse, these lopsided votes might be the norm. If board members come from different industries, have different identity backgrounds, possess diverse knowledge, and rely on different models, they will be less likely to agree on their rankings of candidates. Their initial vote among three candidates might be 5–3–3.

A unanimous vote could mean that one candidate clearly dominates the others, or it could signal a lack of diversity. A mixed vote, on the other hand, reveals the existence of diversity. Paradoxically, that could mean a better decision, as it guarantees that not everyone applied the same model. Pushing this logic further, if you never find yourself on the losing side of a vote, then the group cannot be making better decisions than you would on your own. For the committee to be improving choices, you have to be on the losing side sometimes.

The Bonus of Being on the Losing Side

A committee that makes decisions can only be more accurate than a member of that committee if that member is sometimes on the losing side of votes. If not, the member could make every decision on her own and be equally accurate.

THE BUSINESS CASE AS MULTIPLE TASKS

Most business and organizational decisions occur within complex environments and include multiple tasks. A team may predict outcomes, solve problems related to implementation or engineering, generate ideas, and work through logic. Nobel laureate Herb Simon partitions decision making into three stages: information gathering, design, and choice.[71] Creativity guru Edward de Bono describes six necessary factors or dimensions involved in careful thinking that he calls *thinking hats*. These include "facts and figures," "emotions and feelings," and "speculative and positive."[72]

Juliet Bourke of Deloitte identifies six core dimensions that overlap somewhat with de Bono's thinking hats.[73] Bourke finds that good evaluations consider *outcomes, options, process, people, evidence,* and *risk.* Bourke does not believe that each person needs to be adept at each of these. She finds that most people excel at two or three and often ignore the others. Hence, the need for diverse teams.

Bourke describes empirical evidence that businesses ignore any of these dimensions at their peril. She finds that many organizations' leaderships place too much emphasis on outcomes and options. The 1998 McDonald's investment in the Chipotle burrito chain provides an example. McDonald's executives evaluated the potential returns they hoped to achieve (outcomes) and considered alternative purchases (options). Chipotle proved a good buy. McDonald's earned $1.6 billion on their $360 million investment.

Despite this rate of return, McDonald's sold their stake. Media accounts describe tension on the people dimension. The founders of Chipotle shared a commitment to organic, locally sourced food. McDonald's espoused more of an efficiency mind-set.

The loss of cognitive diversity proved costly to Chipotle. Chipotle's commitment to organic suppliers required elaborate supply chains. McDonald's had decades of expertise organizing and operating supply chains. Chipotle did not, and that lack of skill in process led to failures. In 2015, Chipotles were responsible for *E. coli* poisonings in eight states, a salmonella outbreak in Minnesota, and a norovirus in Boston, leading to the Internet meme "You can't spell Chipotle without *E. coli.*"

Bourke's framework demands a certain type of cognitive diversity. A decision-making team must take into account all six dimensions (see figure 3.9). Here again, we see the link between complexity and diversity bonuses. On a simple problem, a team might not be needed. A single person could work through all six dimensions. The correct decision as to whether to buy a new delivery van would require asking the following questions: Will the car serve our needs (outcomes)? What other cars might we buy (options)? How will we finance the car (process)? Can all of our employees drive the car (people)? What is the market value for the car if we have to resell it (evidence)? And finally, what's the worst-case scenario (risk)? By answering these questions, the person has covered all six dimensions.

Strategic choices in more complex environments require teams because no one person could possibly cover all six dimensions. Suppose that the federal government wants to create incentives for more charter schools. They must think about how the outcomes might range between efficiency and corruption, and what types of corruption might emerge. They must think about the possible policy changes. Do they offer grants or subsidies? Do they push to change

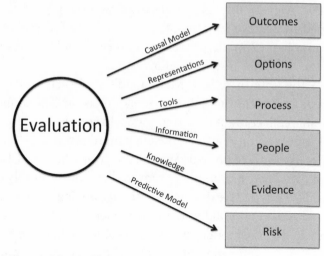

Figure 3.9 Expanded Bourke Model

laws? They have to consider the process by which schools and teachers are accredited. Does this happen at the local, state, or national level? Other process questions concern the allocation of students to schools and the transportation of those students.

Policy makers would also need deep understandings of the populations being served. How will people be informed of their options? Do they have the capacity and means to make good choices? In making these decisions, policy makers should pull together the best evidence. That evidence may be diversely held. And last, they must consider the risks, not only the political risks but also the potential implications for communities if the experiment fails.

To answer each of those questions would require diverse cognitive repertoires. Some, like the evidence questions, would require information diversity and knowledge diversity. Others, namely the questions pertaining to the responses within communities and the associated risks, would benefit from the types of category and mental model diversity attributable to identity. How will, for example, various racial and ethnic communities respond to the new program? Some of those same questions would benefit from disciplinary cognitive diversity. Economists, sociologists, historians, political scientists, and civil engineers would all bring useful knowledge and mental models.

DOMAIN-SPECIFIC BONUSES

Diversity bonuses can also arise in a broad array of task domains including analytic tradecraft, presidential appointments, venture capital investments, drug discovery, product design, and classroom discussions. Here, I present brief overviews of how bonuses occur in those settings.

Analytic Tradecraft

The practice of analytic tradecraft by the intelligence community has been designed to deal with complexity and limited, vague information. Failures in the intelligence community can often be traced back to not challenging assumptions or information. In the 1950s the intelligence community assumed limited Chinese support of North Korea. In 1974 they assumed that the Arabs would not attack Israel. In 1989, they did not think the Soviets would allow German unification, and in 2003, they thought Saddam Hussein was developing nuclear weapons.[74]

To overcome errors in the evaluation of evidence (representations and categorizations), the estimation of probabilities (prediction), and perceptions of causality (mental models), tradecraft enforces diversity through the use of devil's advocates who take the opposite position. Devil's advocates add value, but they are not a perfect solution. Obliging someone to take the opposing position may not be as effective as including someone who actually holds that position.

On the CIA's website, a director and senior adviser for cyber security (who is, needless to say, unnamed) writes, "Truth isn't resident in a single perspective or the product of one mind. To discover it means to come at it from several directions, to question what is seen to be certain that it is what it actually is. The more we question, the more we look, the more we consider, the closer we will get to the wisdom we are being asked to offer."[75]

Selecting Candidates

Hiring and nomination procedures also require multiple distinct tasks and multiple possible diversity bonuses. A president selecting a nominee to the Supreme Court might first consider the direction she would like the court to move (outcomes) and then identify a set of potential candidates (options). She will then task a team with gathering evidence about the candidates. This entails digging into past writings and opinions. The president will then interview those who rise to the top. She will think through the nomination process. How will potential nominees deal with the media and perform during confirmation hearings? She and her team will include possible responses of the Senate Judiciary Committee and the Senate at large. To be prepared for what might happen during the nomination process, a president may even sound out members of the opposing party. Outcomes, options, evidence, process, people, and risk all enter. Failed nominations, such as Ronald Reagan's nomination of Robert Bork, might be chalked up to not considering evidence and process. Bork's record was attacked from the left, and he had a negative affect, which hurt him in the media.

Venture Capital

In evaluating a proposed startup, venture capitalists apply their knowledge of technology and markets to make predictions. They apply mental models of adoption curves. And they apply categories to management teams.[76] In the event that an investment turns sour, venture capitalists take a more active role. They negotiate contracts that allow them to intervene in the case of poor performance. At this point, venture capitalists become problem solvers.

Cognitive diversity helps at each stage. Billionaire venture capitalist Steve Jurvetson says, "I've actually come to respect the most irritatingly challenging people I've worked with as really valuable in improving group decision-making and what to do and what to invest in."[77]

Drug Discovery

Drug discovery provides an interesting example of how the accumulation of scientific knowledge changed the types of diversity that produce bonuses. Early drug discoveries often derived from folk medicine.[78] The isolation of quinine, an antimalarial chemical compound found in the bark of cinchona trees in the Andes, came about because seventeenth-century European missionaries noticed that the indigenous people would chew the bark as a treatment for fevers. Powdered bark became a popular antimalarial medicine. The French scientists named it *quinine*, a variant of *quina*, the indigenous word for *bark*.

Quinine is not a singular case. According to one study, 119 drugs have been developed from folk medicines.[79] That approach to drug discovery has had diminishing returns with many of the most promising folk medicines having been analyzed. Some produced useful drugs and leads. Others turned out to function only through superstition.

When scientific knowledge was less advanced, drug discoveries were as likely as not to occur through serendipity. British scientist Alexander Fleming discovered penicillin by chance when a culture killed bacteria on the surface of a test tube. The image of a scientist experimenting in a lab, guided by horse sense, intuition, and a bit of luck, captures this period of drug discovery.

Modern drug discovery, though it still relies on one part indigenous plants and one part lab-coated scientists, has become more systematic and sophisticated. Scientists still investigate native plants in search of useful compounds, a process known as *bioprospecting*, but that process is based less on indigenous knowledge. Those naturally occurring compounds, along with synthetic compounds, function as libraries of chemicals. Two decades ago, scientists would explore those chemical libraries compound by compound. Scientific and technological advances now allow chemists to test entire libraries against specific biological targets cloned from human proteins. Think of these protein targets as the pathological structures that cause disease.

These new methods turn the original process of drug discovery on its head. Classical pharmacology first extracts a compound and then identifies the proteins it attacks. Modern (or reverse) pharmacology starts from the protein and then searches for the chemical compound that targets it.

In each era of drug discovery, cognitive diversity produced bonuses, though the type of diversity that produced those bonuses changed. Compounds derived from folk medicines tapped into local, indigenous knowledge. This diversity ties to that part of identity connected to geography. Different peoples live in different ecological niches and develop unique knowledge bases.

The relevant knowledge diversity for the scientists in lab coats somewhat blindly searching the library of compounds probably had few ties to identity. The relevant diversity could be measured with respect to the library of compounds. Each scientist developed expertise with different parts of that library. The breadth of their search increased their collective odds of finding useful compounds. Their collective ability derived from their individual talents being pointed in many directions. Hence, Fleming, a brilliant scientist by any measure, describes his discovery of penicillin as serendipitous.

Modern drug discovery benefits from diversity in disciplinary knowledge and tools. The lone chemist in the lab has been supplanted by large, interdisciplinary teams consisting of experts in proteomics, protein folding, computational chemistry, and structural biology. These scientists possess diverse training, acquire diverse knowledge bases, and master tools ranging from X-ray crystallography to computational modeling.

Similar trajectories exist in other domains. Initially, diverse local knowledge and understandings may be of central importance, which may depend on identity diversity. As knowledge accumulates and as understandings become formalized as models, diversity within the core discipline, be it economics, chemistry, or medicine, becomes more important.

Design

Effective design entails understanding the effects of attribute choices. The design of a microwave oven determines its functionality and its aesthetic appeal. The layout of an assembly facility for a manufacturing process affects cost, quality, and safety. The ad placements in a promotional campaign for a US Senate candidate influence voter turnout and support.

Quality design, manufacturing, and marketing involve multiple choices that must have desirable direct and indirect causes. A positive direct effect can be undermined by negative indirect effects. A sturdier composite circular tray that doubles as a serving dish can overburden the lightweight, rotating motor on a microwave oven.

Making a physical product requires materials, equipment, people, a work environment, processes, and management. Each step in the process must function well. Much like in the previous analysis of evaluating an investment, diverse expertise improves performance. A choice could involve creative thinking or it could involve problem solving.

When the Mazda corporation designed the Miata roadster, it articulated a set of desirable features. Mazda wanted a certain feel. It wanted drivers to be able to rest their elbows on the side of the car. That may seem like an easy feature to ensure. It can be thought of as a problem. Engineers had many solutions. They could raise the seat height, lower the sides of the car, or do a little of each. Each combination of choices influenced aesthetics and safety (lowering the sidewalls made the car less safe) and ultimately sales.

Selecting a Panel

Consider a producer of a public-interest television show who is selecting six teens to discuss creative solutions to reduce recreational drug use among America's youth. She wants a knowledgeable, informed panel. To select among thousands of online applicants, she could assign a test over general knowledge of types of drugs and their effects. The producer might find that the top scorers lack diversity. They might all be Latinas living in Foster City, California, who attend the same elite private high school. They may have scored highest in part because in the previous summer they all worked as interns in the same neurobiology laboratory at the University of California, San Francisco. Though individually the best, collectively these six would not constitute the best group for the producer.

Their discussion, informed as it may be, would be narrow compared to that of a group that included students from other regions of the country who belonged to other identity groups. The types of drug use, the forms that social pressure takes, and the opportunities available vary along identity dimensions. When the producer adds a white male who scored lower on the test, the producer does not sacrifice excellence in favor of diversity. She adds a person with a diverse repertoire who will contribute to a more productive discussion.

To blindly choose those who score best would be to fall victim to the *meritocratic fallacy*: the belief that the best team consists of the best individuals. Selecting on individual merit makes sense for a four-hundred-meter relay team, but not for a discussion of drug use because the discussion can produce diversity bonuses.

Admitting Students

Universities understand this distinction between tasks that have bonuses and those that do not. College cross-country coaches offer scholarships to runners with the fastest times, and school admissions officers attempt to admit a student body that is diverse across a variety of dimensions, including identity.

College and law school admissions have been the focus of a series of legal cases relating to identity-based discrimination. Here is another context in which no single test can identify the best group. A law school wants a cohort of students who can best learn to interpret, apply, and adjudicate the law. Acquiring those skills requires an awareness and appreciation of the diverse lives that people lead, as well as of the various activities that compose our social, political, and economic worlds.

No single test that averages grade points and test scores can best determine that group. This is why law school admissions officers look beyond those metrics and consider life experiences, expertise, and identity. They do so to ensure cognitive diversity and a vibrant cohort. A school will admit people with a mix of college majors. To add cognitive diversity, a school may give a leg up to a medical doctor or an environmental engineer.

Given the salience of identity in so many aspects of the law, schools many also consider identity to the extent that it is legally permitted. Society needs lawyers and judges capable of understanding the disparate impacts of rulings in diverse communities. Similar arguments can be made for admission decisions based on socioeconomic diversity. Having an elite 1 percent supply all of our judges would produce a less fair and effective legal system.

The White Whale, Politics, and the Middle East

The value of diversity for businesses like Boeing or LinkedIn can be measured in dollars and market share. Diversity's contribution to policy can be measured in cost and efficiency. In a classroom, cognitive diversity contributes to discussions and understandings.

Literature provides a good starting point. Great works of fiction can be interpreted through multiple lenses. Various literary scholars have interpreted the great white whale in Herman Melville's *Moby Dick* as representing nature, a dragon, male potency, race, evil, the mystery of the universe, and even God.[80] A discussion that considered only one of these interpretations would lack the richness of a more comprehensive discussion that includes them all.

When engaging with any work of literature, people will draw inferences, construct analogies, and make connections based on their life experience and background knowledge. Their identities will filter and influence how they interpret images and events. At least two of the whale interpretations connect to identity dimensions: seeing the whale (a sperm whale) as representing male potency and as representing the white race.

Identity and cognitive diversity also broadens and deepens discussions of politics. Diversity, in fact, may constitute the fundamental problem of politics. Jack Knight and James Johnson, two leading contemporary political theorists, write, "Any imaginable human population is heterogeneous across multiple, overlapping dimensions, including material interests, moral and ethical commitments, and cultural attachments. The most important implication of this diversity is that disagreement and conflict are unavoidable."[81]

Imagine two classrooms discussing the Black Lives Matter movement and the shootings of unarmed African Americans. The first classroom contains predominately upper-class suburban white and Asian American students. Those students classified as African American are recent immigrants. The second classroom contains students with a more diverse mix of racial identities. It includes poor students. It includes students who live in cities and students from rural areas. It includes students with family members in jail.

Assume that in each classroom, the instructor creates a safe space in which all students openly share their opinions and feelings. We should expect that the students in the second classroom will discuss more dimensions to the movement, will introduce more perspectives, and will produce a more complex discussion.[82]

Or consider a class that discusses the Middle East. Most universities' populations include Muslim students, Jewish students, and evangelical Christian students. Each identity group brings a different perspective on policies and actions in the region. Provided these students feel safe sharing their opinions, the diversity of knowledge, information, and mental models that they bring to classroom discussions results in deeper and broader understandings.

SUMMARY

In this chapter, I have shown how the logical case for diversity bonuses can be constructed by connecting repertoires to outcomes on specific tasks. Diverse categories and mental models improve predictions. Diverse representations and heuristics improve problem solving. Diverse perspectives and categories lead to more adjacent possibles and make groups more creative. Diverse information and knowledge improve a group's ability to verify the truth.

In all of these domains, the right type of diversity can improve outcomes. On complex tasks, the best team will not consist of the best individuals. Teams need diversity. Diversity, though, is no panacea. Only rarely will the best team be maximally diverse. Most often, the best team will balance individual ability and collective diversity.

The relative importance of diversity depends on the corpus of relevant perspectives, knowledge, heuristics, models, and information. If there is much that can be applied to the task, diversity becomes more important. It follows that as we reach the frontiers of any discipline, we should seek diversity. The search for diversity can spur us to look across disciplines. Chemists look to physicists to better understand chemical structures. Ecologists turn to mathematicians to better understand niche dynamics. Economists turn to psychologists and neuroscientists to construct more accurate models of people.[83]

On many of the challenges we face today, we need diversity to span disciplines. As already noted, America's obesity epidemic falls into multiple disciplinary buckets. People may have biological predispositions that are exacerbated by abundant opportunities to choose fattening, unhealthy food. The current transportation infrastructure and zoning laws force more of us into cars and fewer of us onto sidewalks. No single cure exists. Making progress on the obesity epidemic will require thoughtful interventions based on input from doctors, marketers, public health professionals, sociologists, economists, and engineers. Finally, if, on the challenges we face, be they improving educational outcomes or selling running shoes, our identity differences correlate with relevant knowledge bases, understandings, and models, then the logic demonstrates the value of identity diversity.

These models reveal logical truths. They do not guarantee that in the world of people, diversity bonuses will always arise. By revealing logical truths, models enable us to interpret and structure empirical data. More importantly, they delineate the routes we must follow to achieve bonuses and help define the behaviors we must adopt to achieve bonuses. To reorder da Vinci's claim, the models provide a compass and rudder.

IDENTITY DIVERSITY

A man is like a bit of Labrador spar, which has no lustre as you turn it in your hand, until you come to a particular angle; then it shows deep and beautiful colors. There is no adaptation or universal applicability in men, but each has his special talent, and the mastery of successful men consists in adroitly keeping themselves where and when that turn shall be oftenest to be practised.

—RALPH WALDO EMERSON, *Experience*

DIVERSITY BONUSES RESULT FROM DIFFERENCES IN WHAT WE KNOW, how we perceive the world, the frameworks and models we use to organize our thoughts, and the ways we generate ideas. The notion of a cognitive repertoire is an artificial construct. How we think about a problem, make a prediction, or evaluate a strategy depends on complex interactions in our brains within a network of neurons, axons, and dendrites.

A variety of factors cause people to build diverse cognitive repertoires. Nature must play a role, but for many of the contexts covered here, our experiences and formal training matter more. A doctor possesses a cognitive repertoire distinct from that of a plumber or a materials scientist more because of training and experience than genetics.

In this chapter, I take up the question of the extent to which identity differences contribute to relevant cognitive diversity. To the extent that they do, identity differences contribute to cognitive diversity bonuses.

Identity diversity commonly refers to differences in race, gender, age, ethnicity, religion, physical qualities, and sexual orientation. Logically, a bright line separates this from cognitive diversity. One corresponds to how we think, while the other corresponds to categories we use to define people. Empirically, the distinction becomes blurry. Our identities influence what we know, how we perceive events, and how we think.

To connect identity diversity to cognitive diversity requires unpacking the term *identity*. I present three frameworks that can organize our thinking: the *icebergs*, the *timber-framed house*, and the *cloud*. The icebergs (there will be two) highlight the fact that we see some attributes while others lie below the surface. The timber-framed house represents identities as consisting of connected components that combine to form a whole. We cannot decompose a Japanese American woman's identity into a Japanese part, an American part, and a female part. The cloud emphasizes the variation within identity categories.

All three frameworks prove central to the main argument of this chapter. When we try to link identity diversity to cognitive diversity, we lean on categories. Those categories are based on what we see above the iceberg's waterline. They structure the questions we ask and the inferences we draw. Claims that women think differently from men or that African Americans bring a unique perspective rest on crude categorizations. Those categories slice off single dimensions from the timber-framed house. Pulling off just one attribute and drawing inferences will produce errors. And last, no matter how finely we make the categories, within-category variation will remain.

As a starting point, we must keep in mind that any group, even a group whose members possess the same identity attributes, will be cognitively diverse because no two people possess identical cognitive repertoires: no two people possess the same information, apply the same perspectives, or carry around identical collections of mental models. That is true even of people who belong to the same identity group.

However, given that our identities influence how we construct our lives and how others treat us, we would expect identity-diverse groups to be more cognitively diverse than homogenous groups. We would also expect people to behave differently when in a diverse group. Empirical evidence supports both inferences.[1]

Given the importance of identities, they must correlate with how we think. In some domains, the links are obvious. Adding race and gender diversity would enhance a group discussion of the *Roe v. Wade* decision, the significance of Harper Lee's *To Kill a Mockingbird*, or the Barack Obama presidency. On the other hand, identity cannot have superordinate influence in all cases. Teams of materials scientists developing organic solar cells lean more on educational and experiential diversity than on identity diversity.

Though our identities may play a smaller role in driving scientific understanding and discovery than in interpreting the law or making psychological inferences, they may still have an impact in science through the analogies we invoke. Think back to high school biology when you had a test on the various parts of a cell and their functions. One of the cell's parts, the Golgi apparatus, packages proteins within the cell's vesicles and sends them on their way. To recall and explain the Golgi apparatus's function, students invoke any number of analogies—a post office, a sugarcoating factory, a baggage department, or a finishing school.[2] We can connect these analogies to life experiences. Few rural kids would think up the finishing school analogy.

The choice of analogy frames how someone thinks of the Golgi apparatus. The student who thinks of the Golgi apparatus as assigning tags on luggage understates the organelle's function. In her view, the organelle puts proteins in boxes and slaps on addresses. Conceptualizing it as a finishing school hints at a more elaborate function and could spur deeper inquiry.

The investigation of the connections between identity and cognition will not produce definitive answers. Evidence that identity diversity correlates with or causes cognitive diversity need not imply that identity-diverse groups always make better choices, come up with more innovative solutions to problems, make more accurate predictions, or elaborate more creative alternatives. In some cases, identity-diverse groups might perform best. In other cases, identity diversity might add little relevant cognitive diversity.

Identity will prove a complex and fluid combination of attributes that cannot be captured by a set of boxes on an application form or variables in a statistical regression. That complexity undermines any simple causal explanation. We cannot *prove* that identity diversity creates beneficial cognitive diversity. What we can do is explore the possible linkages and gauge their plausibility.

AN IDENTITY PRIMER

When describing identity differences, laypeople and scientists alike rely on six primary categories: race, gender, age, ethnicity, physical capabilities, and sexual orientation. More expansive categorizations include neighborhoods, family structure, diet, forms of artistic expression, social norms, education, socioeconomic status, genes, ancestry, dialect, and power relations. We might describe a friend Gunther as a black, German, heterosexual, Catholic male. These categories differ in their permanence. Gunther will always be black and of German descent. His religion or sexual orientation may change.

Identity categories reduce people to a handful of tags—white, male, differently abled, and so on—that cannot capture in full the rich diversity of individuals they contain. We would categorize some of the world's most gifted artists and athletes as disabled. Beethoven became deaf. Jim Abbott, born without a complete right hand, quarterbacked his high school football team, won the Sullivan Award as the nation's top amateur athlete, and pitched a no-hitter for the New York Yankees.

Despite obvious flaws, identity categories persist. They enable meaning making. They function as a self-reinforcing accounting standard. With them, we can describe human diversity, identify discrimination, and measure inequality across groups.

In the past, people thought of identity attributes as *essential*.[3] Essentialism assumes that identities correspond to innate, unchanging characteristics. Men were believed to possess an innate male essence observable through characteristics. Male characteristics, both physical and cognitive, were thought to differ from the innate characteristics of women, who were thought more caring and sensitive. Similarly, the innate characteristics of Asians were thought to differ from those of Europeans and Africans. Asians were seen as more collectively oriented.

Essentialism derives from Aristotelian foundations: the essence of an orange differs from the essence of a peach, and the essence of a dog is distinct from the essence of a badger. Essentialism predates genetics. Many categories once deemed essential have been found to lack genetic foundations. Racial classifications are a notable example. People who identify as African American can trace, on average, one-fourth of their genes to Europe.[4]

Given that people's beliefs about their racial identity and the identities projected on them by others matter more than genetics, we now think of race as *socially constructed*.[5] Society creates the categories and endows them with meaning.

An analysis of any particular trait reveals the challenges of essential designations. Height satisfies two properties of an essential attribute: it is largely determined by genetics and it varies across groups. Data based on a quarter million people reveals seven hundred genes spread over four hundred gene regions that can explain 80 percent of height variation.[6]

We also see variation across groups. The average height of Dutch men (over six feet) exceeds that of American men by about three inches. That statistic will not surprise anyone who has wandered Amsterdam's Schiphol Airport.

And yet, the tallness among the Dutch is at best temporally essential. Over the past two hundred years, the average height of a Dutch male has increased more than eight inches. Two centuries ago, the Dutch were shorter than Americans. If being tall is now an essential trait of the Dutch, then, in the recent past, being short was an essential trait.[7]

Of course, height is just one characteristic of the Dutch. The Dutch are also thought to be less generous ("going Dutch") and more open-minded. Those attributes seem less likely to be essential than height. If we stereotypically categorize the Dutch as a tall, frugal, open-minded people, we surely err.

By applying frameworks, even at the level of analogy, we can think about identity with greater subtlety and avoid these stereotypes.

We are also better able to think about how and when identity diversity might connect to cognitive diversity.

THE ICEBERGS

The first framework, the icebergs, distinguishes attributes that compose identity diversity—race, gender, ethnicity, sexual orientation, age, and physical capabilities—by their observability (see figure 4.1). We see a person's skin color, gender, and age. We hear her dialect. We see physical qualities. We do not see values, beliefs, religion, history, or ancestry. The traditional identity iceberg analogy categorizes attributes as either above or below the waterline.[8] We observe those attributes above the waterline. We can only infer attributes below the waterline.

The iceberg analogy reveals an inherent *selection bias* in impressions of identity diversity. We construct categories and make inferences based on (or biased toward) observable identity characteristics. Many lump Korean Americans, Chinese Americans, and Japanese Americans into a single category: Asian Americans. That categori-

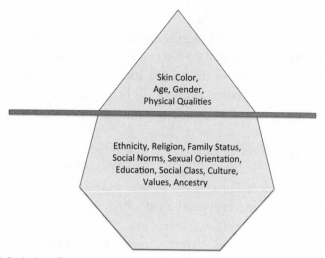

Figure 4.1 An Iceberg Representation of Identity Diversity

zation sweeps ancestry, ethnic identity, and religious practices under the rug. The media emphasizes the disproportionate number of Asian Americans at elite colleges and universities. The large number of evangelical Asian American students goes unnoticed.[9]

If selecting a representative group of students to discuss their experiences at Berkeley based on observable racial characteristics, we might choose two Asian Americans. If both students identify as Chinese American, the two of them may not be that diverse. A more deliberate set of choices, one that looks below the waterline, might select a first-generation Chinese American Buddhist and a third-generation Korean American Christian. This second pair would produce a broader, more nuanced discussion.

The iceberg framework also highlights a distinction among perceived, expressed, and internal identifications. A person may internally feel as though they belong to one identity group, express a different identity through behavior, and be perceived as belonging to either of the two identity groups by different people. For example, self-reported racial categorizations among multiracial adolescents depend on context. Their answers to questions about their race at home in the presence of their parents differ from the answers they give at school when surrounded by friends.[10]

This traditional iceberg model captures impressions of identity in the physical world. The virtual world creates a second iceberg. Data gathered from the web reveal attributes that we may not observe at street level. The virtual iceberg includes criminal records, property ownership, and political donations, none of which we can infer by passing someone on the street.

The differences between these two icebergs have become more relevant because social scientists and human resource professionals increasingly evaluate the effects of diversity by analyzing online data; in other words, the virtual iceberg. A social scientist working with census data might include a person's neighborhood and social class, two attributes that lie below the physical waterline. Social scientists then measure relationships between neighborhood characteristics and performance in school, probability of criminal behavior, and likelihood of drug use.

As more attributes rise above the virtual waterline, we can better avoid the stereotypes we jump to in the physical world: African Americans are more likely to go to jail, Asian Americans perform better in school, white Americans commit more acts of terrorism. Those correlations may be statistically valid, but they lack causal explanations. Any explanatory attributes for criminal behavior or educational performance, such as income, social class, parental education, neighborhood, religious affiliation, or mental health, likely lie below the physical waterline.

To categorize someone as Asian American and make inferences based on that categorization can lead to wrong actions as well as improper inferences. I once met a third-generation Japanese American who had been hired to manage a company's Asian American client list. The company hoped his shared identity would allow him to build trust with clients, improve communication, and increase revenue.

Upon being hired, he found that the company's Asian American clients were Korean Americans. He soon quit, not because he was not successful at his job; he performed above expectations. He left because he believed that any company with such a poor understanding of its clients would not be successful in the long run.

THE TIMBER-FRAMED HOUSE

The second analogy, the timber-framed house, represents a person as possessing multiple, connected identity attributes.[11] Just as two parts of a timber-framed house can be nailed together or lie far apart, so too can pairs of identity attributes. A person's neighborhood and social class connect more closely than her skin color and diet, while her ancestry probably links more tightly to her religion than to her current social status.

The timber-framed house analogy warns against separating out effects of individual identity attributes. A person's entire identity influences her life experiences and therefore her cognitive repertoire. We cannot and should not think that a person's identity-based influences can be decomposed into a sum of effects from individual

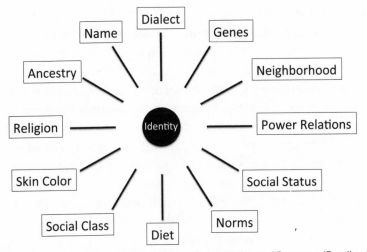

Figure 4.2 Identity as a Timber-Framed House (Sen and Wasow, "Race as a 'Bundle of Sticks'")

identity attributes.[12] The identity influences on the cognitive repertoire of an African American woman cannot be decomposed into an African American effect and a woman effect.

Therefore, we cannot gather data on the opinions of African American women on a proposed educational reform and tease out a woman effect and an African American effect. The effects of gender and race interact and intertwine. A person's identity consists of the whole structure. We can no more understand a person by listing her identities than we can appreciate a house by taking an inventory of the materials used in its construction. We need to know how the parts interact.

This nonadditivity of attributes arises in intersectionality theory.[13] Intersectionality teaches us that considering the effects of race and gender separately can obscure discrimination and miss forms of oppression. For example, a company that hires white and black men and only white women might have representative numbers of blacks and women, even though it hires no black women.[14] Alternatively, a company that hires only white men and black women could have more than a representative number of blacks yet no black men.

Relatedly, the discrimination experienced by black women may differ markedly from that experienced by women or blacks.

The inseparability of attributes implied by the timber-framed house analogy should give us pause when interpreting data sorted by single attributes. Single-attribute correlations obscure richer stories. For instance, women constitute approximately three-fourths of veterinary students. We cannot infer that being a woman makes one more likely to want to be a veterinarian. The vast majority of women veterinary students are white. Therefore, it is not *women* who pursue veterinary degrees, it is *white women*.

The timber-framed house framework is important to keep top of mind because we are prone to crude, inaccurate inferences based on single attributes. These are often wrong. Yes, women make up two-thirds of fund-raisers, but few of those women are Latina. Yes, two-thirds of judges are men, but not many are Asian American.

THE CLOUD

When we invoke a crude category—European American, African American, and so on—we condense diverse populations to a single point. This diversity of cognitive repertoires within any category reveals the impossibility of asking any one person to represent an identity category.[15] This observation leads to the third framework: the cloud. Any short list of identity attributes will be shared by a diverse set of people. The identity bundle that includes the features *educated, heterosexual, Catholic*, and *Irish American* is held by a diverse collection of people including comedians Conan O'Brien and Bill Murray and television correspondent Elizabeth Vargas.

Within any bundle, people differ in diet, skin color, social class, political views, and family structure. That holds true for any identity bundle. Categories do not divide people into clean sets of identical people; they create neighboring clouds.

The variation with the cloud also problematizes inferences. We cannot claim that someone brings a woman's perspective. There is no such thing. The set of women is too large and diverse to have a unique shared perspective. The most we could say is that the set of ways in which women look at a particular problem differs from the set of ways in which men frame it.

As we move forward, we must keep all three analogies in mind: identity consists of multiple dimensions, some of which we see and others of which we don't (the iceberg); these attributes cannot be separated because they connect (the timber-framed house); and within any category, we find a diverse group of people (the cloud).

CONNECTING IDENTITY DIVERSITY TO COGNITIVE DIVERSITY

We are now in a better position to explore potential links between identities and cognitive repertoires. That those links exist should be obvious. Our identities influence what we value, whom we know, and what we experience. They also influence how we make sense of those experiences.[16]

We live in segregated communities defined by identity categories, so those categories correlate with the knowledge, models, information, representations, and heuristics that constitute our repertoires. Our communities influence our opportunities and how we represent the world.[17]

A similar path of logic can explain differences between westerners and easterners. Easterners (and here I mean Asians, not New Yorkers) more often rely on relational representations, while westerners focus more on individual objects.[18] An American will say, "Look at that fish." A Japanese will say, "Notice the pattern of fish." These differences derive from history, cultural practices, and experiences. They are not essential.

In thinking through the effects of identity on our cognitive repertoires, in places it will be helpful to distinguish between *fluid intelligence* and *crystallized intelligence*.[19] Fluid intelligence corresponds to problem-solving skills and logical reasoning. Tests of fluid intelligence ask subjects to match patterns or solve logic puzzles. Tests of crystallized intelligence ask for the definition of *cosine*. A person with high fluid intelligence can acquire knowledge quickly. If he does not retain it, then he lacks crystallized intelligence.

Including this distinction complicates and enriches how we think about the components of a repertoire. Some parts of our cognitive repertoires, namely heuristics and representations, contribute to fluid intelligence. Other parts, like information, knowledge, and models, contribute to our crystallized intelligence.

It is worth noting that scores of fluid intelligence have risen over the past ninety years, and a majority of those gains occur among the lower half of the distribution.[20] This rise in fluid intelligence may result from greater exposure to logical and abstract reasoning; that is, children learn heuristics and representations that enable them to score more highly on tests of fluid intelligence. Thus, we should think of fluid intelligence as dependent in part on life experiences.

How Identity Might Matter

The claim that members of identity groups have special understanding of their own groups can be supported by multiple strands of evidence. Data on friendships proves particularly convincing. People tend to hang out with people from the same identity group. One study finds that a typical white American has but a single black friend and a single Latino friend.[21] It involves, therefore, a rather large logical leap to presume that most people possess deep knowledge of the preferences and beliefs of people with different identity classifications.[22]

Whether identity diversity plays a direct or indirect role, or no role at all, will depend on the situation. Often, we have no idea what type of diversity will come to bear. Entire books can be filled with anecdotes of these idiosyncratic diversity bonuses.

Here's a favorite of mine, based on a physical difference told to me by Laszlo Bock, a former senior vice president of Google. After acquiring YouTube, Google found that approximately 10 percent of people uploaded their videos upside down. This was a puzzle. Well, it was only a puzzle to the 90 percent of people who are right-handed. When a left-handed Googler heard the problem, she knew the cause: lefties. A left-handed person tips her smartphone to the right to take a horizontal video. A right-handed person tips his smartphone to the left. What's upside down to a righty is right side up to a lefty.

The smartphone anecdote sticks.[23] It is simple, unexpected, concrete, credible, and uplifting. It also oversimplifies. It maps a single identity attribute or experience to a particular solution, masking the complex, mysterious relationship between who we are and how we think.

Such stories function better as motivational impetus than as guides to practice.[24] Could Google have known that a left-handed person was needed? Should they make sure every programming and problem-solving team has a lefty? To build a logic of diversity bonuses from identity, we need to think through the mapping between identity bundles and cognitive repertoires. A good place to start that process is with (inappropriate) stereotypical mappings from identity characteristics to cognitive repertoires.

Stereotypical Identity-Based Cognitive Differences

Recall from the iceberg analogy that identity attributes—woman, Asian American, visually impaired—differ in their observability. We can make inferences based only on the attributes we see. We infer that identity diversity implies diversity of thought. We infer that Asian Americans think differently from European Americans, and that men think differently from women.

This assumes that we can take the parts of our cognitive repertoires and trace them back to individual components of our identities (see figure 4.3). We do this when we say, "We need a woman's perspective on this," or, "Our group includes no people of color. We're missing out on valuable ways of thinking." Though well intended, these statements lack precision (and border on offensive).

Unpacking the reasoning reveals the imprecision. Start with a population of people. Each person has multiple dimensions to her identity. Focusing on a single attribute puts her in a box with everyone in the population who shares that attribute. That could be the African American box. It could be the woman box. If the latter, the arrows oblige us to identify the parts of her cognitive repertoire that result from being female.

Let's focus first on information and knowledge. A person's information and knowledge includes everything she has acquired over

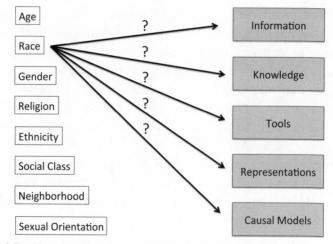

Figure 4.3 The (Oversimplified, Problematic) Single-Attribute Mapping

her lifetime, what she has learned at school and in her vocation and avocations. Some of the information will be organized. Some will be idiosyncratic.

Some will depend on our identities. Identity-based categorizations—gender, race, religion, sexual orientation, and such—correlate with differences in books read, movies watched, websites visited, college courses taken, and so on by people who vary on that dimension.

Imagine convening a large group of women and men and asking everyone to list everything they know, all their information and knowledge. Each person would create a large set. We could label each set with an *F* or an *M* to denote gender. If a statistician compared those two collections of sets, she would find substantial overlap. Some information would be in almost every set. Almost everyone knows that cars run on gasoline, that New York City has tall buildings, and that horses have four legs.

The statistician would also find information and knowledge that reveals geographic location and educational background but provides no clue as to gender. Information on the capital of Kentucky and knowledge of mitosis and meiosis might well be equally present in the sets labeled *F* and *M*.

The statistician would also find bits of information and pieces of knowledge that do correlate with gender. She could identify statistical differences between the two sets. Those differences would allow her to evaluate someone's set and predict the person's gender. With enough data, she would classify correctly with a high degree of accuracy.

In my thought experiment, the statistician can see a person's entire information and knowledge set. With far less information, algorithms can predict a person's gender, age, and ethnicity. For instance, Google Ads' settings page predicts your gender, age, and interests based on your search history.[25] It pegs me as male.[26] These algorithms exploit the fact that members of different identity groups differ statistically in the books they buy, the websites they visit, the movies and television shows they download, the health issues they research, and the sports and hobbies they pursue. These differences produce statistically distinct distributions over the websites searched by identity groups.

Men compose 60 percent of whiskey drinkers, 70 percent of baseball fans, 80 percent of private investigators, 90 percent of hunters, and 100 percent of vasectomy patients. A person who knows that Old Forester Classic is 86 proof, that Lou Whitaker was the 1978 American League Rookie of the Year, that it is easier to lift fingerprints from a golf ball than from a gun,[27] that Washington and Idaho preclude the removal of the sex organs when gutting a deer so that the state can verify gender, and that residual pain from vasectomies can last more than a year would be statistically far more likely to be a man.

If the statistician had access to people's full cognitive repertoires and again created two collections of sets, one labeled M and one labeled F, the two collections would again be internally diverse, overlap substantially, and exhibit enough statistical differences for the statistician to predict gender out of sample with a high degree of accuracy.

Similar results would hold if we considered classifications based on race. The cognitive repertoires of people labeled African American or Latino will be diverse, overlap with those of other racial groups, and have identifiable statistical signatures.

Subclusters also exist within each cluster. The people classified as Asian American include Japanese, Korean, Chinese, and Filipino Americans. Each of these groups possesses distinct histories and cultural practices. Variation within the set of Asian Americans may be clustered by country of origin. A Japanese American may have little knowledge of Korean American culture and vice versa.

This way of thinking of the connection between identity and cognitive diversity accords with the timber-framed house analogy. Second-generation Chicanas combine three identity groups: Chicano, female, and second-generation American. The cognitive repertoires of second-generation Chicanas consist of the intersection of the cognitive repertoires of those three groups.

That intersection property does not imply that a characteristic of each of those three groups is also a characteristic of Chicanas. It could be that Chicanos, women, and second-generation Americans disproportionately attend comedy clubs and know recent comedic tropes. If second-generation Chicanas do not go to comedy clubs, they would lack that knowledge. The failure of characteristics to apply to intersections is analogous to the problem identified by intersectionality theory. A firm can hire women and African Americans but not hire African American women. Here, a characteristic can be common among Chicanos, women, and second-generation Americans but not be common among second-generation Chicanas.

Given that within each identity category, people vary in their repertoires, we cannot expect token representatives to speak for an entire group. If the Ford Motor Company wants to market cars to the growing Latino population, it should hire a cohort of Latino employees, not a single Latino in marketing. Similarly, if the University of Delaware wants students with diverse cognitive repertoires to create a rich intellectual environment, they require more than one person from each identity group.

Points in the Clouds

The cognitive repertoires of people within any identity category differ. No single person can represent her identity group. A cohort of people can function as a representative sample.

Can't a Homogeneous Group Be Diverse?

The cloud analogy applies to any group with a common identity attribute—even the proverbial group of all white men. They too will be cognitively diverse. The information, knowledge, mental models, representations, and heuristics within their heads will differ. A group of older white men who attended Exeter and Dartmouth in the 1960s, majored in economics, and pursued careers in investment banking will be cognitively diverse: no two the same.

But they will not be that diverse. Their collective repertoire will contain holes. For example, the group may lack knowledge of the educational aspirations of second-generation Latinos or frameworks for explaining the cultural acclimation process of Somalian immigrants. Or they may bin all Asian American women within a single category, limiting their ability to predict the efficacy of many public health interventions.

These older white men would not be the first people we would turn to for heuristics for debugging Python code, writing hip-hop lyrics, or predicting trends in fashion. Nor would we expect them to be experts on women's health concerns, to be familiar with the video game market, or to understand the financial concerns of recent widows.

I am purposefully stereotyping here. Some men may be experts in those domains. My point is that their clouds of information and knowledge, their clouds of heuristics and mental models, and their clouds of representations differ statistically from the clouds of twenty-five-year-old Latinas.

Whether it is then a large leap to infer that the lack of identity diversity on Wall Street contributed to the home mortgage crisis is an empirical question. It is probably fair to say that investment bankers

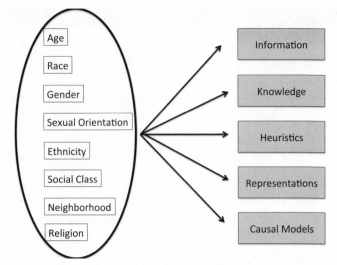

Figure 4.4 The Identity-Bundle-to-Cognitive-Repertoire Mapping

had less knowledge of the financial models carried around in the heads of the diverse people flipping houses than they would have had if the investment bankers had been more diverse.

Whatever mapping does exist goes from identity bundles, from our whole selves, to our full repertoires (see figure 4.4). Each person's unique bundled identity combines with experiences and training to produce her unique cognitive ensemble, situated somewhere in the cloud.

IDENTITY-BASED COGNITIVE DIFFERENCES BY TASK

The pragmatic question remains as to the amount to which identity differences in repertoires map to performance differences. Inferring the extent of identity's influence is difficult because the mapping is complicated. If we represent people as timber-framed houses of identity attributes and represent identity groups as clouds, then, as already discussed, the concept of a woman's perspective is not well defined. That term cleaves identity bundles and ignores the gestalt of repertoires. It isolates gender and representation. Applying similar logic, we should not put much stock in the notion of a Latino mental model, a heterosexual categorization, or an Asian American heuristic.

That said, empirical correlations between identity bundles and cognitive repertoires do exist. As mentioned, Google knows our identity attributes from our searches.

A first step in determining the relevance of the identity-driven components of our repertoires is to recognize that it varies by task. We expect the identities of city council members to influence their positions on educational reform more than we expect the identities of students to correlate with the techniques they use to invert matrices in linear algebra class.

Identity also interacts with geography. Each person has someplace she lays her head down on a pillow at night. If she also worships, works, organizes, and plays near that place, she will know the people who live there with a depth and granularity that outsiders cannot match. Given a seat at the table, she can add her information, knowledge, and mental models to policy choices. Following similar reasoning, health services providers who understand the lifestyles, community structures, and ways that information spreads within a community will be necessary parts of a health services team. We cannot just roll out a bunch of doctors with degrees from elite schools and expect them to improve health outcomes.

As a rule, we should expect identity-driven differences to matter in any domain that serves people: education, finance, entertainment, or health. Thus, a strong case can be made for the potential contributions of cognitive diversity correlated with identity diversity to the areas of product design and marketing, to policy creation, and to media production.

Identity diversity can also matter in less weighty social contexts. Careful thought and elaborate efforts enter into casting decisions. Interns, midlevel executives, and producers all read scripts and suggest actors. After someone has been selected, she may not accept the part. In the movie *Gravity*, Sandra Bullock stars as a lone astronaut who attempts to return to Earth in a failing space module. Angelina Jolie had been director Alfonso Cuarón's first choice. Jolie opted not to pursue the project.

To find a replacement, Cuarón sought out other A-list Hollywood stars. He considered actresses he thought capable of carrying an entire film. His set included Natalie Portman, Blake Lively, and Scarlett Johansson.[28] He made a wise choice in Bullock. The movie won six Academy Awards, and Cuarón was awarded the Oscar for Best Director.

Mitt Romney, the 2008 Republican candidate for president, described how he would use a similar process to populate a diverse cabinet by creating a binder of qualified women. Romney was pilloried for this in the media. That criticism is ironic given that creating lists of qualified women candidates guards against an implicit pro-male bias when making hires. Binders are a standard strategy for improving the representation of women.

To see why binders—or some systematic method for constituting a pool of candidates—are necessary because of our biases, I created an experiment I called Tom Hanks Is Busy. In the experiment, I describe the following scenario: Tom Hanks has been cast in a Hollywood drama as an everyman who rises to the occasion to rescue a group of teens in peril. For personal reasons, Hanks steps out of the role. The director needs to find a replacement. The experiment asks that you replace Tom Hanks.

Stop reading for a moment and think. Who would you choose to replace Tom Hanks?

I have posed this question to many people. Common answers include Liam Neeson, George Clooney, Adam Sandler, Hugh Grant, and Brad Pitt. These actors can be thought of as adjacent possibles to Tom Hanks. They are all white men.

To see how a systematic approach reduces bias, list some adjectives that describe Hanks. You probably chose terms like *huge star*, *dependable*, *kind*, *sensitive*, *middle aged*, *funny*, and *artistic range*. Now suppose I gave you that list of adjectives and asked you to think of actors with those attributes.

You might now think of Denzel Washington.

Is Denzel a good replacement for Hanks? Hanks was born in the mid-1950s and won two Academy Awards. Ditto for Denzel. Hanks has starred as a war hero and an everyman. Hanks played a pilot who crash-lands a plane in *Sully*, as did Denzel in *Flight*. Both are huge celebrities who star in movies that have grossed more than $2 billion. Both also direct and produce.

The have similar off-screen images. Both are quietly religious. Both have been married for more than twenty-five years and both have four children. Both donate to multiple charitable causes and both are active in politics. If Denzel did not jump to mind, that does not mean you are racist, but it does reveal that race plays a large role in the adjacent possibles. If you did not think of Sandra Bullock or Meryl Streep, then gender does as well.

This thought experiment should not be dismissed as lighthearted fun. The history of racial inequities in casting decisions within the film industry suggests casting directors rely on racially and gender-biased adjacent possibles. Identity-diverse casting teams would be one way to correct for those biases, that is, if African Americans would be more likely to think of Denzel.

A similar logic extends to strategic decisions for consumer products. A brewer wants to sell beer. Soft-drink companies want to sell soda. Knowing the occasions that bring people together and the foods that people eat informs marketing, packaging, and pricing. Paper companies want to sell diapers. In 2016, Pampers released a hilarious video of babies caught in the act, so to speak. In the initial release of the video, every baby was Caucasian. The majority of babies born in the United States are not.

Can Identity Diversity Matter for Science?

The relevance of identity diversity is less obvious on scientific and technical problems. We know that in some cases, our identities can have large effects. I begin with a well-known example in which identity played a role in scientific research.[29]

Fifty years ago, descriptions of the process of human egg fertilization characterized the sperm as conquering a passive egg. The people who wrote those descriptions were men. The film of attacking sperm that I watched in seventh-grade science class with a roomful of boys might have featured Richard Wagner's *Ride of the*

Valkyries as a soundtrack. In that version, the egg waits passively as the conquering sperm swarm. A more gendered analogy would be difficult to construct.

Later, a research team including both men and women showed that the egg actively selects from among the many sperm attacking its outer wall. They discovered that the egg's selection depends in part on genetic diversity.[30] Understandings of the sperm and the egg show how identity diversity can influence how people represent and model a phenomenon.

To dig deeper, let's engage in a prototypical thought experiment regarding homogenous and diverse groups that goes as follows: a NASA administrator must select a group of scientists to increase the lift capacity of the new Space Launch System (SLS). She must choose between two groups. The members of both groups have similar ability as measured by IQ tests, college grades, and college entrance scores.

The first group consists of eight Muslim men between thirty-eight and forty-three years of age. All earned aerospace engineering degrees from Georgia Tech and have worked at the Marshall Space Flight Center in Huntsville, Alabama, for at least ten years.

The second group (the diverse group) consists of men and women belonging to a variety of ethnic and racial groups. They also vary in age, education, and work experience. Some earned aerospace engineering degrees. Others studied mechanical or electrical engineering. This group includes two outsiders on loan from Boeing and Ford. Should the administrator choose the homogenous group or the diverse group?

This experiment stacks the deck in favor of the identity-diverse group, whose members possess more diverse technical repertoires. Even if their identity diversity had no influence, the second group would be the stronger choice.

A more informative thought experiment varies identity diversity and training diversity independently. This requires four groups. The first would consist of people from the same identity group with similar experiences and training. A second group would include identity-diverse people with similar training and experiences. A third group would consist of people from the same identity group who have different educations, training, and experiences. The fourth group would be diverse in every possible way, like the second group from the previous example. We could then think through which group would perform best. That would be difficult if not impossible for any one person to do.

These types of thought experiments do not resemble real-world choice processes. A NASA administrator choosing a group of scientists to increase the lift capacity of the new SLS would not be given a binary choice between a "homogenous" group and a "diverse" group. Nor would she choose among four types of groups like those just described.

Instead, she would form a group from a set of applicants. In selecting that group, she would ask herself a series of questions including the following: What types of training will be relevant for the problems the team will face? What educational backgrounds might I consider? What experiences? Does the group include people with applicable knowledge bases? Does it include people who bring different frames—someone who will think of costs, someone who will think of risks, someone who will think of novel possibilities, and so on?

The answers to those questions will not be independent of identity diversity. Recall how the clouds overlap and differ statistically. Leaving out people from an identity group means selecting a non-representative set of cognitive repertoires. If we have no evidence either way, should our default position be that those parts of the repertoire that correlate with identity matter or that they don't?

To answer that question, we must think through the parts of a repertoire. The information and knowledge pertinent to designing a propulsion system might be thought to have the weakest correlation with identity. Most of that knowledge would come from engineering, though perhaps a piece of knowledge from biology, kinesiology, or chemistry could improve the design. Ideally, we would pull academic transcripts when forming the group to get a team with diverse knowledge.

Identity-based heuristics and mental models and frameworks surely matter more. When a problem becomes difficult, we seek analogies drawn from past experiences. Identity contributes to how we represent systems. One of the proposed designs for an SLS booster was named the Dark Knight.

Identity may also influence how we think about power and balance. Take the experience of learning to scull. Single sculling shells are over twenty-five feet long and less than eighteen inches wide. Those dimensions do not promote stability. Men are on average taller than women, and they have broader shoulders, which distributes more of their weight to the upper part of their bodies. The typical man placed in a shell struggles to balance. One good solution is to start rowing. Most women, who on average have a lower center of mass, can achieve balance by relaxing. Placed in the same situation, men achieve balance through power and women by, well, balancing. Those different experiences could translate into frameworks and heuristics for achieving balance when designing spacecraft and satellites.

Thus, a wise NASA director would consider identity diversity as contributing to cognitive diversity. To tap into as diverse a set of cognitive repertoires as possible, she would want teams with men and women. She would also want a variety of types of engineers who attended different schools. Standard engineering courses like advanced fluid dynamics may cover different topics at different schools. MIT covers windmills in its fluid dynamics course. The University of Illinois does not.

Though the direct influence of identity diversity on germane cognitive diversity in technical fields should be less pronounced than in domains that involve people, a lack of identity diversity may well correlate with less cognitive diversity. The NASA director's mission, perhaps to get people to Mars and back, requires brilliant, diverse thinkers. She would be reluctant to put together a team of people who all belonged to the same identity group.

Furthermore, we must keep in mind that on unsolved problems, where we lack a heuristic or do not know what knowledge, model, or representation might lead to the breakthrough, we want as much relevant cognitive diversity as possible. Where a solution might come from, or where a person might acquire it, could be serendipitous.

Add to the mystery of the source of breakthroughs the evidence that the presence of diverse others causes us to think differently, and we have even more reason to err on the side of identity diversity.

Identity-Based Opportunity Bonuses

Here, I tell three stories of how a unique way of looking at the world resulted in an innovation or a new product. In each case, the person recognized a dimension that others had overlooked. One recognized a medical disparity based on race. The other two saw unmet community needs. In each case, the dimension aligns with the person's identity. All three people created diversity. I refer to these as opportunity bonuses because these diverse ways of seeing created new opportunities. They were not solving an existing problem.

Patricia Bath: Medical Innovator

At an early age, Patricia Bath displayed uncommon scientific talents. Her precocity as editor of the Charles Evans Hughes High School's science paper led her to be invited to a 1959 National Science Foundation summer cancer research workshop held at Yeshiva University. While there, she derived a mathematical equation describing cancer cell growth. She was only sixteen years old.[31]

She went on to study chemistry and physics at Hunter College in New York and, at age twenty-six, earned an MD from Howard University. Bath later became the first African American resident in ophthalmology at New York University Hospital, the first African American woman surgeon at UCLA Medical Center, and the first woman to head a residency program at the Charles R. Drew School of Medicine and Science. She would later receive a medical patent for the Laserphaco Probe, a tool that removes cataracts while simultaneously irrigating the eye to facilitate surgical lens replacement.

At first glance, Patricia Bath's story appears to be one of the millions of examples of the larger-pool logic. Had Bath not been invited to the summer workshop, had she not been allowed to study chemistry and physics and to earn an MD, the world would have been denied an accomplished surgeon and a medical innovator. Her success reminds us that talent knows no color or gender.

If we dig deeper, we find diversity bonuses. Bath worked at both Harlem Hospital and the Columbia University Eye Clinic Hospital. She held the former position partly because of her identity. Having these two windows on the world, she noticed a disparity in blindness rates among African Americans at the two hospitals. She was able to identify the lack of access to care as a cause. The research stemming from this observation led to the development of community ophthalmology. Her identification of the disparity—the differences in blindness rates—originated a new opportunity to improve health care that others did not see.

Robert Johnson: BET

Billionaire businessperson Robert L. Johnson was born in Hickory, Mississippi, on April 8, 1946, and raised in Freeport, Illinois. Johnson earned a BA in social science at the University of Illinois and an MA in public policy at Princeton. His work experience included stints as a public affairs director for the Corporation for Public Broadcasting, a communication director for the National Urban League, and a vice president of the National Cable and Television Association.

By 1980, he had built a unique and powerful repertoire of skills and knowledge: academic training in social science, an understanding of public and cable television markets, experience communicating through media to the African American community, and an awareness of the distinct viewing patterns of African Americans. In that year, he launched a cable channel, BET (Black Entertainment Television), that catered to the interests of African Americans.

Beginning with a two-hour block of programming on Nickelodeon, Johnson offered content ignored by the white media. He noticed that the music video channel MTV relied on a largely British collection of extant videos. Other than Tina Turner, few black artists received airtime on MTV. In a 1983 on-air interview, David Bowie observed, "It occurred to me having watched MTV over the last few months that it's a solid enterprise. It's got a lot going for it. I'm just floored by the fact that there's so few black artists featured on it. Why is that?"[32]

Johnson was already two steps ahead. He had launched *Video Soul*, a half-hour show featuring R&B and soul music. Johnson also produced *Black College Football*, broadcasts of games between all-black powerhouses like Jackson State and Grambling. Though these schools sent as many players to the NFL as traditional schools like the University of Southern California, Ohio State, and Florida, their games received no airtime on major networks. Johnson rectified that and launched a media empire that propelled him to riches.

Johnson became the first African American billionaire and the first black majority owner of a major sports franchise. He succeeded because he knew music and sports, because he had developed strong analytic skills, because he had a range of experience in television and broadcasting, and because he had developed tools to communicate to black audiences. He had the right repertoire.

Johnson's story embodies how a person's identity and experiences can reveal an opportunity that others miss. Emerson wrote that "people only see what they are prepared to see," a sentiment echoed by Canadian playwright Robertson Davies, who wrote that we only see "what the mind is prepared to comprehend." Johnson comprehended a large, untapped market of African American viewers and accumulated the skills to leverage that opportunity.

Christy Haubegger: Latina Magazine

Christy Haubegger provides another example of how an identity-based perspective created a new market. Christy, a Mexican American, grew up in Bellaire, Texas, as the adopted daughter of "tall blond people." After graduating from the University of Texas, she completed her law degree at Stanford in 1992, where she edited the *Stanford Law Review*.

Law degree in hand, Haubegger looked around and saw no role models from her identity group. She had no Anthony Kennedy or Sandra Day O'Connor whose footsteps she could follow. Sensing an opportunity, she founded *Latina* magazine. She would create her own role models by profiling Latina astronauts, authors, judges, and entrepreneurs.

Today, *Latina*'s circulation exceeds a quarter million and has garnered many honors, including being named best magazine by *Advertising Age*. The stories of Johnson and Haubegger demonstrate how a person's identity can influence the opportunities that one sees. It is not coincidental that Johnson started BET or that Haubegger founded *Latina* magazine. The opportunity bonus they produced stemmed in part from their identities.

Interactions and Identity Diversity

Up to now, I have considered the direct effect of identity diversity on cognitive repertoires. Identity diversity can also indirectly influence how people tap into their cognitive repertoires. Evidence from controlled experiments shows that the presence of a person from a different identity group causes people not from that identity group to generate more ideas and construct more complex arguments.[33]

As a thought experiment, imagine a group of people evaluating designs for a public garden. Add to this group a person in a wheelchair. That person will almost surely cause his fellow group members to pay attention to lane widths and curb heights. Add a blind person to the group and others will be more aware of physical boundary markers. Differently abled people contribute to the cognitive diversity of the group without saying a word.[34]

The presence of diverse others can also lead to more critical thinking. In a simulated stock market experiment, traders were assigned to either homogeneous or ethnically diverse groups. The members of diverse groups questioned price deviations more critically and produced fewer, and smaller, bubbles. An analysis shows that their market prices were nearly 60 percent more accurate.[35]

Full Inclusion

The logic of diversity bonuses demonstrates how diverse cognitive repertoires contribute to better outcomes on a variety of tasks. As we think about what causes people to differ in what they know, how they represent problems, the models and frameworks they apply, the categories they use, and the techniques they master, we cannot but conclude that education and life experiences play major roles.

As we contemplate that question more deeply, we realize that our identities play a significant role on many problems. They influence the categories we construct. They influence the dimensions on which we focus. When analyzing a topic like economic inequality, women are more likely to consider gender effects and members of minority groups are more likely to bring up racial disparities. They do so because those dimensions are salient.

To some extent, our identities influence how each of us goes about any task. We bring to it our unique standpoints. We also apply ways of thinking we learned in school and technical skills we learned on the job. We cannot separate out the beams of the timber-framed house, nor can we necessarily assign how a person thinks about a problem to either her identity, her experiences, or her education. On some problems, they may all matter.

Last, as we think about the influence of identity diversity, we cannot forget that our identities also influence what we value and deem worthy of our time and attention. The decision about what problems we address, which is itself a complex question, therefore requires an identity-diverse team. We must be inclusive in deciding our goals if we want to create effective inclusive groups and teams to achieve them.

THE EMPIRICAL EVIDENCE

True ideas are those that we can assimilate, validate, corroborate and verify. False ideas are those that we cannot.

—WILLIAM JAMES

EMPIRICAL EVIDENCE OF THE BENEFITS OF COGNITIVE AND IDENTITY diversity takes multiple forms. It includes correlational data, controlled experiments, and case studies. In this chapter, I summarize some of that evidence, paying particular attention to diversity bonuses. In some domains, prediction in particular, the evidence of significant diversity bonuses will be unequivocal. As would be expected from the theory, direct evidence for identity diversity bonuses will be more mixed. It will exist in some cases but not in others.

In addition to presenting direct evidence of bonuses, I also describe other evidence consistent with diversity bonuses, such as the growth of teams. For more than two decades, organizational scholars have noted the increased predominance of team-based work.[1] Teams now manage a majority of mutual funds, write most software and apps, and provide input into most high-value business decisions. The shift to teams may be most pronounced in the academy. A generation ago, the model academic paper had a single author. Today, a scientific paper is three times more likely to have six or more authors than be composed by an individual.

The trend toward teams has even occurred within creative endeavors. Teams of three or more songwriters now write a majority of the Billboard 100 hits.[2] Many people are aware that Paul McCartney and John Lennon, who often wrote as a duo, sit atop the list of songwriters with the most number-one Billboard hits. Few people know that in third place on that list sits a forty-five-year-old

Swede, Martin Sandberg (aka Max Martin), although many know Martin's songs. He wrote "I Want It That Way" for the Backstreet Boys, "That's the Way It Is" for Céline Dion, "DJ Got Us Fallin' in Love" for Usher, both "Roar" and "I Kissed a Girl" for Katy Perry, and Maroon 5's "One More Night."

I should say, he *cowrote* those songs. Martin did not compose any of the aforementioned songs by himself. He was a member of songwriting teams credited with those hits. His career reflects the broader industry trend toward collaborations.

Why teams? Simple: teams perform better. When teams compete against individuals on difficult tasks, teams generally win. That is no idle claim. Later in this chapter, I present studies of more than fifteen million research papers, a decade of mutual fund returns, and the largest prediction contest ever conducted.[3] In each case, teams outperform individuals by a substantial margin.

Teams win because they can draw from larger cognitive repertoires. A team possesses more information, more ideas, more knowledge, and more ways of thinking than a single person. A team can access more perspectives and more tools. This abundance of cognitive tools allows them to produce more ideas and to find improvements in the ideas they encounter. It allows them to partition reality more finely and avoid blind spots. This abundance depends on the team consisting of individually accomplished individuals who are collectively diverse.

Consider Max Martin's collaborators: Cuban American rapper Armando Christian Pérez (better known as Pitbull), Swedish DJ Denniz Pop, Indian American record producer Savan Harish Kotecha, Canadian record producer Henry Russell Walter (aka Cirkut), classically trained American songwriter Bonnie McKee, African American rapper Juicy J, and British songwriter Cathy Dennis—a talented lot no doubt, but what jumps out is their diversity. They specialize in different musical styles, they come from diverse backgrounds, and they belong to different identity groups. Their diversity enables them to write songs that appeal to wide audiences.

In examining the evidence, we should not expect diversity bonuses on all tasks or from all diverse groups. Cognitive diversity does not produce bonuses on all tasks. To add value, cognitive diversity must be germane. Writing computer code requires skills that are different from those required to write hit songs or identify subatomic particles. The CEO of CERN, the European Organization for Nuclear Research, would be wise to pass on an application by Max Martin. Martin's repertoire of songwriting skills, as impressive as it may be, would not be applicable to furthering our understanding of subatomic particles. Even in cases in which diversity could produce a bonus, say, asking Max Martin to help create music for a video game, a collaboration could fail to produce bonuses if the team lacks a shared mission, fails to create an inclusive culture, or cannot communicate effectively.

In this chapter, I engage four disparate literatures. I first look at aggregate correlative data relating employee and leadership diversity to organizational success. Those data make a strong correlative case for diversity bonuses. Next, I look at a specific case, the change in Norwegian law that required increased gender diversity on boards.

I then look at academic studies of groups and teams. That research leads to more nuanced and modest conclusions. Diversity bonuses appear on some problems and not all. And too much diversity can be a problem. Last, I look at evidence showing a trend toward more team-based work. This last set of studies reveals strong evidence of diversity bonuses. It may be a best-case scenario for identifying diversity bonuses. The teams studied pursue common goals, they have good information about the repertoires of potential team members, and their performances can be measured quantitatively.

We should not view this empirical evidence as a final arbiter. We must keep in mind that the data reveal the world as it is, not as it could be. With experience, diverse teams could perform even better, a point I take up in the next chapter.

THE VIEW FROM TEN THOUSAND FEET

The empirical evidence for diversity bonuses includes compelling correlations, confusing causal studies, large N evidence from teams, and over a half century of conflicting experimental studies. The cor-relational evidence from ten thousand feet appears unequivocal. These studies include a 2015 McKinsey analysis of top management teams of 366 companies in the United States, the United Kingdom, Canada, and Latin America that finds a positive linear relationship between diversity and financial performance. Companies with man-agement teams in the top quartile for gender diversity outperform those in the bottom quartile by 15 percent. Companies in the top quartile for ethnic diversity outperform those in the bottom quartile by 35 percent.[4]

The correlations between diverse leadership and performance are even more striking. A 2014 analysis of twenty-seven thousand senior managers at three thousand large firms revealed positive correla-tions between the percentage of women in leadership roles and firm performance. In a continuation of that study covering the two and a half years from January 2014 to July 2016, firms found even stron-ger correlations. The market values of firms at which women compose more than one-fourth of senior leadership grew at nearly 3 percent over market averages. Firms at which women filled more than half of senior leadership positions beat the market by more than 10 percent annually.[5]

An earlier, more intensive McKinsey analysis of 180 companies in France, Germany, the United Kingdom, and the United States in 2012 compared return on equity (ROE) and earnings before inter-est and taxes (EBIT) for companies in the upper and lower quartile in their executive board diversity. Here, they measure diversity by the percentage of women and foreign nationals on the executive board.[6] For Germany and the United Kingdom, ROE was over 66 percent higher for firms in the top quartile than for those in the lowest quartile. In the United States, ROE was nearly 100 percent higher. For France, the difference in ROE was not significant.

The results on EBIT reveal different country-level patterns. In Germany, the most diverse firms had an EBIT 82 percent higher than the least diverse. In France and the United States, the increase was around 50 percent, and in the United Kingdom, the increase was 30 percent. A separate study of the effect of gender diversity on the firms in Standard & Poor's top 1,500 firms from 1992 to 2016 finds that women on boards increase firm value, though only for firms that focus on innovation.[7]

The literature that analyzes city and regional racial and cultural diversity and economic performance also shows strong correlative evidence. Racial diversity significantly increases performance in advertising, finance, entertainment, legal services, health services, hotels, bars and restaurants, and computer manufacturing.[8] A one standard deviation increase in racial diversity (relocating from South Dakota to Michigan) increases productivity by more than 25 percent in legal services, health services, and finance and results in an increase of more than 10 percent in advertising.

The industry-level analysis suggests that racial diversity improves performance when workers solve problems, think creatively, and must understand their customers. As would be expected from the diversity-bonus logic, increased racial diversity does not increase performance in industries that involve physical labor. Firms that produce aircraft parts, fabricated metals, machinery and nondurable goods, paper products, and transportation do not become more efficient by increasing the racial diversity of their employees.[9]

Studies also show that city-level productivity increases in the diversity of professions.[10] Not surprisingly, professional diversity also scales with city size, which may contribute to why workers in larger cities are more productive.

As powerful as they may seem, all of these studies can be challenged on the grounds that they only report correlations. In the studies that show that diverse firms earn higher profits, the causal effect could well run in the opposite direction: successful firms may be able to afford diversity. If that were true, the firms would need some reason for pursuing diverse workers—perhaps to promote social justice, or in anticipation of demographic trends. More likely, it might be that firms with more inclusive cultures attract more diverse employees and earn higher returns. If so, diversity would correlate with firm performance but not cause it.

THE CAUSALITY CONUNDRUM

Our goal should be to find a causal relationship between diversity and performance. Correlative results only show how one quantity, in this case profits or market share, varies systematically with another, in this case identity or cognitive diversity. Correlation need not imply causation. A person's blood pressure at age fifty probably positively correlates with having granite kitchen countertops. The granite itself does not cause a drop in blood pressure. A third attribute, income level, causes both. On average, higher-income people have lower blood pressure for reasons related to diet, stress, and exercise. They are also more likely to own homes with granite countertops.

Direct tests for causality entail manipulating the variable of interest. We would need to select a random subset of homes and replace granite with Formica in some and replace Formica with granite in others and then measure the effect of those changes on blood pressure.

If we desired, we could perform the Formica experiment. Unfortunately, we cannot perform an analogous experiment on identify diversity in groups. We cannot manipulate a person's race or gender and rerun a group problem-solving exercise. We would have to swap out the whole person, and that would manipulate more than race.

For this reason, direct testing of the causal effect of race or gender will always lie out of our grasp.[11] We can, however, identify the causal effects of race or gender in discrimination by manipulating identity attributes on job and loan applications. Changing an applicant's name from Emily or Greg to Lakisha or Jamal can result in up to a 50 percent reduction in the probability of a callback for a job.[12]

The impossibility of manipulating primary identity attributes does not rule out other approaches to identifying causal effects, often by evaluating natural experiments in which unexpected events cause identity compositions to change for a random sample. They can then compare that sample to the population not affected by the event.

The 2003 law requiring Norwegian boards of directors to be 40 percent female by 2008 is an example of a natural experiment. By most accounts, the new law was not anticipated. And, at the time the law passed, only 9 percent of Norwegian board members were women. Thus, we have a random change in gender composition that we can test for gender effects.

Kenneth Ahern and Amy Dittmar interpret that random change as a natural experiment to estimate gender effects. When the law passed, some firms had 0 percent female board representation, others had 10 percent, and others had 20 percent. Those firms with no women on their boards had to increase their percentage of women more than the firms that already had 20 percent women board members. The complete data set consists of more than two hundred firms, each of which had to add some percentage of women to comply with the law.

In an ideal natural experiment, the women who joined the boards would be identical to the male board members on other relevant characteristics such as experience levels or educational backgrounds. Unfortunately, the women were younger and had less experience. Half as many of the new women board members had been CEOs as the men they replaced. Differences in experience contribute to board dynamics and decision making. Furthermore, some appointees were family members of the owners, raising the possibility that some firms tried to skirt the law.[13] One would expect that dismantling or expanding an existing board and adding younger, less experienced people, regardless of gender, would hurt performance in the short term.[14]

Though not perfect, as few natural experiments are, the Norwegian example provides a solid test case. If those firms that added relatively more women performed worse, then we can infer that adding women to boards hurt performance. If those firms that added more women performed better, then we can infer that adding women to boards improved performance. The evidence from the Norwegian case reveals a negative effect of gender diversity. The boards that most increased their gender diversity performed less well after the law was implemented. The decrease in return on equity was found to be as high as 20 percent for some firms.[15] That finding has been corroborated in other studies.[16]

These findings should not be surprising, except to those people who believe that diversity bonuses occur by magic. To see why, we need to return to the logic. For cognitive diversity to produce a bonus, it must be germane to the task. That same logic applies to identity diversity. For women, by virtue of being women, to create immediate diversity bonuses, women's repertoires—their knowledge, information, models, heuristics, and representations—would have to produce more accurate predictions, more creative ideas, better solutions to problems, or more comprehensive evaluations of projects. A female policy maker crafting legislation for education reform or a public health official developing wellness protocols to reduce health disparities may well possess information or knowledge that stems from her identity. A chemist studying amyloids may not.

With that logic in mind, we can return to the case at hand. Norway's main industries are petroleum, natural gas, metals, fishing, pulp paper, chemicals, machinery, timber, textiles, and mining. Two features stand out. First, these are all capital-intensive industries competing in commodity markets. Unlike fast food, retail, tech, entertainment, or media, these industries cannot or do not roll out new product lines each quarter. Furthermore, companies that manufacture chemicals, drill for oil, harvest timber, and build machinery do not sell directly to consumers, nor do they need to understand the tastes of diverse consumers. With the possible exception of textiles, none of these industries would seem situated for identity diversity bonuses in their primary markets.

Gender would and surely does matter in these industries on operational, cultural, and strategic dimensions. Over the past decade, I have spent some time at a leading Scandinavian manufacturing company. A few decades ago the great majority of their engineers and management were native men. Now, they find that a representative percentage of the top students are recent immigrants and women.

The process of on-boarding young immigrants and women into a predominantly male firm involves complex personnel issues. Building an inclusive culture that enables women and the growing immigrant population, currently 12 percent of the Norwegian population, to contribute as well is, unlike building an oil platform, a task for which we might expect board gender diversity to add substantial value.

Women on boards could influence these long-term strategic and organizational actions. Even if they had, we would not expect an immediate positive effect. The increase in women on boards must have had some effect on action. Otherwise, the empirical differences in performance would be inexplicable. It just must be that in the short run, those actions hurt performance.

Analyses show that firms that added more women directors made more acquisitions and added more employees. Given that this occurred during an economic downturn, we should not be surprised by the negative market impact.[17] Those actions can be read as evidence of poor monitoring or as prescient long-term strategic thinking.

The evidence that supports the poor-monitoring argument may have little to do with gender directly. Whether because of risk aversion or adherence to existing norms of what constituted a qualified candidate, boards overselected from a small set of women. One woman served on eighteen boards. Her effectiveness, as well as that of others, must have been compromised. Second, to comply with the law, boards either had to expand in size or remove existing members. On average, nearly a third of board members changed. That percentage turnover would disrupt any deliberative body.[18]

In sum, if we evaluate the Norwegian policy change objectively, we should not be surprised by the findings. The law implemented a bang-bang approach to increase the number of women on boards. The women appointed had less experience and were spread thin. Their addition disrupted boards during a downturn. And, finally, the primary industries affected do not jump to front of mind as those for which gender could produce immediate bonuses. Had the large increase in board gender diversity produced anything but an immediate downturn, it would have been astounding.

The Norwegian policy should be seen for what is: the planting of a large, golden carrot for future consumption. Mid- and early-career Norwegian women now have greater opportunity. The guarantee of near-equal opportunity on boards will encourage them to build repertoires that make them valuable board members. In the long run, Norway will be able to draw from a larger talent pool and achieve diversity bonuses. Given seats of power and wealth, women may also diversify Norway's economy into industries in which gender diversity would be expected to produce larger bonuses.

FIFTY YEARS OF EMPIRICAL RESEARCH

The next strand of research I cover consists of empirical studies of team performance that span more than fifty years. It encompasses experiments, case studies, and industry-level studies. While a few generalities emerge, this strand produces less clarity than would be expected given its scale and scope.

When evaluating any experimental study, we must take into account its replicability, which will depend on the size of the sample, the quality of the data, and the magnitude of the result. Small magnitude effect sizes found in small samples may be artifacts of time and place and not an empirical regularity. Even the most careful studies need not hold up in replication. A recent effort by 250 scholars to reexamine one hundred psychology experiments reproduced significant results in fewer than 40 percent of the replications.[19]

Replicability aside, there have been so many studies on diversity that we can still draw inferences. Much of that literature tests for direct effects of diversity. The literature, for the most part, distinguishes between *informational, knowledge, and skill diversity* and *social category diversity*. The first category corresponds to what I call cognitive diversity and the second to identity diversity. A typical study treats one of the two types of diversity as the independent variable and takes team performance, job turnover, or job satisfaction as the outcome variable.

The inseparability of identity and cognitive diversity implies that the same study can support both cognitive and identity-based diversity bonuses. For example, one study involving 699 participants found that a measure of collective intelligence predicts group performance in solving difficult problems better than the team members' individual IQs, a finding that corroborates the *no test exists* claim for problem solving.[20] In that study, team success correlates with the number of women. But that effect is largely washed out when one accounts for the ability to read emotions, a cognitive skill.

The complexities of interpersonal behavior imply that nearly anything can and does happen. One study might show that newly formed
teams fail to create sufficient trust and thus perform poorly. Another
study might find that people in long-standing teams think alike and
lose the potential benefits of diversity. We are left with evidence
showing that newly formed teams perform worse than established
teams and that they also perform better.

Nevertheless, generalities do emerge from the data, and they align
with the main theoretical threads developed here. First, as we would
expect from the theory, identity diversity does not improve performance on routine tasks.[21] That finding, though negative, aligns with
what the logic implies.

Second, both cognitive and identity diversity increase perspective
taking, which correlates with but does not guarantee better group
performance. The experiments, on the whole, show that cognitive
and identity diversity produce more, though not necessarily better,
solutions and that cognitive diversity improves outcomes when making predictions and solving problems.[22] Evidence from crowdsourced
innovation sites shows that cognitively diverse communities often
solve problems that perplex groups of experts.[23]

As mentioned, one study finds that gender diversity improves performance on difficult tasks and does so through improved communication and social perceptiveness.[24] The best teams consist of a mix
of men and women.[25] Findings on the effects of racial and ethnic
diversity are more mixed. Our analysis would suggest they might
have a negative effect when coordination plays the dominant role
and a positive effect on more creative and innovative tasks.

Industry studies find that increasing social category diversity correlates with higher job turnover. And some studies find that too
much diversity of any kind can hinder performance on almost any
task, at least initially.[26]

Another conclusion that jumps out from the thousands of studies
of diverse groups is that all types of diversity have costs. Cognitive
and identity diversity create challenges. A diversity of perspectives
or models can produce misunderstandings. Identity diversity can undermine trust, personal validation, and commitment to a group's goal.

It can result in less communication and engagement. All of these effects make managing diverse groups a challenge.

Given how much sand diversity tosses into the gears, we might expect that diverse groups would always perform worse than homogenous groups. The fact that diverse groups often perform better should thus be seen as especially strong evidence of bonuses. One might even claim that when an experiment yields equal performance between an identity-diverse group and a homogenous group, the results do not reject diversity bonuses, because without some bonuses, the diverse group would have performed worse.

That inference becomes even stronger when one takes into account the fact that a majority of the experimental papers and many of the observational studies analyze groups meeting for the first time. Effective diverse groups need time to gel.[27] Effective teams consist of people who believe that diversity will improve outcomes and therefore validate each person's membership in the team.[28] All of these conditions held for the teams in the Netflix Prize competition.

Some of the most convincing evidence comes from studies of predictive tasks. Here, I highlight two studies that reveal diversity bonuses. The first study concerns a forecasting contest run by the Intelligence Advanced Research Projects Activity from 2011 to 2014. More than twenty-five thousand forecasters, who collectively made more than a million predictions, participated. Many of the forecasts concerned international politics: Would Vladimir Putin remain in power? Would North Korea test nuclear weapons? Would Scotland leave Great Britain?[29]

Unlike in the Netflix Prize competition, participants did not work from a common data set. They relied on their own knowledge and on qualitative models to make probabilistic estimates. They did not, as a rule, construct empirical models fitting parameters to data. The Good Judgment Project headed by Barb Mellers and Phil Tetlock won the tournament. The most accurate individuals were 36 percent more accurate than random. With training, some of these participants could increase their accuracy to 41 percent better than random.

After the first year, the researchers identified a set of sixty superforecasters. The superforecasters were found to have high *fluid intelligence*. They could recognize patterns, solve logic problems, and reason from data better than most people.[30]

In the second year, they randomly assigned these superforecasters to five teams of size twelve. When formed into teams, these super-forecasters shared more information and articles than members of other teams. These teams of superforecasters then possessed even more information and knowledge and engaged with more predictive models. These teams subsequently performed 66 percent better than random and significantly better than teams comprising the top individuals not categorized as superforecasters.[31] The increase from 41 to 66 percent resulted from the team being able to tap into their diversity.

The second study consists of a meta-analysis of twenty-eight thousand predictions on six economic indicators by professional economists. The mean prediction of all forecasters was 21 percent more accurate than a randomly chosen forecaster and 10 percent more accurate than the best individual forecaster up to that time. Averaging the prediction of the six most accurate forecasters to date resulted in predictions 25 percent more accurate than an average forecaster and 15 percent more accurate than the best forecaster.[32]

Without knowledge of the diversity prediction theorem, these results would be counterintuitive. By adding in the predictions of the second-, third-, fourth-, fifth-, and sixth-best forecasters, who are demonstrably less accurate, we improve on the best forecaster. This can only happen if those other forecasters add diversity. They do. And they produce a substantial diversity bonus.

THE TEAM, THE TEAM, THE TEAM

The first strand of data shows correlative evidence of greater diversity at leading firms. The second strand, consisting of thousands of studies, paints a mixed, though broadly supportive, picture. In the past decade or so a third strand of literature on team performance has emerged that provides some of the strongest evidence of diversity bonuses.[33]

This strand leverages enormous data sets based on academic research, patents, economic forecasts, and returns on equity funds.

The data sets encompass tens of millions of academic papers, millions of patents, and thousands of teams of portfolio managers. The tasks covered in these studies are challenging: advancing knowledge, coming up with innovative ideas, forecasting economic growth, and managing an equity fund.

These studies show substantial benefits to teams and significant contributions to team success attributable to diversity. The undeniable success of teams contradicts a widespread belief that scientific, technological, and artistic breakthroughs originate from the minds of singular geniuses. As John Steinbeck writes in *East of Eden*, "Nothing was ever created by two men. There are no good collaborations, whether in music, in art, in poetry, in mathematics, in philosophy."[34] While Steinbeck and others can point to Isaac Newton, Thomas Edison, Marie Curie, Albert Einstein, and Wolfgang Amadeus Mozart, data show these great minds to be the exceptions, not the rule, particularly in recent times.

To be fair, Steinbeck was writing in 1952, before Francis Crick and James Watson uncovered the structure of DNA, before Lennon and McCartney redefined popular music, before Steve Jobs and Steve Wozniak changed the meaning of the word *apple*, before Ben and Jerry mixed up Cherry Garcia, and before Sergey Brin and Larry Page launched Google. And, in further defense of Steinbeck, he did say "two men," allowing for the collaboration between Marie and Pierre Curie and leaving open the possibility of Patti Smith and Bruce Springsteen.

Then again, maybe we should be less generous. Steinbeck surely knew of the Wright brothers. He also must have been aware that even history's most lauded individuals had assistants. Raphael and Michelangelo worked with teams of assistants. Marcel Grossmann helped with the foundational math for Einstein's general relativity theory.[35] Steinbeck's contemporaries F. Scott Fitzgerald, Thomas Wolfe, and Ernest Hemingway all benefited from the wisdom of the same editor, Maxwell Perkins, whose sharp pencil improved on their prose.[36]

This flurry of anecdotes is drawn from overwhelming aggregate evidence. Studies of patents reveal that teams, not individuals, dominate and that the notion of the "heroic lone inventor" lacks empirical support.[37] The same holds for academic research. The most influential papers are written by teams.[38]

Furthermore, the teams that make the most significant scientific advances, construct the investment portfolios that generate the highest returns, and construct the most accurate predictive models are not arbitrary assemblages. They agree on a mission. Their members trust one another enough to challenge ideas. And, most important, they are *diverse*, both cognitively and in their identities.[39] They consist of people who bring diverse experiences, perspectives, knowledge, and training.[40]

Unlike the teams thrown together in experiments, these teams work together for sustained periods of time. They therefore develop trust. And they play for real. They race for patents, they compete for academic prestige, and they try to make the most money.

Studies of the academy, research labs, and the financial world reveal strong support for diversity bonuses. In science and engineering research, 90 percent of published papers are team efforts. In social science, 60 percent of papers are coauthored.[41] Similarly, more than half of all patents are now written by teams.[42] Last, more than three-fourths of equity mutual funds are managed by teams.[43]

The data on academic papers show the dominance of teams within subfields as well (see figure 5.1). Social science can be divided into 54 subfields. In every one, coauthored papers outnumber single-authored papers. Science and engineering papers can be divided into 171 subfields. Coauthored papers outnumber single-authored papers in 170 of these subfields. In medical research, the ratio of coauthored to single-authored papers exceeds three to one. The same subfield dominance holds for patents. Stefan Wuchty, Benjamin F. Jones, and Brian Uzzi evaluate the more than two million patents issued by the United States since 1975.[44] Teams predominate in all thirty-six categories of patents.

Data from a National Academy of Sciences report on team-based science show the marked increase in coauthored papers from 1960 to 2014 (see figure 5.2).[45] A similar trend can be found in investment teams. Twenty-five years ago more than two-thirds of equity funds were managed by individuals; now more than 70 percent are managed by teams.

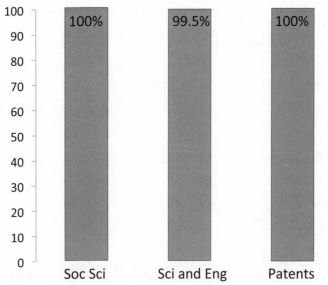

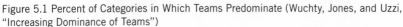

Figure 5.1 Percent of Categories in Which Teams Predominate (Wuchty, Jones, and Uzzi, "Increasing Dominance of Teams")

Teams Win

The growth of teams requires an explanation given that teams cost more money and take more time to reach decisions because they require coordination. We can thus infer that teams would not be so prevalent if they did not outperform individuals. Direct comparisons show that to be the case. Teams win.

In science and engineering and the social sciences, coauthored papers earn more citations. This is also true within subfields. Coauthored papers have higher average citations in every one of the 54 social science subfields, and in 167 of the 171 scientific subfields. The same holds for patents. Team-authored patents earn more citations overall and do so in thirty-two of the thirty-six patent categories.[46]

For patents written between 1986 and 1995 from inventors based in the United States, a sample with more than half a million patents, citations increase with team size. Solo-authored patents earn on average nine and a half citations, patents written by teams of size three receive twelve and a half, and patents with more than six authors

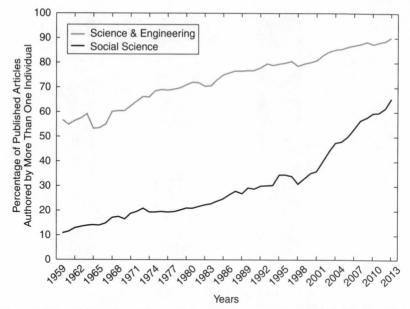

Figure 5.2 Trend in Coauthored Papers in Social Sciences and Science and Engineering (National Research Council, *Enhancing the Effectiveness of Team Science*)

receive on average more than seventeen citations.[47] Few people co-author for the fun of it. They coauthor to produce better research.[48]

These findings describe averages. Analysis of the best papers and patents shows that teams also perform best. Team-authored papers are four and a half times more likely to receive more than one hundred citations (a common benchmark for excellence) in both science and engineering and the social sciences. Team-authored papers are more than six times as likely to earn one thousand citations in science and engineering.[49] Team-authored patents are 28 percent more likely than sole-authored patents to be in the top 5 percent and 9 percent less likely to receive no citations.[50]

The data from equity fund managers also show that teams win. Accounting for risk, the gains for funds run by three people outperform those for funds run by a single individual by about 60 basis points.[51] This fact goes a long way toward explaining why teams, not individuals, now run most funds.

Diversity and Team Performance

The data leave little doubt that teams are outperforming individuals in the academy, in scientific research, and on Wall Street. The question remains as to whether we can attribute any part of that team success to cognitive diversity. The increase in team-based work and team success could be the result of teams taking on bigger projects. One person cannot build and operate a particle collider. Bigger teams can dissect more sea slug brains, run more model specifications, and conduct more experiments. Teams might be winning because of scale, not cognitive diversity.

We can start with qualitative accounts which support diversity bonuses. Steve W. J. Kozlowski and Bradford S. Bell, in a survey of studies of team-based work, note the value of a diversity of "skills, expertise, and experience."[52] The quantitative evidence is also compelling. High-impact papers include deep, diverse thinkers.[53] Jones, Uzzi, and Wuchty's analysis of collaborations among researchers using the same data set of nearly twenty million papers finds that two scientific researchers employed at different institutions have a 7 percent greater chance of writing a high-impact paper than if they work at the same institution. Two social scientists from different schools have a nearly 12 percent greater chance than two colleagues from the same school.[54]

Richard Freeman and Wei Huang study one and a half million scientific papers written from 1985 to 2008 in the United States. They find that the number of citations a paper receives increases with the number of authors, the number of e-mail addresses with distinct institutional domains, and the number of references contained in the paper: *more authors from more schools result in more citations.* Freeman and Huang also find that increased ethnic diversity of authors correlates with more citations, controlling for other factors.[55]

The fact that people work at different schools or come from different ethnic backgrounds does not ensure cognitive diversity, though it's more likely, a point discussed in previous chapters. A more direct approach for identifying cognitive diversity relies on the references in patents and papers. References provide a proxy for the knowledge domains of a paper's authors. If a paper references species-area laws from biology, we can assume that an author knows or at least speaks to the literature on that topic. If a paper references papers that use some analytic tool, say spectral analysis, we can assume an author knows that tool.

Two other studies use this approach and find evidence consistent with the claim that the best teams consist of accomplished diverse thinkers. One study examines the 5,529,055 patents filed between 1976 and 2006 in the United States.[56] It develops a *proximity* measure for each patent based on whether it cites patents from common or uncommon combinations of categories. The most-cited patents have low proximity, that is, they reference rare combinations. The same technique applied to a sample of nearly two million papers shows that the best papers also have low proximity.

The second study applies random sampling to predict the likelihood of each pair of references appearing in the same paper.[57] It is more likely that two papers on social behavior in communities of naked mole rats would be cited together than it is that either paper would be cited with a paper on fast oscillations in cortical-striatal networks in the brain. The analysis assigns a *conventionality score* to each pair of papers in a reference list. This captures the likelihood that the two papers would be cited together. Each paper can then be assigned a *median* conventionality for each pair of papers in its list of references.

A paper is classified as *conventional* if its median lies in the upper half of all papers. This divides the twenty million papers into approximately two equal-size groups: those with high median conventionality of pairs and those with low median conventionality of pairs. For each paper, it is possible to calculate the conventionality threshold for the bottom 10 percent of pairs of references. Papers with a lower-than-average 10 percent threshold are classified as *novel*, as those papers cite pairs of papers that are infrequently cited together.

These two categorizations bin the papers into four types: *conventional and novel, conventional but not novel, novel but not conventional,* and *neither conventional nor novel.*[58] Conventional and novel papers combine atypical pairings with conventional pairings. An economics paper that contained forty standard economics references and twenty references from theoretical biology would fall into that group. The many pairs of references from economics and pairs from biology would be likely. The combinations of economics and biology references would be unlikely.

For each of five decades, the researchers compute the probability of a paper from each group becoming a hit paper. They define hit papers as those that produce the top 1 percent, 5 percent, or 10 percent of citations. All fifteen analyses (five decades, three thresholds) produce similar results: Papers that are either novel or conventional but not both become hits at slightly above expected rates: 1.2 percent of novel but not conventional papers in the 1950s fall in the top 1 percent, as do 1.2 percent of conventional but not novel papers published in the 1990s. Papers that are neither conventional nor novel become hits at about half their expected rates.

Papers in the novel and conventional category produce hits at *twice the expected rate.* In every decade, more than 2 percent of novel and conventional papers belong to the top 1 percent of papers, almost 10 percent belong to the top 5 percent, and about 18 percent belong to the top 10 percent. A similar analysis of a selection of highly cited papers in social science finds that atypical combinations increase the likelihood of a hit.[59] We might replace the words *conventional* and *novel* with *coherent* and *diverse.* We can then restate their result as follows: the best papers address existing literatures and combine diverse ideas.

That same analysis examines the isolated effect of adding authors, taking into account the number and diversity of papers. It finds that adding authors *decreases* the likelihood of a hit paper. All else being equal, adding an author makes the paper less successful. Working in teams can be difficult. Miscommunications can arise. Coauthors can differ in writing style. Though significant, that effect is small compared to the bonus created by more and new ideas.

We might expect that more authors would imply more citations because people cite their friends' and colleagues' work. They may, but whatever additional citations arise through friendships are more than wiped out by the difficulty of working in a team. The sizes of the teams that write papers and patents and manage equity funds and the diversity of those teams are chosen strategically. Teams may add or drop members along the way to improve performance. So, though these studies reveal benefits from diversity, they do not imply, much less prove, that more diversity is always better. Nor did the logic presented earlier. Too much diversity can cause problems.

Data support that intuition. An analysis of the publication records of recipients of National Science Foundation grants using the number of publications as a measure finds that adding more researchers increases the number of publications.[60] However, as the number of authors increases, the addition of people from other institutions and other disciplines decreases the number of publications. This interaction effect is small relative to the direct effect of larger teams. Nevertheless, the finding aligns with the intuition that too much diversity can hinder large teams.

Taken as a whole, the third strand of studies provides powerful evidence of the effectiveness of diverse teams. In evaluating any data, we should consider the possibility of selection bias. Team-based work surely exhibits selection bias. Teams choose people whom they expect to make the team better. They do not select randomly. Nor should they: randomly selected teams would not perform well. What should perform well are mindfully constructed diverse teams of talented people. And they do; they significantly outperform talented individuals who work alone.

SUMMARY

As a rule, we place greater weight on empirical evidence than on theoretical claims. And, taken in its entirety, the evidence weighs strongly in favor of diversity bonuses in many contexts. The success and growth of teams and the corresponding indications that those teams leverage diverse knowledge bases and tools is compelling evidence that cognitive diversity contributes to team success.

In some cases, diversity bonuses have to exist. On predictive tasks, the only way not to have a diversity bonus is if there exists no diversity. It is therefore the magnitude and not the existence of the bonus that catches our attention. The 5, 10, and 20 percent improvements in the accuracy of economic forecasts are meaningful, as are 60 basis point increases in returns.

Even in those cases in which we do not see bonuses (most notably the lack of immediate gender diversity bonuses in the Norwegian board case), we find support for the core logic. None of the major industries jump to mind as domains in which gender might produce immediate gains.

Finally, to tee up the final chapters, I reiterate that these data reveal where we are now. They come from segregated societies with histories of exclusion. With practice guided by theory and evidence, diverse teams should produce larger bonuses. Many of these results come from teams working without rudder or compass.

CHAPTER SIX

DIVERSITY BONUSES AND THE BUSINESS CASE

My main purpose in life is to make enough money to create ever more inventions.

—THOMAS EDISON

HAVING PRESENTED LOGIC FOR HOW DIVERSITY BONUSES ARISE and presented evidence that they exist, I now widen the aperture and evaluate their contribution to the broader business case for diversity and inclusion. The direct implication requires little elaboration. Diversity bonuses can lead to higher profits, larger market shares, and faster rates of innovation. That potential creates an incentive to hire, support, and promote people with diverse cognitive repertoires.

The second-order implication, that identity diversity creates the same opportunity, necessitates thinking about when and how germane cognitive diversity correlates with or is caused by identity diversity. As already noted, identity diversity may be more relevant in some domains than others.

Throughout this chapter, I emphasize that every business or organization exists for a reason. It has a mission. McDonald's aspires to produce "good food," create opportunities for "good people," to be a "good neighbor," and to be its "customers' favorite place and way to eat and drink."[1] The outfitter REI is "dedicated to inspiring, educating and outfitting for a lifetime of outdoor adventure and stewardship."[2] The University of Michigan, where I work, strives to provide an uncommon education for the common person. The business case for identity diversity depends on leaders, managers, and rank-and-file employees believing that identity diversity can produce mission-relevant bonuses and on everyone taking actions to reach that goal.

Diversity bonus thinking is not the only reason an organization would promote inclusion. Historically, business conversations about diversity and inclusion have emphasized legal compliance and the advancement of normative ideals. Often, companies promote diversity and inclusion as core values without any reference to diversity bonuses. They situate being inclusive, like being honest or courageous, as the right thing to do.

Recent demographic trends create a business case for diversity and inclusion that relies on market logic of supply and demand. To the extent that members of an identity group have special knowledge of that group, firms that attract diverse employees will be more successful selling to diverse consumers. Given that the pool of potential workers and consumers will soon be majority minority, organizations unable to hire diverse employees or sell to diverse consumers will suffer in the long run.

In this chapter, I argue that the link between identity diversity and better outcomes gives the diversity-bonus logic a special power within the business case.[3] As I touched upon in the prologue, legal and normative arguments frame diversity and inclusion efforts as counter to performance. The demographic argument frames them as necessary and painful. These other frames create a reluctance to embrace diversity, save for those who believe in the cause. In contrast, the diversity-bonus logic implies the contrary assumption that diversity drives excellence. It places inclusion in a company's self-interest.

Even leaders who create diverse teams for legal or moral reasons or out of demographic necessity would like those teams to succeed. If diverse teams fail, support for inclusion will wane. An understanding of how diversity bonuses arise increases the chances of realizing bonuses. The logic provides a rudder and compass.

The diversity-bonus logic does not make an unequivocal case for diversity. In some cases, cognitive and identity diversity produce bonuses. In others (see the US Congress), they contribute to conflict. The logic implies that tasks will differ in the extent to which identity can produce bonuses. They will also differ in the extent to which any form of cognitive diversity can produce a bonus.

Organizations like NASA, Boeing, and Google that seek technological breakthroughs place a huge emphasis on cognitive diversity. Cognitive diversity is also front of mind for financial firms and the homeland security industry, which traffic in large amounts of data. Both those industries also emphasize identity diversity, though for different reasons. Financial services firms must attract investors. They need to understand a diverse customer pool. Homeland security analysts need to understand the motivations of potential terrorists. To do so, they need to understand marginalized people. Identity diversity is relevant to both those tasks.

The logic also implies that a supporting organizational culture is key to success. It is not enough to just have diverse people in the room. People must feel comfortable sharing their ideas, engaging the ideas of others, and responding to challenges. People who share a strong sense of mission, be it taking people to Mars or making the best yogurt in the world, will be better able to achieve bonuses.[4] One would hope that the same cultural features that encourage cognitive diversity—openness, tolerance, a commitment to facts, and so on—would also be welcoming to people from diverse identity groups.

Though I refer to the business case, I mean to address the broader class of organizations. The analysis will not always carry through unchanged. Universities place more weight on the normative dimension than most businesses because creating an inclusive society or serving the entire society may be part of their mission. While universities seek bonuses in the advancement of knowledge, their role in creating opportunity and creating a well-functioning multicultural society creates a demand for representation of diverse identities for its own sake.

The final two lines in the mission statement of the University of Wisconsin–Madison, "to provide a learning environment in which faculty, staff and students can discover, examine critically, preserve and transmit the knowledge, wisdom and values that will help ensure the survival of this and future generations and improve the quality of life for all," speak to a direct benefit from diversity and inclusion. In contrast, the missions of for-profit entities may be less directly linked to identity concerns. To connect Goodyear Tire Company's global purpose, "delivering the highest quality tires, related products and services for our customers and consumers," to diversity and inclusion is not as straightforward.[5]

The remainder of this chapter consists of five parts. In the first part, I dig deeper into the possibility of and potential for identity-based diversity bonuses. In the second part, I describe the normative and demographic arguments. In the third part, I comment on how diversity bonuses position inclusion to be in a company's self-interest and show that this reinforces the normative and demographic arguments for inclusion. In the fourth part, I describe the full business case based on bonuses, normative concerns, and demographics, using the financial sector as an exemplar. I also comment on board diversity. In the last section, I expand on how the weights allocated to the components of the business case can, and should, vary by industry.

THE GROWING BELIEF IN DIVERSITY BONUSES

The contribution of the diversity-bonus logic to the business case for diversity and inclusions rests on identity diversity correlating with or causing relevant ways of thinking. Put more informally, our identities must influence our repertoires in ways that produce better outcomes.

The idea that organizations should hire and consult with people with diverse cognitive repertoires has begun to take root. The litany of quotes that lead off this volume demonstrates that leading organizations believe in diversity bonuses. The actions of those same companies back up their prose.

They all seek diverse talent. They hire graduates from a variety of schools and colleges. Rumors that Alphabet, the parent company of Google, only hires from Stanford and the Ivy League are false. They hire more people from Berkeley, Michigan, Carnegie Mellon, Illinois, and Washington than from any Ivy League school. In fact, Alphabet hires more people from the University of Waterloo and Georgia Tech than all Ivies except Harvard and Cornell.[6]

Leading companies hire college graduates who major in diverse topics. Investment banks hire philosophers. Tech companies hire linguists. And pharmaceutical companies hire computer scientists.

Until recently, many of these efforts to hire diverse employees might have been classified more as experimental than strategic. The nascent field of people analytics, pioneered in Silicon Valley and on Wall Street, bring evidence to bear on hiring.

Increasingly, I find that companies are abandoning the use of standard rubrics to evaluate candidates. They realize that hiring by a common criterion results in homogenous employees. Organizations are learning that the best team does not consist of the people who score best on some test. What is happening in organizations is aligning with what was found in the labs: the best teams are diverse.[7]

The aforementioned widespread use of teams provides further evidence of the growing belief in cognitive diversity bonuses. Genentech makes decisions to push research forward using diverse teams. Google makes hiring decisions with teams. Government agencies and universities do as well. US attorney offices use teams to decide on the cases to file. The Federal Reserve relies on a committee to deliberate on interest rates. The University of Michigan uses multiple diverse teams to decide tenure cases. They all use teams because teams perform better than individuals.

ORGANIZATIONS AND IDENTITY DIVERSITY BONUSES

The business case for identity diversity bonuses depends on the general case of cognitive diversity bonuses. Achieving identity bonuses requires more effort. People must believe that these bonuses can exist. People must be willing to engage across identity groups. If not, they cannot achieve the bonuses. Identity-diverse groups must also overcome additional obstacles. Stereotype threat, implicit bias, and a host of other factors impede group success.[8]

Owing to these extra frictions and costs, organizations must make a strong case for identity diversity bonuses. Claiming that identity diversity improves outcomes does not make it so.

An organization can proceed from one or two standpoints. It can start from a position that identity can play no role and demand that advocates of identity diversity bonuses refute that position. Or it could take the opposite position and assume that identity diversity does matter and demand that opponents prove that it does not. My experience has been that most organizations find themselves somewhere near one of those two extreme positions. Most people either believe that identity is relevant or they believe that it, at most, has a marginal influence.

A more thoughtful and productive approach takes each task as it comes. Any organization faces a variety of challenges and opportunities. On some, identity diversity has the potential to produce bonuses. Effective leadership makes people aware of the potential for identity diversity bonuses so that managers consider identity when forming teams.

The intelligence community provides a useful starting point for contemplating the identity diversity bonuses, given its reliance on cognitive diversity.[9] Within a few minutes of talking to an intelligence analyst, you hear about the necessity of diverse information sources and categorizations, the value of applying a variety of tools, and the usefulness of multiple models of human behavior.

To remind people of the potential of identity to produce bonuses, the United States' intelligence community hands out silver-dollar-size medallions. One side of the medallion resembles a gold coin and features the familiar liberty eagle with an olive branch in one set of talons and arrows in the other. Around the circumference it reads, "Office of the Director of National Intelligence." The flip side features a white-enamel background with a blue, orange, and periwinkle geometric design. Around the outer edge, written in gold print, is the statement, "Intelligence Community Equal Employment Opportunity and Diversity."

The implicit claim could not be any clearer. *National intelligence and identity diversity: two sides of the same coin.* If everyone within the intelligence community saw identity diversity as contributing to germane cognitive diversity, the medallions would be unnecessary. To back up the medallion's implicit claim involves showing that people from different identity groups acquire unique information and knowledge, create distinct categorizations of the world, or bring different analogies and models to bear that produce diversity bonuses.

Those arguments are easy to make for some problems, such as trying to understand or predict who becomes a terrorist. Members of underrepresented minority groups or religious minorities have experiences in feeling marginalized that may give them special insights. My impression has been that the default position within the intelligence community is to seek out identity-diverse people on these tasks.

That said, the intelligence community does not naïvely assume identity diversity to be a proxy for relevant cognitive diversity on all tasks. Identity diversity likely receives little weight for teams that study how to dismantle bombs.

The key takeaway is that as long as there exist some tasks for which identity diversity can produce bonuses, and clearly there do, the intelligence community needs identity diversity in house. It also needs to build a culture in which identity-diverse teams function well.

As with the intelligence community, businesses find that the magnitude and extent of identity-based cognitive diversity bonuses vary by task. Any task that involves selling or marketing products to consumers could have significant identity-based diversity bonuses. That claim will hold true if people possess finer or special knowledge of their own identity groups, making diversity bonuses possible.

Advertising may be the domain where the link to identity-based repertoires is clearest. To say that women better know their own preferences for cars, antiperspirants, or 401(k)s oversimplifies a bit. We must keep the cloud, the timber-framed house, and the icebergs in mind. For example, we cannot expect coverage through overlap. A team consisting of black women and white men would lack full understanding of how white women and black men might respond.

Evidence of the perceived value for identity diversity in advertising can be found in the actions firms take. In the fall of 2016, Verizon, General Mills, and HP pressured their advertising agencies to diversify their employees. Verizon's chief marketing officer, Diego Scott, sent a letter to firms that manage the company's advertising accounts that read in part, "Marketers are expected to have a deep understanding and insight about their markets."[10] Verizon took this action for business reasons. It wanted to maintain and build market share. It was not acting solely on social justice grounds.

Marketers believe that identity-based knowledge reduces the likelihood of culturally insensitive actions. The long list of corporate blunders resulting from demographic blindness supports that belief: the coffee company Beaner's, whose name infuriated segments of the Latino community; Sprint, who ran a video clip featuring a consumer's description of a competing firm as "ghetto"; IHOP, whose cash register receipts for egg-white omelets read "whites only"; and even Google, whose image search algorithm generated pictures of only middle-aged white men when asked to display CEOs.[11] While a middle-aged white male may find humor in the "whites only" receipt, someone who lived through the civil rights movement likely would not.

Identity-based knowledge can also contribute to product design. IDEO teaches storycentric design. Designers follow and observe consumers. If commissioned to design a popcorn popper, IDEO goes into people's homes (with permission, of course) and watches them pop and eat popcorn. IDEO observers make note of where people store their poppers, how they clean them, and whether they use or ignore available features and settings. Close observation may reveal that people make popcorn in two batch sizes: either a small, personal bowl or a party size. IDEO then designs a minimal viable solution to meet those needs. To make rich observations, IDEO seeks out identity-diverse consumers. They hire identity-diverse employees to better classify observed behaviors as idiosyncratic or representative: Is a Japanese family's decision not to refrigerate soy sauce unusual or typical?

Given how our identities influence how we construct and order our lives, identity-diverse teams may also be better able to provide services as well. Diverse medical practitioners provide more culturally aware health services to minority communities. Practitioners who know a community may make more accurate predictions about patient behaviors. Evidence shows that people share more medical information with health care professionals from the same identity group.[12]

Identity diversity may also help teams understand more fundamental behaviors. Evidence shows that women and men differ in their attitudes toward risk.[13] Women who are certified financial analysts may have more accurate understandings of what drives those risk preferences. Relatedly, African Americans, Asian Americans, and Latinos differ in how they value education, family, and honor. We cannot expect ten smart white guys in a room to develop products, services, and technologies that meet those needs.[14]

Last, identity-based bonuses are not limited to tasks that require understanding or predicting the preferences or behavior of diverse people. Our identities correlate with our experiences and how we model problems. Think back to the example of the typical experiences of men and women who learn to scull and how that influences how they think about balance.

Overall, the argument that identity diversity correlates with relevant knowledge, categorizations, and models for advertising, product design, and the provision of services seems compelling. We might even summarize that case by reference to appeals made by political activists from underrepresented groups who chant, "Nothing about us without us." The corporate version might be something like "Nothing sold to us without us."

IDENTITY AND REPERTOIRES

To glimpse the full potential of identity diversity bonuses entails thinking beyond knowledge-based identity bonuses and considering individuals' entire cognitive repertoires. While identity diversity surely correlates with information and knowledge about one's own identity group, it also correlates with the categories and representations we construct for any product domain: books, apps, restaurants, movies, or music. Identity also correlates with the models we carry around in our heads about how people live their lives, respond to information, or react to incentives. Our identities also correlate with the heuristics and rules of them that we apply and the set of analogies and experiences we draw from. For those reasons, if we add two Latinas to a group of white men, the possible diversity bonuses extend far beyond the Latina market.

The expansion to full repertoires has significant consequences for inclusion as well. Limiting identity's expected contributions to knowledge-based bonuses has the undesired effect of siloing diverse employees in identity- and diversity-related jobs.[15] Thus, we find that minorities disproportionately take positions in charge of marketing to their own identity group, as chief diversity officers, and as professors of American culture. To assign people jobs limited to their own identity groups skates on the edge of exploitation: come tell us about your people so that we may sell them more soap. It also misallocates talent. A woman assigned to market cars to women may have greater potential to add value given her experiences in supply chain management.

NORMATIVE AND DEMOGRAPHIC ARGUMENTS

The diversity-bonus component of the business case rests on improving the bottom line. Normative arguments for diversity and inclusion rest on economic, social, and political disparities. Those disparities have been well documented: In 2014, the median African American household earned $43,000, compared to $71,000 for whites. Even among the college educated, a substantial gap remains. The median African American household earned $82,000. The median white household earned over $106,000. The median white household also had sixteen times the wealth of the median African American household and fourteen times the wealth of the median Latino household. Gender gaps also persist. In 2014, women earned 80 percent of what men earned in the United States.[16]

Racial and gender disparities in education and employment in technical fields contribute to these income disparities. African Americans earn degrees in engineering at one-half the rate of whites. Latinos and African Americans each make up only 4 percent of biomedical researchers and 6.5 percent of the STEM workforce, despite being, respectively, 10 percent and 15 percent of the total workforce.[17] Some of the most prestigious STEM firms employ far less than representative numbers of minorities. As of 2015, Facebook and Twitter each employed fewer than one hundred African Americans. Only 2 percent of Google's workforce and 3 percent of Yale's faculty are African Americans, and an even smaller percentage work as executives in the financial services industry.

At the top of the business pyramid, the numbers are even less representative. Only fourteen African American men have ever served as CEO of a Fortune 500 company. In 2017, no African American women and only twenty-five women total served as Fortune 500 CEOs. The 114th Congress includes only twenty-one women US senators and only two African Americans and three Latinos.

The causes of these disparities are manifold. As noted, education is one. More than 80 percent of white students graduate from high school, as compared to fewer than 65 percent of African Americans and Latinos. Six-year college graduation rates for whites exceed 60 percent, while fewer than 50 percent of Latinos and 40 percent of African Americans graduate within that same time frame. The white students also attend more highly ranked colleges.

Even accounting for educational differences, in many jobs and in many professions women, African Americans, and Latinos enter at lower rates and leave with higher probability. Some who grasp the gold ring—who earn jobs at Google or Goldman Sachs—do not enjoy the ride and leave. Others are forced out, unable to overcome formal and informal barriers to success

Demographic changes amplify the potential effects of these disparities. Within thirty years, demographers predict that the majority of Americans will be nonwhite. To remain competitive in the labor market, organizations must appeal to diverse employees. Businesses must understand the needs of a diverse consumer base.

The diversification of the labor pool means that even firms in industries where we would not expect diversity bonuses to exist must seek diversity. Consider the canonical no-bonus team: a track-and-field relay team. The best team consists of the four fastest people, regardless of their race. Thus, the 1936 US men's Olympic four-by-one-hundred-meter relay team consisted of the four fastest men. Two, Jesse Owens and Ralph Metcalfe, were African American. The other two, Foy Draper and Frank Wykoff, were Caucasian. That racial diversity produced no bonus.[18]

The same logic applies to firms that perform routine cognitive tasks. They too need to diversify the talent pool. In the introduction to this volume, Earl Lewis and Nancy Cantor refer to the movie *Hidden Figures*, which tells the story of how, when faced with a shortage of mathematicians during World War II, the National Advisory Committee for Aeronautics (now NASA) hired African American women to make scientific calculations.

The women profiled in the movie computed trajectories. Some of that, such as the development of heuristics to simplify calculations and identify errors, undoubtedly produced bonuses.[19] Those bonuses were most likely not attributable to identity. However, by dipping into the large talent pool, the government found people who could produce bonuses. As the racial profile of America changes, these narratives will become the norm. Our workforce will include large numbers of Latino mathematicians, Arab American biostatisticians, and African American pilots. Given the growing diversity of the talent pool, in the long run, employers will need to hire diverse employees.

THE SPECIAL POWER OF DIVERSITY BONUSES

The three justifications for diversity and inclusion differ: normative arguments for diversity and inclusion policies seek to redress past wrongs or create a more equitable future; the demographic argument frames greater workforce diversity as a necessary market response; and the diversity-bonus logic shows that cognitively diverse teams perform better on complex tasks.[20]

The demographic argument and the bonus logic rely on more pragmatic concerns. A claim that diverse perspectives create distinct sets of adjacent possibles and result in better solutions to complex problems lacks the rhetorical or moral force of normative appeals, such as the one offered by Franklin Delano Roosevelt in a 1932 speech in Detroit, Michigan: "We Americans everywhere must and shall choose the path of social justice, the path of faith, the path of hope, and the path of love toward our fellow man."

Fortunately, the path to 1.2 percent higher returns on equity follows a similar route to the paths of social justice, faith, hope, and love. To return to the words of Wendell Berry, "What is good for the world will be good for us." That is not to say that the two routes do not diverge in places. When they do, the choice of whether to paint the sign for the business case in bright colors or to adhere to normative principles may not be easy.

As noted earlier in the book, while diversity bonuses offer direct benefits, tying diversity and inclusion efforts to higher profits, better policies, more novel innovations, and more scientific breakthroughs, equity-based normative arguments imply a cost. In doing so, they frame inclusive efforts as a *collective action problem*. The collective (society) benefits from inclusion. The organization or individual pays a cost.

This tradeoff thinking—the idea that diversity harms performance—is widespread. In his dissenting opinion in the University of Michigan's affirmative action case, Supreme Court Justice Antonin Scalia wrote that schools and employers face a choice. They can choose diversity, or they can choose to be "super duper."[21]

Scalia makes an imprecise claim; he provides no conditions. On additive tasks, he is correct. Replacing a member of a relay team with a slower runner or hiring a data analyst who makes errors at a higher rate based on identity considerations sacrifices quality on the altar of social justice. In those cases, hiring based on diversity precludes becoming super-duper. On complex tasks, Scalia is wrong. The logic and evidence of the previous chapters shows that to be so.

Tradeoff framing contributes to why affirmative action policies lack broad support.[22] Asking people to turn over income or accumulated wealth to others based on historical injustices and current disparities proves a tough sell. Efforts to create inclusive behaviors can suffer from a similar problem if framed only as the right thing to do. Engaging in civil discourse involves difficult conversations. We must confront biases. We must consider dimensions that we have previously ignored or contemplate novel adjacent possibles. Those activities come at a cost of time and mental effort. Inclusion can also be seen as a collective action problem. An individual may desire a trusting, multicultural society but find it easier to build a homogenous team, to heed the "siren call of sameness."[23]

Tradeoff framing also contributes to the lack of support for affirmative action in the courts, a forum in which normative considerations often rise above self-interested motivations. A sequence of rulings stretching from *Fisher* to *Bakke* have all but ruled out affirmative action based on historical injustice. In *Grutter v. Bollinger*, in which the court upheld affirmative action policies at the University of Michigan Law School, Sandra Day O'Connor, writing for the majority, argued that past discrimination was not sufficient justification for affirmative action. She based her support on a broader compelling interest in classroom diversity.

Bottom-Line Thinking

The special power of the diversity-bonus logic becomes evident if you place yourself in the shoes of the CEO of a large corporation like AB InBev, Boeing, Allstate, Bloomberg, or Ford, and then you ask yourself what you would do in the area of diversity and inclusion. Suppose that you adopt an entirely normative justification for diversity and inclusion. You recognize your company's long-run interests in an integrated, robust society. For that reason alone, you want to promote social justice. However, your core mission is not advancing social justice. It is building the world's best cars, brewing great beer to bring people together, or insuring lives, homes, and autos.

Also, keep in mind that advancing social justice lies outside your formal job description and contributes little, if anything, to your compensation, which is based on revenue, profits, stock price, and market share. Nor does it align with your fiduciary responsibility to its shareholders to generate profits.

This framing positions advancing social justice in opposition to your mission and your company's bottom line, two goals that in an ideal market economy will align almost perfectly. That is the genius of markets: if Ford and GM make safe, efficient, stylish, high-quality cars at a good price point, they earn profits. If Gilead and Genentech develop antiviral drugs that cure diseases, they generate a positive return to their shareholders. Profits enable companies to survive and grow. Companies that fail to turn profits will not long survive.

The danger of normative thinking alone should be apparent. If policies that equalize opportunities for women and people of color reduce profits or market share, they will lack support. A failed business cannot advance any social causes. You know this as CEO, so your primary commitment will be to carry out the company's mission. Thus, if you were the CEO of, say, Boeing, you would want the diverse, talented men and women who work with you to get up every morning thinking about how to design, engineer, and build the world's best planes. Building a fair and just society will be secondary.

The evidence showing that teams that position inclusion efforts as normative goals produce worse outcomes only compounds the lack of alignment.[24] The prophecy becomes self-fulfilling: diverse teams perform worse because they are expected to do so. In sum, the normative argument alone lacks sufficient force within a market economy, where profits drive behavior, to be the lever on which you can stand as CEO.

Alternatively, you might adopt the demographic argument or some hybrid of the normative and demographic argument. In that case, hiring diverse employees and building an inclusive culture could be accepted as a long-term investment: a short-term loss that produces a higher return in the long run by creating access to a larger talent pool. That strategy could work, albeit at a rather slow pace.

Last, you might adopt an approach that seeks diversity bonuses. Now, to the extent to which identity diversity can generate bonuses, no tradeoff exists. You want diverse teams and you want to create an inclusive environment because you expect those teams to perform better. The signposts to achieving mission, generating profits, and creating a diverse and inclusive work environment all point in the same direction.

This almost-too-good-to-be-true alignment becomes problematized when we go more deeply into the workings of the organization and the nature of the mission, and begin to think with more care about the types and magnitudes of potential diversity bonuses. Before critiquing it, we should take a moment to appreciate the triple alignment.

Neoclassical economics shows that firms that perform best earn the highest profits, implying that efficient fulfillment of mission and maximal profits align. The diversity-bonus logic states that diverse teams can perform best on cognitive complex tasks. Thus, on those tasks, creating a diverse workforce, pursuit of mission, and profits align. Firms need not choose between being super-duper and being diverse.

People and Profits

In a knowledge economy, a firm's long-term profits depend on its people. That is less true in a manufacturing economy, in which routine workers are often interchangeable. The same logic applies to universities, research centers, and government agents. The concern for long-term success implies an emphasis on attracting and retaining talented and diverse people.

Firms care about profits, to be sure, but those that maintain long-term success also care about developing future leaders. An executive remarked to me that it was not a coincidence that "succession management" embeds "success." We see these in the actions executives take. In the first weeks of the Donald J. Trump administration, Tim Cook (Apple), Jeff Bezos (Amazon), Sheryl Sandberg (Facebook), and Larry Page (Google) all posed with President Trump in support of a proposed policy change that would allow US firms to repatriate monies held overseas.

At that time, American corporations held more than $2.5 trillion overseas and sought to reduce the 35 percent corporate tax rate to 10 percent. The result of that policy change would be over $500 billion extra in profits. Apple alone had more than $200 billion overseas at that time. Their $50 billion in savings would exceed their 2016 profits.

Less than a week after that photo was taken, the Trump administration issued an executive order limiting immigration and travel to and from the United States. Apple's CEO, Tim Cook, spoke out against this policy. He did so because Apple employs people from all over the world and needs those people to be able to travel and communicate freely. Other CEOs made similar critical comments.

These CEOs took the expected positions on both policies. A concern for short-term profits led to their support for the proposed tax changes—what CEO would not want an extra $50 billion in profits? A concern for their long-term success and its dependence on a diverse, talented workforce led them to criticize the changes to immigration policy.

Two clear impressions emerge from visiting successful firms and organizations. First, they focus on their core mission, and second, they seek and value talented workers. These are not just my takeaways from visiting hundreds of corporations, universities, and organizations. They can also be found in any number of management and strategy books.

Given those impressions, if diversity and inclusion are framed as the right thing to do, they cannot have much force. In addition to a misalignment with the main goals, that framing positions diversity and inclusion as one of many do-good policies a corporation might pursue. This places diversity and inclusion initiatives in competition with other "oughts," such as sustainability, charity work, and service to the local community.

Thus, as lofty as the normative goals may be, we cannot expect corporate leaders to make promoting a multicultural society or correcting social disparities their primary concern. Corporations look to the bottom line. As much as advocates might want corporations to privilege normative desires for shared understandings and social justice above base concerns for profits, that will be a hard sell. Normative-based inclusion efforts not linked to a business case run the risk of degenerating into halfhearted, symbolic, feel-good gestures. For corporations to take meaningful action, they must see diversity and inclusion in their self-interest. They must believe in the business case.

An idealist might dismiss these arguments as overly cynical and argue that we should work toward creating a world in which the normative arguments carry the day, in which individuals have climbed sufficiently far up Maslow's hierarchy of needs to commit to economic reparations and affirmative action policies, and in which we all embrace and pursue inclusion and integration.

Let us suppose we get to that place, that we live in a world where people support affirmative action on normative grounds. I will argue that even in that world—in fact, especially in that world—the diversity-bonus logic is necessary, as it shows how to make inclusion successful.

If we do not understand how diversity produces bonuses, we cannot put our diverse repertoires to best use. We might even put them to improper use. Bonus logic informs emergency room doctors to put lots of eyeballs on novel and critical presentations and to apply checklists for sprained ankles. On the difficult problems, we should seek medical professionals with diverse training, case experiences, and identity attributes. Social justice logic offers no such guidance. If anything, normative logic argues for identity-representative panels of doctors on all cases. That would waste time, cost money, and result in worse health outcomes.

Diversity-bonus logic provides insights into how to constitute teams and how large those teams should be. How many doctors should we assign to a patient? How many economists, business people, and lawyers to a federal bailout program?

The diversity-bonus logic also points to useful behaviors. On creative teams, people must be willing to share their ideas, no matter how crazy. On predictive tasks, we need people with novel categorizations and causal models. When problem solving, people must take proposed solutions seriously and look to recombine them to create even better solutions. These behaviors require trust and personal validation, characteristics found in successful groups.[25]

While trust and validation align with social justice thinking, other behaviors that can generate diversity bonuses need not. On critical decisions, asking someone to play the role of devil's advocate and to challenge every idea can add value. That may not be seen as normatively inclusive.

Even worse, an overemphasis on normative concerns can result in satisficing, in which every decision or action must be approved by each individual. Thus, a team tasked with coming up with a new design or policy can wind up with an incoherent collection of parts meant to satisfy people with different goals. The saying that a camel is a horse designed by a committee is meant to capture this type of group failure. One person wants the horse to have long legs to go fast; another wants the horse to have big strong feet to be sturdy; and a third wants the horse to be able to travel long distances.

Set aside for the moment that these attributes make for an animal well suited to the desert, and focus on the fact that they make for a lousy horse. What we learn is that if people have different goals, diverse groups will not produce good outcomes. We need only look to Congress to see this to be true. Elected officials who must satisfy multiple constituencies to remain in office often fall victim to the camel problem. Diverse groups that evaluate solutions according to a shared set of criteria avoid the camel.[26]

The contrast should be clear. The bonus logic promotes reasoned, outcome-focused, inclusive diversity, and that can require challenging people's ideas and sometimes making choices that favor one person over another. The normative logic promotes representative diversity and fair, rather than efficient, outcomes.

Thus, to the extent that normative arguments offer incomplete and counterproductive guidance for how to achieve bonuses, they make inclusion appear to be less in our self-interest than it could be.[27] So while bonus-logic thinking may produce less immediate representativeness than normative thinking, evidence shows it generates better outcomes.[28] And if people experience direct benefits from diversity and inclusion, then those policies will have more support. Thus, paradoxically, a long-term goal of inclusion on normative grounds may be better attained by also promoting inclusion on pragmatic grounds.

Colleges and universities pursue this approach. Almost all university and college diversity and inclusion statements mention some form of diversity bonuses in addition to their normative interest. They emphasize how interactions among groups of diverse students produce deeper understandings (a bonus), better solutions to problems (a second bonus), and new areas of inquiry (a third bonus). These potentials for direct benefits, even for universities and colleges that have a strong normative commitment to inclusion, endow the bonus logic with a power that normative arguments lack.

THE BUSINESS CASE IN FULL

The diversity-bonus logic plays a powerful role in the business case by producing direct benefits. That does not mean that demographics do not matter or that social justice is not relevant. Any given organization will weigh the three parts of the business case—the nomative, the demographic, and the bonus logic—differently.

The talent pool part of the business case, as well as diversity bonuses, will be relevant for large employers that confront complex supply chain problems like Wal-Mart or McDonald's. A small engineering firm in Duluth, Minnesota, will be less worried about the broader talent pool and may care more about diversity bonuses.

Large corporations see value in each of the three parts. Waste Management Corporation, a waste and environmental services company with 2016 revenue of $14 billion, serves more than twenty million consumers. We might think that the first part of the business case, diversity bonuses, would not exist at all for a company picking up and emptying dumpsters. That characterization ignores the part of their business related to operations. Waste Management Corporation hires thousands of analysts and engineers. The analysts measure costs, determine pricing strategies, determine routes, and solve general logistics problems. The engineers manage more than a dozen waste-to-energy plants and more than one hundred landfills. These are all difficult tasks on which diversity bonuses surely exist, though they may be more due to cognitive than identity diversity.

Waste Management Corporation also needs access to a large labor pool. At present, they employ over forty thousand employees, so they see value in the demographic arguments. While promoting social justice may be a concern, we would not expect it to be central. As might be expected, while Waste Management does include diversity and inclusion as a core value, they list it fifth on the company web page, after *honesty*, *accountability*, *safety*, and *professionalism*. That ordering is what we might expect.

Microsoft Corporation, as would be anticipated, gives diversity and inclusion higher billing, listing it third after *growth mindset* and *customer obsession*. Given the dynamism of the software and gaming industries, Microsoft's primary emphasis on growth and customer services makes business sense. The justification for listing diversity and inclusion third on Microsoft's site is as follows: "We don't just value differences, we seek them out. We invite them in. Microsoft is a place where employees can be who they are. We value diverse perspectives. And as a result, we have better ideas, better products and happier customers."[29] Their language summarizes the diversity-bonus logic in which inclusion is less about social justice than about performance.

The same differential weighting of the business case applies to board diversity. Boards of directors could see value in all three parts of the business case. Board diversity, particularly gender diversity, has become a political concern, with more than a dozen countries, including Germany, France, Australia, and Italy, following Norway's lead and passing laws mandating quotas. In the United States, women do not hold representative numbers of seats on boards of directors or positions of leadership in Fortune 500 companies. A 2016 report by the United States General Accounting Office found that women held 16 percent of the seats on boards of directors of S&P 1500 firms. Those numbers represent a doubling from 1997.

Though women are underrepresented on boards, the distribution of women across industries does align with diversity-bonus thinking. It reveals more women on boards of companies that sell products to women and fewer women on boards of more technical companies. The boards of companies that sell household and personal products have over 20 percent women, as do food and beverage companies and retail companies. The boards of semiconductor and related companies and energy companies are 9 percent and 10 percent women, respectively.

The first two parts of the business case help us to make sense of the relative distribution of women on boards. We might expect the contributions of identity diversity bonuses to be larger for household and personal products than for the semiconductor industry. The available pool of talent in consumer goods may be less gender biased as well.

The normative part of the business case applies to boards as well. Boards that do not promote equity and social justice may lack full wind in their sails. Effective boards rely on active diverse members. Board members may give that little bit extra if they see the corporation as doing good as well as turning profits.

DIVERSITY AND INCLUSION ON WALL STREET

The most successful diversity and inclusion programs move beyond a check-the-box, get-the-numbers-right mentality. Forward-looking business leaders now construct their business cases around diversity bonuses, tapping into a larger talent pool and the contributions of an inclusive culture. The details of that business case depend on the industry. The business case for Wall Street differs from the business case for Wal-Mart.

Here, I consider the financial management sector, including large firms such as Credit Suisse, Goldman Sachs, and BlackRock that promote identity diversity. The scale of these firms can be mind-blowing. BlackRock, which I use as an exemplar, manages $5 trillion in assets, an amount that exceeds the GDP of every country other than the United States and China.

At a July 2014 retreat, BlackRock CEO Larry Fink and the company's global executive committee challenged their human resource department to increase minority and female representation in the leadership pipeline.[30] To understand why one of the most successful and technically savvy investment firms on Wall Street would push diversity and inclusion, we can look to the three components of the business case: diversity bonuses, demographics, and social justice.

Significant diversity bonuses can occur in two of the primary activities of a financial services firm: analytics and client services. Financial firms rely on teams of analysts to evaluate complex markets. On those teams they want cognitive and identity diversity: team-run funds outperform individuals and gender-mixed teams outperform all-male teams.[31] Wall Street executives also look to the data from science and research. They see the growth and success of teams in cracking difficult problems. They know that long-term success requires having the smartest teams.

The bonuses in client services stem from the ability to understand a diverse set of investors. Pension funds for state employees and unions are some of the larger institutional investors. Both groups invest funds for identity-diverse people. Those people are more likely to trust their life savings to and ask questions and share opinions with people who resemble them.

The second component, access to a large diverse pool of talent, likely also contributed to BlackRock's decision. BlackRock now employs over twelve thousand people, so it needs to be attractive to all identity groups. White men compose fewer than 30 percent of recent college graduates. In the long run, Wall Street needs to attract the 70 percent in the majority as well. The current situation offers ample space for improvement. At present fewer than 3 percent of Wall Street executives identify as underrepresented minorities, and fewer than one in five senior managers are women. Hiring more diverse employees is just a first step. The culture must change as well. Wall Street does not want to lose the diverse talent it hires.

BlackRock, Goldman Sachs, and Credit Suisse see themselves as meritocracies. They hire and promote top performers. If data show that only white men succeed, then the firms' leaderships know that they are operating under a myth. In a true meritocracy, everyone has an opportunity to succeed, regardless of her background or identity. A lack of success for members of some identity groups can imply a less than fully inclusive culture, a bad omen if your business model depends on its people sharing information, ideas, models, and insights.

Thus, any company staking a claim to a meritocratic culture must promote equity. In his 2017 annual letter to CEOs, BlackRock chairman Larry Fink wrote, "Environmental, social, and governance (ESG) factors relevant to a company's business can provide essential insights into management effectiveness and thus a company's long-term prospects. We look to see that a company is attuned to the key factors that contribute to long-term growth: sustainability of the business model and its operations, attention to external and environmental factors that could impact the company, and recognition of the company's role as a member of the communities in which it operates."[32]

BlackRock's assessments of a company's value include evaluations of a company's efforts on social dimensions such as diversity and inclusion efforts, worker training programs, and engagement in local communities because they provide a signal of that company's prospects for long-term success. In his letter, Fink makes clear that he considers social factors crucial within a financially relevant window and not in some infinite long term. It represents the type of forward thinking that enabled BlackRock to attract $5 trillion in assets.

That same logic applies to BlackRock itself. Its efforts suggest that its leadership believes that a diverse, inclusive workplace offers the possibility of wiser investments, more compelling pitches to clients, and more informative analytic tools. An inclusive culture that promotes social factors, including community engagement, will continue to make BlackRock an attractive employer to the changing demographic of college graduates.

In seeing the full case based on diversity bonuses, demographics, and equity, BlackRock is not alone. The leadership at Credit Suisse, Ford, Boeing, Genentech, Gilead, Alphabet (Google), Microsoft, Cummins, PepsiCo, IBM, Caterpillar, and Bloomberg also see the potential bonuses, know the demographics, and share the normative values. They too seek diversity bonuses.

SUMMARY

In this chapter, I have demonstrated the importance of the diversity-bonus logic within the broader business case for diversity and inclusion. The diversity-bonus logic aligns efforts to increase diversity and create inclusive environments with an organization's core mission. In contrast, normative arguments for inclusion can position diversity efforts as orthogonal to or even counter to mission. Demographic arguments as well can be seen as costly, at least in the short run.

I do not mean to imply that organizations should abandon the normative or demographic arguments. To the contrary, if more people accept the normative arguments and if the demographic argument proves compelling to the organization, diversity and inclusion initiatives roll out more smoothly, resulting in more equitable distributions of wealth, income, and opportunities.

CHAPTER SEVEN
PRACTICE: D&T + D&I

If there is no struggle, there is no progress.

—FREDERICK DOUGLASS

IN THIS FINAL CHAPTER, I ELABORATE ON THE PATH TO CREATING effective diversity and inclusion programs, programs that produce diversity bonuses. This is not an easy task. Once, in presenting the logic of diversity bonuses to NASA employees, I commented that social science was harder than rocket science because social science must understand people, and people are an unpredictable, diverse lot.

The difficulty of creating an effective diversity and inclusion program should be apparent to nearly everyone. Each year, corporate America spends billions on diversity and inclusion. In 2015, Google planned on spending $150 million on diversity initiatives, and Apple spent $50 million. A preponderance of evidence suggests that all of this spending barely budges the needle on numbers and that efforts to reduce discrimination often result in backlash or diversity fatigue.[1]

At this point, a quick summary of what we know, and what it appears we have to do, goes as follows: On a variety of tasks, diverse teams have the potential to produce exceptional performance; that is, better performance than individuals or homogeneous groups. As a rule, on complex tasks, the best team will not consist of the best individual performers. The best team will instead consist of people with diverse, relevant repertoires.

It then follows that organizations should apply their best judgment, informed by theory and data, to create diverse, high-potential teams; that they should also create a culture of trust and a shared sense of mission; and that they should design practices and procedures to achieve bonuses. Given that diverse teams add costs in effort and time, diversity should be applied to high-value, complex tasks. The easy, low-margin stuff can be left to individuals. The goal is obvious: inclusive teams with germane diversity on the hard high-value problems, strategic diversity, and inclusion on complex tasks.

Attaining that goal requires effort and practice. To arrange different thinkers wrapped in diverse identities around a conference table and expect a bonus is to engage in the type of magical thinking that has been the Achilles' heel of diversity initiatives. Success does not depend on how diverse the people in the room look; it depends on the team's ability to leverage their diverse repertoires. Tossing diverse people in a room and asking them to be innovative will more often produce a dog's breakfast than an iPhone or a breakthrough app like Pokemon Go.

At a minimum, any successful diversity and inclusion policy must include six Ms. Organizations must *message* from the top and link diversity to *mission*. The organization must *manage* teams with the goal of achieving diversity bonuses. That means creating an inclusive culture. It also means applying germane diversity on complex high-value opportunities. Organizations must also *measure* performance and provide *mentors* for underrepresented employees. And, last, organizations must tie inclusive behaviors to *merit*; that is, they must reward people who advance diversity and inclusion.

These six Ms work in concert with one another. A CEO who presents glorious imagery of how differences lead to better outcomes has greater impact if she also puts in place policies and norms that enable bonuses to arise—that is, if she manages to produce bonuses.

These six Ms must be taken seriously. Among the companies I have visited, I have been struck by the correlation between success in diversity initiatives and buttoned-down, effective management practices on the other aspects of their businesses.

How any given organization builds good practices depends on the challenges they face, their current employees, and their employee pool. There can be no one-size-fits-all solution. There do exist a few areas where almost all organizations need to improve: bias reduction, the creation of inclusive cultures, and developing people and team analytics. First, though, I will talk about practice.

WE *ARE* TALKING ABOUT PRACTICE

In *The Difference*, I wrote of the *parable of the bikes*. I asked readers to imagine asking a group of five- or six-year-old children to run as far as they can in ten seconds and then to place those same kids on bikes and redo the experiment. I noted that while the average distance traveled in the two cases would be about the same, the very best performers would be children on bikes, and so would the worst.

Homogeneous groups perform like the kids who run. They produce the B-pluses. They rarely do anything amazing. Identity and cognitively diverse teams of people perform like the children on bikes. They produce exceptional results. We saw that in the data on academic papers and teams. Look into most great success and you find diversity. For example, the creative team behind the record-breaking musical *Hamilton* includes Lin-Manuel Miranda, a New Yorker of Puerto Rican descent, Jeffrey Seller, a gay, white, male Jewish adoptee from Detroit, and Jill Furman, who grew up in a wealthy Manhattan family.

But diverse groups, like the children on the bikes, can also fail miserably.

Creating successful diverse teams and inclusive organizations requires practice. That practice is made easier when we know that bonuses exist. Permit me an extended analogy. In 1979, the National Basketball Association introduced the three-point shot. Teams that could make the three-point shot earned a bonus: three-point shots were worth 50 percent more than normal shots. No one needed to write an entire book explaining the three-point bonus.

What was needed was practice. Though the best players in the world by most metrics, NBA players lacked the ability to make the longer shots. In that first year, NBA teams took on average three shots per game from behind the arc, making a paltry 28 percent. Multiplying that percentage by 1.5 corresponds to 42 percent for a two-point shot. In 1979 NBA players made two-pointers at a 48 percent clip. The three-point bonus went unrealized.

Practice took time. Two years after the introduction of the three-point line, the 1981–1982 NBA champions, the Los Angeles Lakers, starred Magic Johnson, James Worthy, and Kareem Abdul-Jabbar, three of the greatest players in the history of the NBA. They made only thirteen three-pointers out of ninety-four attempts. That translates to about 14 percent. Those Lakers did not realize a three-point bonus. To their credit, they did not even try for one.

Had NBA players relied only on empirical analysis, the three-pointer would have remained a minor part of the game. It was not producing any bonuses. And yet, every general manager, coach, and player saw the potential 50 percent bonus. That led to practice. If we jump ahead to 2015–2016, we see the residue of that effort. In 2015–2016, NBA teams averaged more than twenty three-point shots per game. In a single playoff game in 2016, the Cleveland Cavaliers torched the Atlanta Hawks with twenty-five three-pointers, a number that nearly doubles what the 1981–1982 Lakers made over the entire season.

Three-pointers now produce a bonus as well. League-wide, players connect on over 35 percent of three-point attempts. This equates to more than 50 percent accuracy on two-point shots. In addition, the very best teams shoot more three-pointers on average and make them with higher accuracy.

Knowledge of the three-point bonus provided a rudder and compass. Players spent hours in the gym—or, in the case of 2015 and 2016 league MVP Stephen Curry, on a dirt driveway—firing from long range. In 2016, Curry made more than four hundred three-pointers and connected at a rate above 45 percent.

Organizations need practice as well. They need to learn how to compose teams, and how to engage in behaviors that produce the bonuses. And they need data and theory to guide practices. Unlike basketball skills, which can be honed individually, the skills needed to produce diversity bonuses require participation in teams.

Practice, and therefore inclusion, entails cost. Schools, colleges, and universities can allay some of that cost by providing environments for young people to learn behaviors that produce diversity bonuses. Failure in the classroom—a botched homework assignment—won't lower anyone's profits or harm the environment. And, as might be expected, studies show that students who engage in diverse groups at school encounter more ideas and see the value of inclusivity. They continue to seek diverse groups. As adults, they are more likely to live in and work in integrated communities.[2]

BIAS REDUCTION

To learn behaviors that produce bonuses within diverse teams requires that the organization include diverse people. Our workplaces must be diverse, so must be our universities. Efforts to create diverse workforces must overcome biases that disadvantage women and members of minority groups. This is step one.

To get diverse people on the bus, so to speak, diversity and inclusion training programs often begin (and sometimes end) with bias-reduction training. Reducing discrimination is the low fruit in the business case for diversity as these programs receive little pushback from employees. My experience has been that this is true even for people who reject normative arguments based on historical and current discrimination.

People who work at Boeing want to hire the most talented engineers. The employees at PIMCO want to hire the smartest market analysts. Everyone prefers to choose from a larger pool of talent. That larger pool of talent also consists of a more cognitively diverse pool of talent. That is true even if identity diversity does not correlate with relevant cognitive diversity.[3]

Bias training is needed because even though the law prevents discrimination based on (some) identity characteristics, discrimination persists. As Thurgood Marshall noted in a 1988 speech to the American Bar Association, "A child born to a Black mother in a state like Mississippi . . . has exactly the same rights as a white baby born to the wealthiest person in the United States." He then added, "It's not true."[4]

He was correct in 1988. He would also be correct now.[5] Evidence shows that discrimination occurs at multiple layers across a variety of contexts. Women and applicants with African American–sounding names receive fewer job callbacks, lower salary offers, and lower competency rankings, despite identical resumes.[6]

Acts of bias can be unintended, and even unconscious.[7] When making hiring decisions, people err in the direction of homogeneity. We falsely believe that people who share our identity are smarter and more capable. We are not as connected across identity groups as we need to be.[8] Even if people did not prefer their own group, discrimination could still arise if people could more accurately evaluate people from their own identity group.[9] For these reasons, unconscious-bias training has become a staple of diversity training.

Nepotism and social network effects also contribute to bias. People pull strings for their children and their friends' children. They help get them summer internships. They arrange college interviews. These people's friends and their children tend to belong to the same identity groups and have similar experiences. Both reduce cognitive diversity.

Last, as mentioned in the previous chapter, many companies apply a common rubric to applicants. This can also produce bias. If members of an identity group enter college less prepared, they may earn lower grades. Or they might not go to the "right" school or have the same opportunities.

The full list of biases—direct, unintended, unconscious, social network based, and rubric based—combine to disadvantage some groups. Attracting and maintaining a diverse pool of employees requires not just reducing them but eradicating them completely. Getting close is not good enough. Small biases accumulate to form large biases. That is not a moral prescriptive. It is based on the mathematics of bias accumulation.

The Accumulation of Bias

That mathematics of bias accumulation can be best understood through an example. As a first step, we need to calibrate the magnitude of racial and gender biases. Single-study biases range from 5 percent to 25 percent for salary offers.[10] Similar-size biases seem to exist in other contexts. Manipulating the race of the seller of a baseball card from white to black lowers the price on eBay 20 percent.[11]

These one-shot measures reveal small biases. I believe that to be accurate. Bias exists but not at horrible levels. However, these measures understate the accumulated effects of biased decisions. A person's career consists of dozens if not hundreds of evaluations and perhaps dozens of opportunities for success.

Suppose that to make senior partner at a law firm or to reach the executive suite in a Fortune 500 company, a person must pass ten hurdles. These could be performing well in an interview, attracting a new client, or excelling in a leadership role. Each hurdle is an up or out, a win or lose.

A person with a 50 percent chance of success at each juncture stands a one-in-a-thousand chance of passing all ten and reaching the C suite. If we assume women and minorities are 10 percent less likely to earn a promotion, so they pass 40 percent of the time, then they reach the C suite at a rate of one in ten thousand. That's one-tenth the chance. In a ten-level hierarchy, 10 percent discrimination produces 90 percent fewer women and minorities at the top.

Bias training counters these pernicious accumulated effects of small biases. It can increase awareness so that people ask themselves, Am I selecting this candidate or taking a risk on this candidate because she looks like me, or because she's good? Bias training can also involve instituting changes in process. Process solutions include requirements to interview minority candidates, mandating at least one woman or minority on each panel or committee, or requiring more than one evaluation rubric.[12]

Eradicating bias is not as simple as it might seem. A university postdoctoral hiring committee might disproportionately hire faculty who attended elite graduate programs where students are thought to receive better training and to have cleared a higher admissions hurdle. A candidate who excelled at Thomas Jefferson High School for Science and Technology and Yale College, and then earned a PhD at Caltech, is perceived to be better coached by stronger scholars than someone who attended Middleville Thornapple-Kellogg High School in rural Michigan and Ferris State College, and earned a PhD at Western Michigan University.[13]

The committee should neither ignore the second candidate nor feel compelled to hire him under an inclusion initiative. Instead, the committee has to do the hard work of looking at the candidates' repertoires as well as their accomplishments. If the university already employs two postdocs from the same lab that produced the first candidate, they might well give the second candidate a much longer look.

INCLUSIVE CULTURES

Once a company has diverse people in the room, those people must act to produce bonuses; that is, they must act inclusively. Creating an inclusive culture demands more than listing inclusivity as a core value and rewriting a few sentences on www.ourcompany.com. Meaningful inclusion requires a more organic bottom-up process guided by managers who shape behavior, motivate and inspire employees, guide actions, and create meaning.

Adding inclusion as a core value is still a good thing, and hundreds, if not thousands, of companies ranging from U.S. Steel to Cold Stone Creamery to Better Homes and Gardens Real Estate do so. Better Homes and Gardens Real Estate replaced innovation with inclusion to encourage employees to become better listeners and to be more open to new ideas. Ironically, that change could make the firm more innovative.

Inclusion can take a variety of forms. Here, what I mean by an inclusive culture is one in which people have the ability to apply their full repertoires. A lack of inclusion means that someone feels that she has something to add and does not or cannot. An inclusive culture need not involve people sharing their personal narratives and beginning each sentence with the phrase, "I appreciate and respect your position." That said, people will be more willing to share ideas if they feel safe, respected, and validated.

Recall that if people share ideas, a team can be as good as its best member, so better than the average. If, in addition, ideas are challenged and combined, they can be better than those of their best member. Those challenges and deep engagements with ideas are a necessary component of the type of inclusive culture that maximizes bonuses.

Kim Scott, a management consultant, refers to the practice of challenging and improving as "exercising radical candor." She sees this as a necessary behavior for a successful manager. Scott categorizes the behavior of managers on two dimensions: caring personally and challenging directly. Managers who care personally but do not challenge directly fall into the ruinous empathy box. To practice radical candor, a boss must be both caring and challenging. Caring gets the diverse idea into the room. Challenging improves it.[14]

The investment firm Bridgewater and Associates relies on an extreme form of radical candor that founder Ray Dalio refers to as a meritocracy of ideas. The firm's culture prizes openness, transparency, and honesty above all. Any and all ideas put forward face stiff challenges. Dalio believes that his principles best advance Bridgewater's core mission of understanding how the world works. Their form of inclusivity may not be for everyone, but it does achieve diversity bonuses.

Google's lessons learned led them to similar policies. They too value dissent and encourage transparency. Dissent, by the way, is also a core value of McKinsey and Intel. Google also relies heavily on teams. Teams hire, promote, assign salaries, and even fire employees. Transparency, dissent, and teams: each increases the likelihood of good actions. Google also seeks talent. They want smart people.[15]

At Google, inclusion also means freedom. In their 2004 initial public offering letter, Larry Page and Sergey Brin described how employees could devote 20 percent of their time to new ideas and projects. Employees could form impromptu teams to leverage diverse talents to create new products and services. The list of in-house successes includes both Google News and Gmail. In practice, not every employee uses her full 20 percent. Less important than the actual percentage of time spent on individual projects is the fact that any employee could allocate one day a week to an idea and could build a team of Googlers to pursue it further. That possibility epitomizes an inclusive, flexible culture.

These types of inclusive practices promote diversity bonuses. That does not mean that they are ideal for every organization. The Nuclear Regulatory Commission does not want its employees experimenting with the reactor. It wants its employees to follow protocols. As a rule of thumb, an organization that depends on stability and control may find that more hierarchical, less inclusive cultures lead to better performance.[16]

Inclusive cultures make sense for companies that operate in fast-changing, that is, complex, environments. Thus, the trend away from routine work and toward nonroutine cognitive work spurs organizations to promote inclusion. The stories of Katherine Johnson and Dorothy Vaughan from *Hidden Figures* again prove illustrative. The advent of computers made hand calculations obsolete. Katherine Johnson became part of a team who applied techniques from analytic geometry to determine the calculations the computers would make. Dorothy Vaughan became a supervisor of Fortran computer programmers. Their transition to nonroutine work helped put people on the moon.

Thus, the trend toward cognitive nonroutine work in the corporate world creates pressure for more inclusive cultures. That trend occurs within organizations as well. A half century ago, Bell Canada made the bulk of its profits from providing phone service. Quality control and the maintenance of service were essential to their business success. Beginning in 1983, Bell Canada began diversifying. Now rebranded as the conglomerate BCE, it competes in a range of markets including wireless, media, and sports. Those markets demand flexibility. BCE CEO George Cope's corporate profile lists his ability to build high-performance teams as one of two primary strengths.[17]

PEOPLE OR TEAM ANALYTICS

The bleeding edge of diversity and inclusion programs rely on cutting-edge analytics. They leverage data to create the best teams. Identifying criteria or attributes of successful groups represents the frontier.

At the moment, almost all hiring practices suffer from a common error. Organizations evaluate people as individuals when those people will work in teams. Some corporate human resource departments and graduate student admissions committees assign scores to grades, letters of recommendation, and so on to produce a cumulative score. Those applicants with the highest score get hired or admitted.

To ensure talent, organizations demand that people satisfy certain criteria to get a job. According to legend, Google's hiring of Vint Cerf, an Internet pioneer who has been awarded the National Medal of Technology, the Turing Award, the Presidential Medal of Freedom, and the Marconi Prize; who has been elected to the National Academy of Engineering; and who has received more than twenty honorary degrees, was delayed because he did not submit an undergraduate transcript.

These practices violate the no-test results discussed in this book. On complex tasks, no single test applied to individuals can identify the best team. Some organizations continue to hire based on grade point averages despite the fact that the organization with probably the most data, Google, has evidence that it does not work. Laszlo Bock has described grade point averages and IQs as far less important than problem-solving ability in predicting success at Google.[18]

The growing field of people analytics seeks to identify characteristics of successful teams. What is known so far is that good managers play a role, as does the ability of team members to read the emotions of others.[19] The aforementioned research on the millions of academic papers and patents implies that strategic team choice works. When academics form teams, they do not walk down the hallway and look for a random smart person. They search their contacts or the Internet for someone with a cognitive repertoire that complements their own. We know that, because the best papers combine diverse, deep references.[20]

If a recipe for success consists of two parts—getting the right people in the room (diversity) and creating the right space for them to produce bonuses (inclusion)—then theory and data can assist us in both parts. Suppose a firm has to make a prediction about the effects of a change in the regulatory environment. Rather than have one person idiosyncratically select a diverse team, a team might be queried to generate ideas about what types of diversity might be relevant. What perspectives, knowledge, and tools might be useful in making an accurate prediction?

If possible, past data could be leveraged. I once visited a company that could trace its success to approximately one hundred up-or-down decisions on whether to advance products down the pipeline. When I asked what the data showed, that is, which people were good at making predictions, who made correlated predictions, and whether the company had evidence that certain pairs of people were never both wrong, the company replied that it did not keep data on people's predictions.

Nor did another firm that relied heavily on in-house evaluations of product features. That firm, which has a market capitalization in excess of $100 billion, did keep data on employees' NCAA basketball pool predictions and was able to tell me that the entry that averaged the selections of everyone was in the top three of over a thousand participants in that year's contest. That success should have led them to average feature evaluations as well.

At both of these companies, the forecasts drive decisions that put tens or hundreds of millions of dollars at stake. To make those decisions, they relied on diverse teams, but they made no scientific effort to build optimal teams. They relied on seat-of-the-pants thinking. If Google's former People Team leader Lazlo Bock were consulting for either of those companies, he would run regressions on the efficacy of decisions and team composition. If Bridgewater's Ray Dalio were running either company, he would go back to the videotape any time an error was made. He would see if people ignored the correct idea or, even worse, if the right idea was not in the room. If the latter, he would look to hire someone whose background would make her likely to have the idea. If Phil Tetlock or Barb Mellers were in charge, they would identify diverse superforecasters and then combine them into a team.

CONCLUSION

Progress toward creating productive inclusion requires practice. The formal models reveal how cognitive diversity can contribute on a variety of tasks. They show how groups and teams whose members possess diverse representations, models, knowledge, and heuristics can make more accurate forecasts, find better solutions to problems, come up with more creative ideas, provide broader and deeper evaluations of policies and strategies, and better discern what is true.

The logic shows that diversity bonuses occur primarily on complex tasks that involve multiple dimensions or variables. Implicit in the claims are assumptions about each participant's willingness and ability to contribute and the potential to contribute across diverse representations and models. We should therefore expect to put in effort if we want to achieve diversity bonuses. Ample empirical evidence shows that bonuses can be achieved: the best academic research, the most innovative patents, and the best investment decisions are all done by teams. And those teams are cognitively diverse and often identity diverse as well.

The potential for diversity bonuses offers an alternative frame. A focus on equity alone leads to a fixed-sum mind-set. We think in terms of tradeoffs. Diversity-bonus thinking enables us to see how our differences can make us more innovative, resilient, and prosperous. It points to how we might enlarge the pie instead of negotiating over the sizes of our current slices.

Progress requires a specific type of practice. We must rid ourselves and our organizations of conscious, unconscious, and structural biases. We must create environments in which everyone has an opportunity to contribute.

Herein lies one of the core challenges in creating effective diverse teams: success requires unity and difference. Successful diverse teams must be united in their goals. At the same time, team members must appreciate, encourage, and engage their differences. They cannot check their identities at the door. They must bring their whole selves—their identities, their experiences, their education and training—to achieve bonuses.

To conclude, I have shown logic and evidence for how germane cognitive diversity produces bonuses on the high-value complex tasks that predominate in our modern economy. I have shown how not any diversity will do. The diversity must be germane to the task. In some cases, differences in education or training may be most relevant. In others, our identities or experiences will have larger effects.

The theory and evidence demonstrates the need for a purposeful and strategic mind-set to group composition, hiring policies, and organizational culture and practices if we hope to produce diversity bonuses. The path will not be easy. Achieving these bonuses is a complex task. There may be few one-size-fits-all solutions. What works for Microsoft may not work for Louisiana Tech. What works for IBM may not work for Disney. Within each organization, thoughtful, diverse teams will be needed to think through how to identify and tap into diverse talent and how to create environments within which all people contribute and thrive.

I end on a hopeful note. Evidence of diversity bonuses becomes more compelling day by day, week by week. We appear to be getting better at creating effective diverse teams. Best of all, the people who belong to the teams and groups that produce diversity bonuses see the synergy between the normative ideal of an integrated, inclusive society and the economic ideal of an optimal team. They see inclusion as necessary to our collective success. May we all reach that place soon.

WHAT IS THE REAL VALUE OF DIVERSITY IN ORGANIZATIONS? QUESTIONING OUR ASSUMPTIONS

KATHERINE W. PHILLIPS

It is hardly possible to overrate the value . . . of placing human beings in contact with persons dissimilar to themselves, and with modes of thought and action unlike those with which they are familiar. . . . Such communication has always been, and is peculiarly in the present age, one of the primary sources of progress.

—JOHN STUART MILL, *Principles of Political Economy*

WHEN PHILOSOPHER AND POLITICAL ECONOMIST JOHN STUART Mill claimed diversity as a "primary source of progress," it was 1848 and his initial concern was trade among nations. He claimed that being exposed to the goods and products of a foreign country served as a mechanism for economic growth. But more importantly he claimed that exposure to other countries served the intellectual and moral growth of the people. Mill's concerns with difference did not stop there. Some have claimed Mill was the first feminist, as he advocated for the equality of women in society as well. Now, in 2017, we are having the same conversation about the "value . . . of placing human beings in contact with persons dissimilar to themselves" (that is, diversity) for organizational and team performance, educational development, technological advancement, and other important outcomes in society. The so-called business case for diversity has consumed the attention of scholars and practitioners alike as they seek to justify efforts to diversify organizations and open opportunities for a broader swath of society—women, racial minorities, persons with disabilities, the aging population, and other "nontraditional" and often undervalued society members. The fact is, this question of "What is the value of diversity?" is not a new one. Mill made proclamations about it in 1848, and now Scott Page's treatise provides a compelling answer to this question through logic and empirical research on the promise of cognitive and identity diversity.

Page's contribution to Our Compelling Interest has offered us an in-depth explanation of *how* diversity can provide a bonus under the right circumstances—when problems are sufficiently difficult. He has used simple and compelling logic, and provided numerous examples from the boardroom to the classroom to Hollywood studios, to explain how bringing a set of people with cognitive and identity diversity together *can* lead to better performance on complex tasks or difficult problems. Important to note is that Page does not use the word *will* or the word *should* in his statements. This is not an exercise of precision or guarantees, nor is it an exercise of morality. Instead, it is an exercise of functionality and utility—when and where is it possible for diversity to provide unique benefits over homogeneity? By understanding the possibility of diversity's benefits, we might then understand what society is striving toward, so we can make some assessment of whether it is worth it to try to get there. I believe the logic and the evidence support the potential for a "diversity bonus," and there is no doubt that it is worth it for organizations and for societies to try to capture that bonus.

I would like to add to the discussion of Our Compelling Interest and Page's diversity-bonus premise by providing three contributions. First, Page mentioned that identity diversity's bonus might emerge not from the direct connection between identity diversity and cognitive diversity but instead from indirect effects of the mere presence of diversity. Empirical research in this area reveals that identity diversity has an effect that is independent of its connection to cognitive diversity.[1] I believe this is worth exploring further here, as it relates to the assumptions we tend to make about the value of diversity. Page argues that organizations must open opportunities for those who have traditionally been underrepresented in organizations so that cognitive diversity can enter, as in the example Page used about disabled employees being integrated into the federal government. I expand on one argument that goes a step further to say that identity diversity also benefits organizations because of the influence it has on every individual in the organization. Diversity makes people work harder, and that benefit can happen even if the identity diversity is not directly connected to new cognitive perspectives. My comments here lead to the fundamental question, what is the resistance to diversity in organizations? If diversity bonuses exist and *can* be captured, as postulated by Page and supported by empirical literature, why is it so hard for organizations to achieve them consistently?

Second, I believe it is important to recognize that diversity is hard. Diversity bonuses do not automatically emerge simply by putting diverse groups together. Groups are composed of people, and people are far from perfect. The people have to engage with one another in some meaningful and productive ways to garner the benefits of that diversity. Moreover, these groups of people are embedded in systems, in organizations, in historical times, that influence the potential for that diversity bonus to be reached. Even under the best of circumstances, when cognitive and identity diversity is in abundance, there are numerous factors that may facilitate or undermine the emergence of a diversity bonus. I use the example of functionally diverse groups—filled with cognitive and identity diversity to work on difficult problems, the basic prerequisites of Page's model—to explore a few situational factors that might be important for facilitating diversity bonuses in organizations. In many of the successful examples used throughout Page's book, I would postulate that an examination of those situations would find many of the features that are fundamentally built into the best practices of cross-functional teams. Without the right set of situational circumstances, it is difficult for any team to succeed. Teamwork is hard, and many teams fail to reach their potential. This is especially true when the teams are dealing with complex, difficult problems that require interdependence, coordination, and collaboration between a diverse set of individuals. Although organizations strive to facilitate these circumstances, they often fall short and might erroneously conclude that diversity does not work. It is not diversity that has caused the failure; it is a lack of organizational leadership, implicit and explicit biases, improper structures, and poorly designed processes that have caused the team to fail. The potential of the diversity bonus is still there.

Finally, I will challenge the reader with my own, somewhat philosophical, set of questions and assumptions: Why is it necessary to prove the benefit of diversity? Is there an equal push to prove the benefits of homogeneity to organizations and society? Why do some people (for example, women, minorities, the disabled, the old, the young, transgendered people, homosexuals, and so on) have to prove that their presence in a given environment is "beneficial" for the bottom line and others (that is, white people, males, cisgendered people, and heterosexuals) do not have that same burden of proof? There is power in framing and in the questions we ask. This raises explicit issues of representation, power, and status that are often left untouched by diversity researchers, including myself. The reality is that there is a power in the status quo that motivates the desire for "proof" of the business case for diversity—we all see homogeneity as the norm, which perhaps gives it more power than it deserves.[2]

DEFINING DIVERSITY

Before jumping into my contributions, I think it is important to link Page's conceptualization of diversity with past research. Page divided the world of diversity into two main categories: cognitive diversity and identity diversity. This distinction aligns with distinctions often used in the organizational diversity literature. There has been a proliferation of labels used to distinguish different sources of diversity from one another—demographic diversity, value diversity, task diversity, surface-level diversity, deep-level diversity, and so on—but they all make the same basic distinction. In my own empirical research I have gravitated toward the use of the terms *informational diversity* and *social category diversity* to distinguish between diversity that results from what people know (that is, cognitive diversity) and diversity that results from how people identify themselves and others (that is, identity diversity). Importantly, I highlight in my work that informational and social category diversity coexist in groups. It is not possible to characterize a group as having only a level of informational diversity or only a level of social category diversity—a group constantly has some level of each of these types of diversity. Hence, you cannot study one without considering the other.

"*Informational diversity* captures the differences in information, opinions, perspectives, and modes of thought and action that are relevant for the task at hand being completed by a group."[3] This definition is consistent with the distinctions Page makes regarding cognitive diversity. The careful consideration of information, knowledge, heuristics, representations, mental models, and frameworks discussed explicitly by Page in the latter half of the book provides a logic and precision to our thinking about how informational or cognitive diversity influences groups. When individuals are brought together to solve problems in groups, they often possess different information or knowledge structures that can be utilized to inform the group. In fact, for many problem-solving and decision-making groups, the very reason they are brought together is to capture the diverse knowledge and perspectives that are uniquely held by different group members.[4] However, in many cases there is no way to effectively measure cognitive diversity—what people actually know about the current problem. One does not know what another person knows until he or she shares that information. Page compels us to consider the fact that each person who comes to a group has a set of abilities and tools, knowledge, and mental models. These are shaped by a myriad set of experiences and identities possessed by the group member. Although not explicitly stated, Page and I share in the fundamental assumption that every group has some level, even if very small, of informational or cognitive diversity, as no two individuals are exactly the same. As groups work together, the goal should be to increase the presence of that cognitive diversity and the willingness to express those differences to capture the diversity bonus in groups that are facing complex, difficult, and uncertain problems.

Social category diversity exists alongside cognitive diversity in task groups. In my work I have used the term "social category diversity to refer to those distinctions that serve as a salient basis of categorization into in-group (people who are like me) and out-group (people who are not like me)."[5] Salient demographic characteristics such as race, gender, nationality, or age are considered social category diversity, but this diversity may also stem from any characteristic that may not be immediately visible yet can be rendered salient in the context and thus be used to categorize group members. For instance, minimal distinctions such as an ostensible preference for a type of painting or for wearing a red shirt versus a blue shirt can be used to examine the effects of social category diversity, allowing for a connection of this research to the long tradition of social categorization and social identity research dating back to the 1970s.[6] The critical feature here is that people use these social characteristics to tell themselves that some subset of the group of people is "like me" at a deeper level, in terms of what we know and how we feel about problems we are facing, and that some of them are not.[7] For the rest of this chapter I will use the terms coined by Page, *cognitive diversity* and *identity diversity*, for consistency.

THE BENEFITS OF IDENTITY DIVERSITY

Page spent much of his treatise explaining how groups benefit from cognitive diversity. This is compelling and without much controversy. We can believe that if two people who aren't necessarily the best at a task come together to share their specialized knowledge, they might benefit from the full complement of knowledge necessary to be successful on that difficult task. Diversity bonuses that stem from cognitive diversity can occur. However, the role of identity diversity in groups is often what people are thinking about when they ask the question, what is the business case for diversity? This question is a nice way of asking, why do we need people who look different from the majority of us here to be a part of our organization? Why do we need identity diversity to be successful? Although I find the question itself to be plagued by implicit or unconscious negative intentions (I discuss this further later), Page's logic, along with empirical research on the impact of diversity in teams, provides at least two compelling answers to this question.

The first benefit of identity diversity is that it is a *source* of cognitive diversity. The premise here is that people from different identity groups will bring different knowledge, experiences, and mental models to the table for consideration, allowing for increased cognitive diversity and therefore better outcomes (predictions, creativity, decision making, problem solving, and so on). Just like one's functional training in engineering, psychology, or cultural anthropology shapes one's cognitive identity, so too does one's gender, race, cultural background, (dis)ability, and so forth. If the training one has received for five to ten years in school is important for shaping a cognitive profile, one argument that follows is that the life experiences that are shaped by other identities should also be considered important for shaping that cognitive profile. People who have different identities walk through the world having different experiences, being exposed to different opportunities, different knowledge, and different mental models. Cultural differences, gender role expectations, marital status, parenthood, and a myriad set of other identities all influence the cognitive models an individual develops. Moreover, it is not unreasonable to believe that identity makes it possible that, for example, by virtue of being a woman, there may be some common experiences that shape one's cognition in predictably different ways from the cognition of men. For example, women might have different insights about the design of a car because of predictably different ways that women might use the car in comparison to men. Here it is critical to recognize that *representation* may provide different benefits from diversity itself. When creating a product for women, it is critical to have a woman's perspective represented, as she might have insights that a man could not. Likewise, if an American company is moving into the Chinese market, it is in their interest to work with Chinese people who have local knowledge to ensure development of a product that fits customers' needs.

There is a caution here we must consider. No identity, even one's functional identity, is 100 percent predictive of one's cognitive profile.

This is the beauty and the flaw of this logic about the congruence between identity and cognitive diversity. We should not assume that people from the same identity group have exactly the same cognitive perspective to bring to a group for a given problem, just as we should not assume that two people who are different necessarily have different cognitive perspectives.[8] We use identity diversity as a proxy for cognitive diversity. It is not a perfect proxy. Page is essentially suggesting that if some people are kept out on the basis of identity, then organizations are potentially leaving out very valuable cognitive perspectives that could benefit groups, organizations, and society. It is better to err on the side of inclusion, given the complex and difficult problems often being faced in organizations.

It is easier to swallow the logic that identity diversity is important when we are talking about functional differences, but harder for people to accept that a female engineer and a male engineer, both trained at the same schools in the same "right" ways of doing things, might have different approaches to a problem by virtue of their gender. Functional background matters, but so do all of the other myriad identities that shape experiences in life—gender matters, race matters, nationality matters, and so on. The compelling example Page used about a person in a wheelchair having a different vantage point and seeing the world from a different perspective is apropos here. There are times when *representation* from different types of people is the only way to ensure that cognitive diversity is not only present in the group but also communicated and sought after by others in the group.[9]

A second benefit of identity diversity is simply that seeing differences on the surface makes people assume that there are more cognitive differences there in the group, prompting them to seek out this information. Even if the person who looks "different" does not bring any new cognitive differences to the table, his or her mere presence has been shown to change the behavior of the group's members.[10] People work harder in identity-diverse environments than they do in homogeneous environments when it comes to benefiting from cognitive diversity.

Let me review some of the psychological processes that support these claims. First, individuals *expect* individuals with the same identity to agree with them more on both task-relevant and task-irrelevant issues than people who are different.[11] In particular, Katherine W. Phillips and D. L. Loyd's findings support this psychological process in two experimental studies in which they examined two different sources of identity diversity (functional background and geographic affiliation) and argued that expectations can cause diverse groups to benefit from the mere presence of people who are different, regardless of whether those different individuals have unique perspectives to share.

In their first study, they told MBA students that they would be working in a three-person team that included the participant and either two other MBA students or one fellow MBA student and a medical student. This led to two conditions: the homogenous condition, in which all members of the team were MBA students (same functional identity), and the diverse condition, in which one of the members was a medical student (different functional identity). Given the composition of the groups, there was always a majority of MBA students, so the participant was always a member of the majority identity group. The participants were then told that their opinions about which market to target for a medical device were in disagreement with the opinions of the other two members of the group, who were in agreement with one another. Thus, the participant was always bringing some cognitive diversity to the group in the form of a unique opinion. The findings of this first study revealed that participants expected greater task perspective similarity with identity-similar individuals (that is, MBA students) than with identity-dissimilar individuals (that is, medical students). In addition, when their expectations for similarity were violated, participants were more surprised and irritated by disagreement from the identity-similar individuals in homogeneous settings than with the identity-similar individual in diverse settings—that is, they were more tolerant of cognitive diversity and disagreement in identity-diverse settings. Furthermore, participants in diverse groups expected a more positive and accepting group experience than those in homogeneous groups.

One might argue that the results of the first study using functional identity are not that surprising. In their second study, Phillips and Loyd examined the consequences of this assumption of similarity and dissimilarity even when the identity was irrelevant to the task at hand.[12] In this study, the task-irrelevant distinction was the side of campus on which the participants lived (north or south campus); in the diverse condition, there was one group member from one side of campus and two from the opposite side of campus, whereas in the homogeneous condition, all group members were from the same side of campus. This was a meaningful source of identity for the participants, and the experimental methods made that particular identity salient for the participants. In this case, interacting groups were brought together to make a decision about the best company for another company to acquire. The task was an information-sharing task that allowed for the exchange of unique information and opinions about three possible options. In both the homogeneous and the diverse conditions, one of the group members from the majority identity group held an opinion that was different from that held by the rest of the group, just as in the first study. One member of the social majority had information about the companies that was different from that given to the other two members of the group.

The results of this second study suggest that even task-irrelevant characteristics (for example, geographic location) can trigger expectations of similarity. More specifically, Phillips and Loyd found that when a member of the identity majority voiced a different opinion, homogeneous group members had more negative feelings and engaged less in the task than diverse groups (that is, they finished their discussions earlier).[13] Cognitive diversity was more acceptable in identity-diverse environments, even when the cognitive diversity was not aligned with the identity differences. When a member of the identity majority possessed a different opinion, diverse groups were perceived as more positive and accepting of alternative viewpoints, fostered more persistent and confident voicing of dissenting perspectives, and displayed greater task engagement in the same situation. Identity diversity, even when it is not the direct source of cognitive diversity, is beneficial for groups.

Further evidence for how the expression and consideration of cognitive diversity is facilitated by identity diversity in groups can be found in S. Sommers's research on the effects of racial diversity on jury decision making.[14] Sommers compared groups of six white jurors with groups that had four white and two black jurors. In comparing the behavior of the whites in the presence of racial identity diversity or not, Sommers found that whites changed their behavior. White jurors in diverse groups raised more novel case facts, had fewer factual inaccuracies in their discussion of the case, and identified more missing evidence during the deliberation than whites in homogeneous juries. The white participants in the homogeneous juries may have been comparatively less focused on information presented during the case because they expected that the homogeneous setting would be characterized by agreement and easy interaction. Conversely, white participants in diverse settings may have expected more disagreement and divergent opinions about the case, leading them to consider the facts of the case more thoroughly. Thus, Sommers's study indicates that racial diversity in jury decision making can be beneficial, as it may allow white participants to express their opinions and consider information and alternatives that they would otherwise dismiss in homogeneous settings. These claims are also supported by the work of A. L. Antonio and colleagues.[15] Their study directly supports the idea that social category diversity promotes critical thinking by individuals in groups. They found that individuals displayed more integrative complexity when they had been exposed to more racial diversity in their personal lives (as self-reported on a survey) and in their experimental study: following group discussion of a controversial social issue, whites demonstrated more complex thinking in writing an essay when assigned to a diverse group with a black minority-opinion holder than when assigned to a homogeneous group of all whites with a white minority-opinion holder. These results have been further supported by the work of Loyd and colleagues, who showed that even prior to entering a group discussion, people anticipating entering a homogeneous

environment prepare less thoroughly for the meeting than those anticipating a diverse interaction.[16] Even before entering into discussion, identity diversity promotes hard work.

A second psychological process supporting the conclusion that
identity diversity has effects on groups that are independent of alignment with cognitive diversity comes from the fact that individuals
prefer their opinions and beliefs to be more similar to those with the
same identity than to those with a different identity.[17] Ultimately,
this may suggest that identity diversity among group members can
be beneficial, not only because it serves to increase the breadth of
knowledge available to its members but also because expectations
about those identity differences may, under the right circumstances,
facilitate expression and acceptance of differing mental models that
will allow for the emergence of a diversity bonus. For example, Phillips argues that identity-diverse groups may be better able to garner
the benefits of cognitive diversity (that is, opinion disagreement)
when it comes from outsiders rather than members of the identity
majority, because outsiders are more likely to state their dissenting
views with confidence if they do speak up.[18] For identity outsiders,
there is a rationale for having a dissenting view that legitimates its
expression. For identity insiders, it may be harder to justify why one
is disagreeing with one's fellow identity group members, leading to
a dampening of confidence and of the expression of unique viewpoints. Cognitive diversity, even when it is present in an identity-
homogeneous group, is less likely to be voiced with confidence and
less likely to be accepted by others in the group as important and
valid. There are caveats here that will be considered later. For instance,
if the identity outsiders feel they are not welcome in the group, feel
they are not respected enough by others, and expect a high cost for
speaking up, then the benefits of identity diversity—the diversity
bonus—are less likely to be captured.

The third psychological process underlying the value of identity
diversity stems from individuals' motivation to maintain balance in
social relationships with identity-similar others. Specifically, Phillips,
K. A. Liljenquist, and M. A. Neale argue that the members of the
identity majority who agree with identity outsiders feel socially in-

secure because an alliance with outsiders threatens their social ties with other same-identity members in a group—imagine a man agreeing with a woman in a group with other men present.[19] This threat motivates individuals to reconcile the divergent opinions in the group and contributes to better processing of the available information, better decisions, and better problem solving—a diversity bonus. The motivation to restore balance with similar others may ultimately improve group performance as members pay more attention to the task in an effort to reconcile the different opinions.[20] Thus, even when identity outsiders do not bring divergent viewpoints, or cognitive diversity, to the table, their *mere presence* can fundamentally change the behavior of the identity majority and enhance group performance.

Taken together, rather than assuming that people who are different in terms of their identity are beneficial to a group *only* because they can introduce cognitive diversity to the group, the psychological processes just described provide additional explanations about why and how identity diversity can lead to a diversity bonus in groups. Identity diversity triggers expectations that cognitive diversity may be present in groups and legitimizes the expression of unique perspectives and knowledge from both identity insiders and outsiders. In addition, the presence of social category diversity can decrease conformity to socially similar others in a group, which ultimately leads *everyone* to voice unique perspectives more confidently. Finally, the desire to restore social ties with identity-similar others can benefit groups by increasing the discussion of differing information and knowledge.

Page acknowledges that cognitive diversity and identity diversity must both be considered and that identity diversity is important in groups—especially through the opportunity for representation. I have provided insight into the evidence that shows that the mere presence of identity diversity can alter how hard people work, how people think, and how teams perform. Identity diversity has an influence on people's cognition and can paradoxically drive the processing and consideration of cognitive diversity toward more effective outcomes. It may be difficult to fully capture the benefits of cognitive diversity in the absence of identity diversity—this argument adds to Page's claims regarding why we need identity diversity in teams and organizations. My premise is that cognitive differences might go unnoticed and underutilized if there are no triggers from identity differences to let us know that the cognitive differences are there, are valuable, and can benefit the group.

So, if there are so many clear and multifaceted benefits of identity and cognitive diversity in groups, why is there resistance or difficulty around increasing identity diversity in organizations? This question deserves an entire book of its own, but one conclusion I would like to highlight here that I have drawn from my research is that the hard work associated with diversity is not particularly welcomed by group members. Even if the leadership of an organization touts the benefits of diversity, the daily experience of diversity may lead people to feel as though the benefits do not outweigh the downsides of engaging in conflict and disagreement with others, being uncomfortable, working hard, and questioning one's own perspectives and opinions. Diversity is difficult, and it is often hard to see the benefit in performance in organizations right away. How do we know if we have made the right decision, created the best product, or found the best solution to a problem when we are working on a daily basis in organizations? We often do not, especially in the places where Page highlights that diversity bonuses are likely to emerge. This can make it difficult to convince individuals that diversity is beneficial in comparison to the comfortable, more homogeneous environments that they have developed confidence in. In fact, in the Phillips, Liljenquist, and Neale paper, although the homogeneous groups were outperformed by the diverse ones in terms of finding the right answer, when asked how confident they were in their decision and how effective their groups had been, the homogeneous groups reported greater confidence and effectiveness than the diverse groups.[21] There was a misalignment of actual performance and the feelings of the group members. This disconnect is a significant barrier for diversity, making this volume of Our Compelling Interests even more important. There are many other barriers to the acceptance of identity diversity, but it doesn't make it any less true that diversity bonuses can emerge for complex, difficult problems. We should not stop chasing after the benefits of diversity because they are difficult to capture or because some are resistant. Diversity requires us all to work hard, and to embrace the change required in ourselves and in others around us.

SITUATIONAL FACTORS IMPORTANT FOR CAPTURING DIVERSITY BONUSES: THE EXAMPLE OF CROSS-FUNCTIONAL TEAMS

Let's now turn to the example of functionally diverse teams to explore the situational factors that may play a role in the emergence of diversity bonuses. Nearly twenty years ago I wrote a seminal review of the organizational demography and diversity literature with collaborator Charles O'Reilly titled "Demography and Diversity in Organizations: A Review of 40 Years of Research." We explored many, but not all, types of organizationally relevant sources of identity diversity in the paper, guided mostly by the available literature at the time. Of all types of identity diversity we reviewed—race, age, gender, tenure, and educational and functional background— functional background diversity was the most consistently positive for group and organizational performance.[22] Let me be clear: introducing functional diversity was not easy, and it did not always work. Functionally diverse groups also face many of the same problems that other identity-diverse groups face. However, in many ways, the very impetus for creating cross-functional teams was a recognition of the same underlying parameters defined by Page. Organizations were facing difficult problems that could not be solved by one individual, or the best individuals in a given identity (that is, functional) group, alone. There was a recognition that if their organizations were going to be able to innovate the best products and find the best solutions, that all members of the organizations could buy into, they would need to work together across functional silos in the organization. Organizations rapidly expanded their use of functionally diverse teams to solve difficult problems, create new products, and change processes in the 1980s. The theory was that more innovative, efficient, and effective solutions might be found if barriers between

functional groups were broken down from the beginning of a project, creating more interdependence and collaboration across the
organization. Essentially, the use of cross-functional teams was a
precursor to our current conversations about the value of cognitive
and identity diversity. Diversity was being promoted in these organizations, not by bringing new types of people into the organization
but by changing structures, breaking down boundaries, and creating teams of people from different functional groups to benefit the
organization.

With the expansion of cross-functional teams, organizations
began using the diversity they obviously already had within their
walls. Organizations that did this were using the same basic logic of
diversity bonuses introduced here by Page: difficult problems could
better be solved by bringing together an identity-diverse group of
individuals with diverse cognitive repertoires instead of working
within homogeneous groups. People with different functional backgrounds (that is, identities) have been exposed to different information, knowledge, mental models, and representations. Thus, when
exposed to new information in pursuit of a difficult problem, the
diverse members of the cross-functional team might remember different things, encode the information differently, and highlight some
information as important and relevant that others do not see as
such. Cross-functional team members bring both cognitive diversity
and identity diversity to the group in perhaps more predictable ways
than most types of identity diversity. Functional identity differences
serve as a trigger for inferring reasonable and acceptable cognitive
differences that could benefit the organization.

The Congruence Effect

I believe there are a number of instructive reasons these functionally diverse teams were relatively successful when they were first
introduced as a solution to the difficult problems organizations
were facing at that time—factors that might be important for cap-
turing diversity bonuses in organizations today. First, in functionally
diverse teams, the cognitive diversity being brought to bear on the

problem at hand is predictable. Group members know where they might be able to find that cognitive diversity within the group because the identity diversity (that is, functions) is meaningful and trusted. For instance, if a cross-functional team with a lawyer, marketing expert, finance person, and software engineer are put into a group together, there should be little to no concern with assuming that the finance person will be able to answer questions and bring relevant knowledge to the group that stems directly from her identity as the finance person on the team. In functionally diverse groups, identity diversity (that is, one's functional identity) is safe. It is more likely to be aligned with cognitive diversity than in other cases. This alignment or *congruence* between identity and cognitive diversity is an important factor for helping teams effectively identify, share, and integrate disparate knowledge to solve problems.[23]

Page acknowledged that identity diversity is only correlated with cognitive diversity. This correlation should be particularly high for functionally diverse groups. In organizations, individuals who have different functions are supposed to have different information, knowledge, and mental models. The way they approach the problem, the concerns they have when creating a new product, and the perspective they bring to the process being examined all differ *due to* their functional identity. These differences are not only acceptable, they are desired, and this is the very reason the group has been put together. These differences in information, knowledge, and mental models develop deliberately for those with functional background differences. We want our finance colleagues to bring knowledge about finance to bear and our colleagues in marketing to bring marketing knowledge to bear. You would never hear someone lamenting, "I feel like I am representing all finance professionals when I speak up in this group," though you might hear a similar sentiment stated by a woman or person of color when participating in a diverse group.

People like their expectations to be met, so this congruence can be beneficial for the group.[24] As discussed previously, groups are more willing to discuss and accept novel information as useful and relevant when it comes from those they expect to have a different perspective.[25] This use of information can then improve decision making and problem solving in the group. There is no controversy in believing that functional background diversity as an identity should be connected to more cognitive diversity. However, people are often wary when this same logic is applied to other identity categories in society, such as race and gender.

Page's diversity-bonus statement does a great job of dispelling this concern for me, given the many examples he provides, but, for the sake of directly addressing the underlying problem here, let me say that it is one of status, not diversity. For instance, women and men might indeed have relevant cognitive repertoires that differ systematically for a given problem, but this does not have to be true for a diversity bonus to emerge. And if they do differ, this does not mean that men's cognitive repertoires are better (more meritorious) than those of women or that diversity bonuses cannot emerge in gender-diverse groups. The assumption that identity and cognitive diversity will be congruent acts as a constraint on the value some people place on one subgroup's cognitive diversity relative to another's (for example, when Larry Summers was serving as president of Harvard University, he made a statement implying that women cannot succeed at science because their *cognitive repertoires* cannot be as good as the cognitive repertoires of men in this male domain because they are women). For functional background, it is easy to understand how the training, education, and deliberate development of particular mental models emerge. However, it is not so easy for other types of differences, such as race and gender. People may find it more difficult to believe that a female engineer will necessarily have a mental model about how to design a car that differs from that of a male engineer, and this difficulty will make it more difficult to understand the need for identity diversity in the field of engineering. Remember that the benefit of having identity diversity among the engineers arises not only because of the possible cognitive diversity the female engineer might introduce due to her life experiences but also because of the changes in behavior triggered by her mere presence. The bottom line here is that functional diversity is safe. People's expectations about who knows what are aligned with who is from what identity group, and it is okay for people to make that assumption. For many other types of difference, this is more difficult.

What do we do to manage this then? The answer is simple in my mind: all identity groups have to be respected and valued in the same way that functional identities are seen as important. The cognitive diversity contributed to the group must be respected, and the diversity bonus that emerges from mere presence must be embraced for all types of identity differences, not just functional ones.

Common and Clear Goals

The second factor that makes cross-functional teams an interesting case study to consider is the fact that when they are put together, they are usually composed with the express purpose of achieving a particular goal. Having a common goal is one of the most important prerequisites for success in groups. Thus, one might find that as cross-functional teams become routine, and perhaps overutilized, in an organization, their success might decrease—not because diversity is no longer relevant, but instead because the reason for their existence, their common goal, is no longer clear. Tying the composition of a group to its goals may be an important precursor for the emergence of diversity bonuses. In the case of cross-functional teams, not only is there often a clear common goal, but accomplishment of that goal is directly served by the diversity that is present. This allows for the emergence of respect, acceptance, and a valuing of the identity and cognitive diversity in the group. When identity-diverse groups are composed, there is a possibility for cognitive diversity to emerge. The elements for success are there. However, the group members need to explicitly agree on what they are trying to accomplish together in order to harness the diversity bonus. Do not assume group members know what the goal of the group is; always make it explicit, repeat it often, and revise it as necessary to ensure it is understood by all group members.

Diminishing Status Differences

Third, even though functional differences can fuel the same negative concerns in groups that other identity differences can—less cohesion, increased interpersonal conflict, lack of trust, and difficulties with communication, to name a few—when cross-functional teams are put together, each different functional identity group may be more clearly needed for the success of the team. This helps reduce the status differences between different functional groups that might fuel negative effects in other identity-diverse groups. Even if the organization has a natural status hierarchy among functional identities—for example, the lawyers are seen as having a higher status than the marketing members—the team may experience more equality in status and see the value of all members for the team's success. In Page's statement, all cognitive repertoires, even if not all considered "the best," are, within reason, considered important to the success of the team. When unconscious biases and stereotypes stop group members from integrating the cognitive repertoires of their teammates, diversity bonuses are more difficult to capture. When teams are purposefully composed, irrelevant status differences that might stem from identity diversity must be set aside for diversity bonuses to emerge.

Leadership Support

Finally, cross-functional teams are likely to be successful because they have the support of leadership in the organization. Identity diversity requires support by leadership to model appropriate behavior and attitudes about difference. Members of cross-functional teams, when they were initially being used, were often handpicked for participation by organizational leaders who not only believed in the concept of these functionally diverse teams but also invested time and resources in ensuring that the team met its potential. As Page noted, having a diversity bonus emerge is not a guarantee. Even under the best of circumstances, in which cognitive and identity diversity is abundant, there are no guarantees that diversity bonuses will emerge. Organizational leaders have to support diverse teams. Organizations must deliberately shape the environment, provide effective leadership, and support diversity efforts to ensure the success of diverse teams. There must be a regular commitment to the goal of diversity. Are all diverse teams supported by leadership? Are all diverse teams deliberately assembled for the cognitive and identity diversity of the group? Are all diverse teams constituted with a clear goal in mind? These are questions that Page did not pursue in his treatise, but they are important to consider in making diversity bonuses a reality.

CLOSING QUESTIONS AND ASSUMPTIONS

Despite the complexities of diversity, I agree with Page on the conclusion that cognitive and identity diversity *can* produce more ideas and possible solutions. As noted previously, this can happen because people who are different can bring different ideas to the table, but also and importantly because, as Mill proposed back in 1848, being *exposed* to difference changes people, helping them to generate more ideas and think more deeply about problems.[26] The debate should not be over whether diversity can provide bonuses. It can, under the right circumstances. The question really becomes, *will* diversity provide bonuses? And I would say that really depends on us—it depends on how we manage our biases and stereotypes, how we lead in our teams, and how we manage our expectations about difference.

Important from my perspective is also the issue of why we need to answer this question of the business case for diversity in the first place. Why is it necessary to *prove* that diversity has benefits? Is it just as necessary to prove that homogeneity has benefits? The quest for a business case reveals important motivations and defaults in society. The default is homogeneity. People who look like the majority, the incumbent, do not have to justify their existence and presence in organizations. People who deviate from the prototypical majority do. The business case for diversity assumes that diversity is optional, that one could have diversity or one could not. In most organizations this really means that white, male, heterosexual, able-bodied individuals are welcomed as the default prototypical member. There is no surprise when they are members of the organization, when they are leaders.[27] They are expected to be there in the organization. Anyone else who is added to the organization is a "choice," a deviation from the norm, and they must prove that they deserve to be there—women, people of color, disabled individuals, and so on. The logic of the business case for diversity rests on the idea that those who deviate from the norm must demonstrate that their presence in the organization will result in the company making more money. Imagine walking into a company and having the burden resting on your shoulders to prove that you can make the company a million more dollars in profit. That is a heavy burden to bear. We should reflect on how seeking evidence of a business case for diversity reifies the status quo and legitimates the idea that some people belong and deserve to be included in organizations, while other people have to go above and beyond to prove their worth. The questions we ask about diversity have power. They have underlying assumptions that often go unspoken.

As I close this commentary, I would like to highlight fifteen assumptions one should make to help diversity bonuses emerge, though there are many others: (1) assume there is cognitive diversity in the room that just needs to come out; (2) assume that identity differences among group members can promote the expression of cognitive differences; (3) assume that one's gender, race, sexuality, and so on, identities that she may have been walking around with her entire life, will have an influence on the way she sees a problem and what experiences she brings to the table, in the same way that you assume people's functional training will affect them; (4) assume that there is not perfect overlap between the identity characteristics a person possesses and his opinions about a given problem—dig deeper; (5) assume that making difficult decisions, solving complex problems, creating processes, expanding into new markets, and developing innovative products will benefit from both representation of the constituents being served and diversity; (6) assume that people care about maintaining relationships with similar others and sometimes will sensor themselves to maintain harmony—this is just as big a force in diverse groups as the forces that are in operation between people who are different from each other; (7) assume that people will filter how they hear information depending on who is sharing that information; (8) assume people will filter what they are saying depending on whom they are talking to; (9) assume that diverse environments need to be managed to ensure all voices are heard and considered; (10) assume that great ideas may not be recognized as such when they are the product of a diverse group—take a closer look; (11) assume people will be more cautious in their support for diversity because the downsides are often easier to see and feel than the upsides (especially in the short term); (12) assume that status differences exist and that some people in the room are bound to be respected more than others, so group process is critically important for getting everyone's ideas into the room and heard by others; (13) assume that everyone in the room is bringing implicit bias about others with them and that these implicit biases can have detrimental effects on interactions, judgments, and outcomes in the group, even when people have the best of intentions; (14) assume that structures need to be put into place to help combat these biases, as the problem does not solve itself; and, finally, (15) assume that you know something other people don't know and that other people know something you don't know.

Diversity bonuses are real, they can and do occur, and each of us has a role in making them happen.

APPENDIX
THE DIVERSITY PREDICTION THEOREM

I PRESENT HERE A MORE DETAILED EXPLANATION OF THE DIVERSITY prediction theorem. The theorem compares errors. For a numerical prediction, the error equals the square of the difference between the prediction and the true value. Squaring makes all errors positive. A prediction of a sales increase of 10 percent when the true increase equals 7 percent will have an error of nine $(9 = (10 - 7)^2)$. A prediction of an increase of 2 percent has an error of twenty-five $(25 = (2 - 7)^2)$. If one prediction has an error of nine and the other has an error of twenty-five, the average error equals seventeen. One prediction of 10 percent and one prediction of 2 percent produce an average of 6 percent. The *collective error* equals the square of the difference between that prediction (six) and the true value (seven). The collective error equals one. The average error (seventeen) exceeds the collective error (one).

The *average error* equals the average of the predictions' errors. The *collective error* of a set of predictions equals the squared error of the average prediction. The crowd makes a better prediction than its average member. This will always be the case with diverse predictions. In other work, I refer to this as the *crowd-beats-the-average law*.[1] Two effects drive the result: First, overestimates and underestimates cancel out. Second, squaring the differences means the average of two predictions that err in the same direction has lower error than the average error of the two predictions. The error of that average prediction will be less than the average error of the predictions.

We can introduce one more bit of terminology to make an even more precise claim. Define the *predictive diversity* to equal the variation in a collection of predictions. Variation equals the average of the square of the differences between the individual predictions and the average prediction. In our example, the average prediction equals

6 percent. Each prediction differs from that average by 4 percent, making the squared difference of each prediction to the average equal to sixteen ($16 = 4^2$). Therefore, the predictive diversity equals sixteen.

We have computed three numbers: the error of the collective prediction (one), the average error (seventeen), and the predictive diversity (sixteen). Notice that *the collective error (sixteen) equals the average error (seventeen) minus the predictive diversity (one).* This is the *diversity prediction theorem.*[2]

The formal version is written as follows: Assume a collection of N predictors, where *Person$_i$* denotes the prediction of person i. Let *Collective* denote the average of the N predictions, and let *Truth* equal the true value. The following equality holds in all cases:

$$\left(Collective - Truth\right)^2 = \frac{1}{N}\sum_{i=1}^{N}\left(Person_i - Truth\right)^2 - \frac{1}{N}\sum_{i=1}^{N}\left(Person_i - Collective\right)^2$$

The theorem does not imply that more diversity is always better.

For an example, suppose that two people (correctly) forecast the amount of snowfall on June 5 in Phoenix, Arizona, at zero inches. Adding a third person who predicts six inches results in a collective prediction of two, and a collective error of four. The new prediction has an error of thirty-six, increasing the average error from zero to twelve. Finally, the diversity increases from zero to eight (the average of four, four, and sixteen). The diversity prediction theorem reads as follows: $4 = 12 - 8$. Prior to adding the diverse prediction, it read $0 = 0 - 0$.

Suppose that three people predict using an identical model and two other people each use a different model. Suppose also that the three people who use the same model predict with a little more accuracy than the other two. The team of the three best predictors consists of three people who use the same model. The crowd will only be as accurate as each member. If we add the two less accurate predictors and if the gain in diversity outweighs the loss in average accuracy, the diverse group will be more accurate.

To make this more precise, suppose the three people who use the best model have an error equal to ten and that the other two people have errors of fifteen and twenty. The average error of the group of the best equals ten. As that group has no predictive diversity, its collective error also equals ten $(10 = 10 - 0)$. The average error of the diverse group equals fifteen. If the predictive diversity of the second group exceeds five, then the second group will be more accurate than the group of the most accurate individuals.

NOTES

INTRODUCTION

1. Nicholas Kristof, "President Trump, Meet My Family," *New York Times Sunday Review*, January 28, 2017.
2. Vance, *Hillbilly Elegy.*
3. Sugrue, "Less Separate, Still Unequal."
4. Danielle Allen, "Toward a Connected Society."
5. Friedman, *The World Is Flat.*
6. Carnevale and Smith, "Economic Value of Diversity."
7. Frey, "'Diversity Explosion.'"
8. See, for example, Patricia Leigh Brown, "Silicon Valley, Seeking Diversity, Focuses on Blacks," *New York Times*, September 3, 2015.
9. Shetterly, *Hidden Figures.*
10. Gurin, Lehman, and Lewis, *Defending Diversity.*
11. Brief of Amici Curiae, Lt. Gen. Julius W. Becton Jr. et al., Grutter v. Bollinger, No. 02-241 (2003).
12. Carnevale, Jayasundera, and Gulish, *America's Divided Recovery.*
13. Gender Summit North America, *Diversity Fueling Excellence*, 2.
14. Grutter v. Bollinger (02-241) 539 U.S. 306 (June 23, 2003), Sandra Day O'Connor, majority opinion, 3–4.
15. Danielle Allen, "Toward a Connected Society," 90.

PROLOGUE

1. Over the past decade, I have had the opportunity to speak with, among other groups, the US Office of Personnel Management, the Minnesota Association of Independent Schools, Boeing, Google, the Utah Medical Center, Gilead, Northrop Grumman, AB InBev, the US Federal Reserve, the US Treasury, Bloomberg, Microsoft, Yahoo!, Ford, General Motors, Nissan, Caterpillar, Cummins, Molex, Genentech, Legg Mason, the American Medical Association, the American Dental Association, the World Bank, the International Monetary Fund, the World Economic Forum-Davos, the Aspen Institute, Greenhills School, Credit Suisse, First Boston, Motorola, Tyco, the United States Air Force, Louisiana Tech University, Princeton University, MIT, Harvard University, Stanford University, North Dakota

State University, Purdue University, Iowa State University, Sandia National Laboratories, Livermore National Laboratories, TotalSAP, Miller-Coors, DARPA, Johnson Controls, US Cellular, PIMCO, the US Department of Justice, and NASA. I have learned from discussions with thought leaders in and outside the academy. Eric Ball, Jenna Bednar, Jon Bendor, Wendell Berry, Lazlo Bock, John Seeley Brown, Daniel Diermeier, Amy Dittmar, John Hagel, Melody Hobson, Lu Hong, Joi Ito, P. J. Lamberson, Sheen Levine, Katherine Phillips, Jeff Polzer, Carl Simon, Daryl Smith, Omar Wasow, and my editor Eric Crahan offered ideas, comments, and challenges. Andrea Jones-Rooy, Juliet Bourke, Nancy Cantor, and Earl Lewis commented on and emended earlier drafts of the book. My family, Orrie, Cooper, and Jenna, provided unwavering support for this project, as our continuous lives moved along. In addition to debriefing me after every talk and helping to frame the entire project, Jenna made line-by-line improvements to the manuscript.

2. Phillips, "How Diversity Makes Us Smarter."

3. See *Economist*, "Diversity Fatigue."

4. Corey, "More Moderate Diversity."

5. Thomas and Ely, "Making Differences Matter."

6. Ibid.

7. The data also suffer from two identification problems that I cover at length.

8. Mannes, Soll, and Larrick, "Wisdom of Select Crowds."

CHAPTER 1

1. This account is borrowed from historian Robert McNamara's article "Abe Lincoln and His Ax."

2. Goodwin, *Team of Rivals*.

3. Bendor and Page, "Optimal Team Composition."

4. I return to diversity measures when discussing heuristics.

5. Each of his three tools can be paired with each of Barry's four tools for a total of twelve.

6. National Research Council, *Enhancing the Effectiveness of Team Science*, 93.

7. See Foresight, "Obesity System Map," https://www.gov.uk/government/uploads/system/uploads/attachment_data/file/296290/obesity-map-full-hi-res.pdf.

8. Pollack, *Only Woman in the Room*.

9. Data available from the National Science Foundation and the American Mathematical Society. See Vélez, Maxwell, and Rose, "2013–2014 New Doctoral Recipients."

10. Accuracy was measured by the squared distance between the predicted rating and the actual rating. If a person rated *The Shawshank Redemption* as three stars and a participant's model predicted five stars, the squared error would equal four.

11. In the Netflix Prize contest, more than 98 percent of the one hundred million rankings went into a training set. The remaining data were divided into several testing sets to determine accuracy and the contest winner.

12. Van Buskirk, "How the Netflix Prize Was Won."

13. As an exercise, take a moment and write down features of movies that might explain customer ratings. Congratulations if you can think up one hundred.

14. Tetlock, *Expert Political Judgment.*

15. Autor, Levy, and Murnane, "Skill Content of Recent Technological Change"; Autor and Price, "Changing Task Composition."

16. Katznelson, *When Affirmative Action Was White.*

17. Argote and Epple, "Learning Curves in Manufacturing."

18. Bessen, *Learning by Doing.*

19. Knowledge may not transfer across identity groups equally. Reagans and McEvily, "Network Structure and Knowledge Transfer."

20. Reilly et al., "Randomized Trial of Occlusive Wrap."

21. Woolley et al., "Evidence for a Collective Intelligence Factor"; Suroweicki, *Wisdom of Crowds*; Rheingold, *Smart Mobs.*

22. National Research Council, *Enhancing the Effectiveness of Team Science.*

23. See Uzzi et al., "Atypical Combinations and Scientific Impact," and Freeman and Huang, "Collaborating with People like Me." I take up these studies in more detail later.

24. Jehn, Northcraft, and Neale, "Why Differences Make a Difference."

25. See Mauboussin, Callahan, and Majd, *Organizational Structure and Investment Results.* Patel and Sarkissian ("To Group or Not to Group?") find a 58 basis point advantage for teams of size three over funds run by individuals.

26. Ellison, *Invisible Man,* 577.

CHAPTER 2

1. Gardner, *Frames of Mind*; Gardner, *Intelligence Reframed.*

2. Hewlett, Marshall, and Sherbin, "How Diversity Can Drive Innovation."

3. Jehn, Northcraft, and Neale, "Why Differences Make a Difference."

4. Ross and Malveaux, *Reinventing Diversity.*

5. Kahneman, *Thinking Fast and Slow.*

6. Gawande, *Checklist Manifesto.*

7. Johnson, *Where Good Ideas Come From.*

8. Two varieties might both have white petals and yellow cups, flourish in hardiness zones 3–8, and bloom in mid-spring. The USDA Plant Hardiness Zone Map divides the country into zones based on their average minimum winter temperature. Lower-numbered zones have colder winters.

9. Page, *Model Thinking.*

10. Dawes, "Robust Beauty of Improper Linear Models."

11. Tetlock and Gardner, *Superforecasting.*

12. Tetlock, *Expert Political Judgment.*

CHAPTER 3

1. See Clarke and Primo, *Model Discipline,* for a philosophical treatment on the relationship between models and data in the social sciences.

2. Estimates place this between fifty and one hundred thousand feet.

3. Mauboussin, *Success Equation.*

4. Kleinberg et al., "Prediction Policy Problems."

5. I thank Sendhil Mullainathan for these examples.

6. See Page, *Difference.*

7. In the appendix, I present the formal mathematics, along with numerical examples.

8. Romer and Romer, "FOMC versus the Staff." There exists a more sophisticated variant of the theorem called the *bias variance decomposition* theorem. Similar logic to that revealed by the diversity prediction theorem can be found in treatments of Bayesian model averaging and ensemble methods.

9. As an experiment, I predicted outcomes in the 2016 NCAA basketball tournament using alphabetical order. I predicted Xavier, Villanova, and Wisconsin would all lose in the first round. I finished in the bottom 1 percent out of thirteen million people on the ESPN Tournament Challenge. Adding my predictions to my family's pool of predictions reduced the accuracy of the collective prediction.

10. If each of five people predicts that there will be twelve eggs in a dozen and a sixth predicts that there will be only six, then the collective prediction will be eleven. The diversity prediction theorem can then be written as $1 = 6 - 5$.

11. Waldron, "Wisdom of the Multitude."

12. Tetlock, *Expert Political Judgment.*

13. The two students' average guess will be 265 miles, an error of only 15 miles.

14. Goldstein, McAfee, and Suri, "Wisdom of Smaller, Smarter Crowds"; Page, "Not Half Bad."

15. Dietterich, "Ensemble Methods in Machine Learning."

16. Breiman, "Random Forests."

17. These are in the form of if-then rules.

18. Brown et al., "Diversity Creation Methods"; Liu and Yao, "Ensemble Learning via Negative Correlation."

19. Mellers et al., "Identifying and Cultivating Superforecasters"; Satopää et al., "Partial Information Framework."

20. Manski, "Interpreting the Predictions of Prediction Markets."

21. Sobel, *Longitude.*

22. The invention of the mood ring is widely credited to Marvin Wernick, who marveled at thermotropic tape in a hospital emergency room.

23. Weitzman, "Recombinant Growth"; Johansson, *Medici Effect.*

24. Arthur, *Nature of Technology.*

25. Leung et al., "Multicultural Experience Enhances Creativity."

26. McLeod, Lobel, and Cox, "Ethnic Diversity and Creativity."

27. Triandis, Hall, and Ewen, "Member Heterogeneity and Dyadic Creativity." The Internet has expanded the number of possible answers to this second question.

28. Guilford, *Nature of Human Intelligence.*

29. An alternative diversity measure computes the ratio of unique ideas to the total ideas by the group. Two people who come up with the same ideas will have a diversity of zero. Two people who have no overlap in their ideas have a diversity of one because the number of unique ideas equals the number of ideas total. To make this formal, we can let S_1 and S_2 denote the sets of ideas from two people. Let $S_1 \setminus S_2$ be the ideas in S_1 and not in S_2 (define $S_2 \setminus S_1$ similarly) and let $S_1 \cup S_2$ be the union of the two sets. The *diversity*, $D(S_1, S_2)$, can be represented as

$$D(S_1, S_2) = \frac{|S_1 \setminus S_2 + S_2 \setminus S_1|}{|S_1 \cup S_2|}$$

A third measure of the diversity of a group computes the ratio of the total number of unique ideas to the sum of the number of ideas from each person.

30. If we do not know the ideas that people have drawn, then we would expect the group of the most creative people to have the most ideas. For any particular realization of draws, the most creative group could contain someone who is not among the most creative. To identify such a person would require knowing the ideas that everyone drew.

31. Johansson, *Medici Effect*; Padgett and Powell, *Emergence of Organizations and Markets*.

32. To arrive at these numbers of possible pairs, take the number of unique ideas (the first idea) times the number of ideas it can be paired with (the number of ideas remaining) and then divide by two to avoid double counting. The eighteen unique ideas combine to make $18 \times 17 \div 2 = 153$ pairs.

33. Weitzman, "Recombinant Growth"; Simonton, *Origins of Genius*.

34. Von Hippel, *Sources of Innovation*.

35. Kleinberg and Raghu ("Team Performance with Test Scores") prove a technical result in a more general setting.

36. Mokyr, *Gifts of Athena*.

37. Acemoglu and Robinson, *Why Nations Fail*.

38. Gordon, *Rise and Fall of American Growth*.

39. Page, *Difference*; Bendor and Page, "Optimal Team Composition."

40. Hong and Page, "Problem Solving by Heterogeneous Agents"; Kleinberg and Raghu, "Team Performance with Test Scores."

41. Sadoway, "PhD Should Be PSD."

42. Adding zero simplifies expressions. For example, adding zero, written as $(6-6)$, transforms the expression $x^3 - 3x^2 + 3x - 7$ into $x^3 - 3x^2 + 3x - 1 - 6 = (x+1)^2 - 6$.

43. To calculate the probability of solving the problem, take one minus the probability of not solving the problem. The first person solves the problem with any given tool with probability 0.25. The probability that she doesn't solve it with a given tool equals 0.75. The probability that no tools work equals $(0.75)^4 = 0.32$. Therefore, she solves the problem 68 percent of the time. The second person doesn't solve the problem with probability $(0.7)^3 = 0.34$. The third person doesn't solve the problem with probability $(0.7)^2 = 0.49$.

44. Von Hippel, *Sources of Innovation*.

45. Hong and Page, "Problem Solving by Heterogeneous Agents"; Hong and Page, "Groups of Diverse Problem Solvers."

46. To be more precise, the probability that they have identical abilities would be low. Equal abilities would require that each combination of tools has the same probability of solving the problem. If we were to randomly assign potentials to tools, that would be an unlikely event.

47. Hong and Page, "Groups of Diverse Problem Solvers."

48. Weitzman, "Optimal Search for the Best Alternative."

49. If we assume uniformly distributed solution values, the expected value equals a little over 6.8.

50. Kleinberg and Raghu, "Team Performance with Test Scores."

51. One small technical issue arises as well. Their ability measure depends on group size. The most able person for a group of size six may not

be the most able for a group of size eight. That is only true given their assumption that solution values are *statistically independent*. The statistical independence assumption requires diverse repertoires.

52. Tully, Gilmer, and Shugard, "Molecular Dynamics of Surface Diffusion." I have known Mary Shugard for over twenty years but had not known this paper.

53. The term *Brusselator*, coined by Nobelist Ilya Prigogine, combines *Brussels*, the city where the model was developed, with *oscillator*, the phenomenon produced by the model.

54. Daniel T. Gillespie ("Exact Stochastic Simulation") describes how the deterministic approach creates a continuous, predictable outcome.

55. The research of Flo Gardipee, a Cherokee Irish wildlife biologist, provides another instance in which a person's identity contributed to a scientific breakthrough in the case of a constraint. Gardipee studied bison and needed DNA samples. Based on her beliefs, she sought a noninvasive method for collecting DNA samples. She came up with the idea of using fecal samples, now a standard procedure. Gardipee et al., "Fecal DNA Sampling Methods."

56. Hutchins, *Cognition in the Wild*.

57. Boulding, *Economics as a Science*.

58. Sternberg and O'Hara, "Creativity and Intelligence."

59. Campbell, "Blind Variation and Selective Retention."

60. Simonton, *Origins of Genius*.

61. Sternberg and O'Hara, "Creativity and Intelligence."

62. Ahuja and Lampert, "Entrepreneurship in the Large Corporation"; Fleming, "Recombinant Uncertainty in Technological Search."

63. Sarah Kaplan and Vakali, "Double-Edged Sword of Recombination."

64. Youn et al., "Invention as a Combinatorial Process."

65. The analysis by Youn et al. (ibid.) counts the number of patents P, the number of technology codes T, and the number of unique combinations of codes C. Note that given this encoding, a patent that introduces a new technology code and links to no other codes creates a new combination of size one. They find that up until 1860, the number of patents closely tracks both T and C. Since that time, T has fallen off dramatically. Even if it were the case that the patent office now creates fewer categories, the evidence compellingly shows the preponderance of recombinations.

66. Knox, *Lost at Sea*.

67. This part of Lost at Sea is a creative task.

68. My former student Ryan Issacs had the idea of using LSAT-type logic questions to demonstrate the concept of knowledge integration.

69. The probability that the second team makes the correct move can be computed as follows: All five will be correct with probability $(0.8)^5 = 0.33$.

There are five combinations in which four choose correctly and one is incorrect. Each of these has probability $(0.8)^4(0.2) = 0.08$. And there are ten combinations in which three are correct and two incorrect. Each of these has probability $(0.8)^3(0.2)^2 = 0.02$. Combining gives $0.33 + 5$ $(0.08) + 10$ $(0.02) = 0.93$. The same intuition drives Condorcet's jury theorem, which assumes a set of voters, each of whom independently knows the correct answer with the same probability. If that probability exceeds one-half, four results follow: the majority identifies correctly with a higher probability than each individual, collective accuracy increases in individual accuracy and in group size, and large groups approach but never achieve perfect accuracy.

70. Marcolino, Jiang, and Tambe, "Multi-agent Team Formation."

71. Simon, *Administrative Behavior.*

72. De Bono, *Six Thinking Hats.*

73. Bourke, *Which Two Heads?*

74. These examples can all be found in a report on analytic tradecraft. US Government, *Tradecraft Primer.*

75. CIA, *Diversity and Inclusion.*

76. Steven Kaplan and Lerner, "It Ain't Broke."

77. Jurvetson, "Brainiac Steve Jurvetson."

78. Ban, "Role of Serendipity."

79. Chivian and Bernstein, "Role of Traditional Medicine."

80. Hollister, "21 Different Interpretations."

81. Knight and Johnson, *Priority of Democracy*, 1.

82. Gurin, Nagda, and Zuniga, *Dialogue across Difference.*

83. Kahneman, *Thinking Fast and Slow.*

CHAPTER 4

1. Phillips, "How Diversity Makes Us Smarter"; Jackson and Joshi, "Work Team Diversity."

2. These can be found at www.metamia.com, an analogy website.

3. Medin and Ortony, "Psychological Essentialism."

4. Zimmer, "White? Black?"

5. Some identity attributes, including sexual orientation, remain the subject of heated debate within academic, scientific, and religious communities.

6. Wood et al., "Role of Common Variation."

7. How the Dutch got so tall (besides being a good name for a children's book) intrigues scientists. Early evidence supports a genetic contribution. Tall Dutch have been reproducing at a faster rate than short Dutch, meaning that tall genes have been reproducing at a faster rate than short genes. Stulp et al., "Does Natural Selection Favour Taller Stature?"

8. Hall, *Beyond Culture.*

9. More than 80 percent of the students in the more than fifty evangelical student groups at the University of California's two main campuses, Berkeley and Los Angeles, identify as Asian American. Korean Americans represent a majority of these evangelicals. Kim, *God's New Whiz Kids.*

10. Harris and Sim, "Who Is Multiracial?"

11. Sen and Wasow, "Race as a 'Bundle of Sticks.' " Sen and Wasow rely on a bundle-of-sticks analogy. I use the timber-framed house analogy to highlight that some pairs of attributes will be more closely connected than others.

12. Cole, "Intersectionality and Research in Psychology."

13. Ibid.

14. Crenshaw, "Demarginalizing."

15. Setting aside the social maladroitness of such a request.

16. Appiah, "Uncompleted Argument"; Michael James, "Race."

17. Pattillo, *Black Picket Fences.*

18. Nisbett, *Geography of Thought.*

19. Cattell, *Abilities.*

20. Flynn, "Massive IQ Gains in 14 Nations"; Flynn, *What Is Intelligence?*

21. Cox, Navarro-Rivera, and Jones, "Race, Religion, and Political Affiliation?"

22. Anderson, *Imperative of Integration.*

23. Heath and Heath, *Made to Stick.*

24. Bourke, *Which Two Heads?*

25. Google Ads' settings page is located at https://www.google.com/settings/u/0/ads/authenticated.

26. Algorithms that can predict race and gender can discriminate based on those attributes by biasing the ads people see or by offering different interest rates. See Sweeney, "Discrimination in Online Ad Delivery," and Consumer Finance Protection Bureau, *Using Publicly Available Information.*

27. The oil applied to clean guns contaminates the process.

28. Buchanan, "Stars Who Were Almost Cast."

29. I present a similar version of the story in *The Difference.* I repeat it here because it is so provocative.

30. Martin, "Egg and the Sperm."

31. Program head Robert O. Bernard would later include her formulation in an academic paper.

32. Kaufman, "Watch David Bowie." MTV eventually integrated due in part to Michael Jackson's "Billie Jean," "Beat It," and "Thriller" trilogy.

33. Antonio et al., "Effects of Racial Diversity"; Gurin, Nagda, and Zuniga, *Dialogue across Difference.*

34. In 2010, President Obama challenged the federal government to increase its employment of differently abled workers by one hundred thousand. That action will have substantial direct effects given the different cognitive repertoires of differently abled people. It will also have large indirect effects through the increased awareness of others.

35. Levine et al., "Ethnic Diversity Deflates Price Bubbles."

CHAPTER 5

1. Mannix and Neale, "What Differences Make a Difference?"

2. Data from Kopf, "How Many People Take Credit?"

3. Freeman and Huang, "Collaborating with People like Me"; Patel and Sarkissian, "To Group or Not to Group?"; Tetlock and Gardner, *Superforecasting*.

4. Hunt, Layton, and Prince, "Why Diversity Matters."

5. Dawson, Kersley, and Natella, *CS Gender 3000*.

6. Note that foreign nationals should not be equated with underrepresented minorities.

7. Dezsö and Ross, "Female Representation."

8. Sparber, "Racial Diversity and Aggregate Productivity"; Florida and Gates, "Technology and Tolerance."

9. Sparber (ibid.) also analyzes the correlation between the effect of racial diversity and responses to the Department of Labor O*NET survey. He selected four questions that asked whether people make decisions and solve problems, think creatively, serve customers, or work as part of a team. The four questions he used from the O*NET survey were the following: How important is making decisions and solving problems to the performance of your current job? How important is thinking creatively to the performance of your current job? How important is customer and personal service knowledge to the performance of your current job? How important are interactions that require you to work with or contribute to a work group or team to the performance of your current job? He finds that racial diversity improves performance on problem solving, thinking creatively, and serving customers. He finds a negative effect of working as part of a team. Here as well, he finds meaningful effect sizes. The effect of a one standard deviation increase in racial diversity for an industry one standard deviation above average in decision making would produce a 4 percent increase in productivity. He estimates the corresponding effects for creative problem solving and customer service at 2–3 percent and 6–7 percent. The loss for an industry one standard deviation above the mean on the team problem-solving question is also in the 2–3 percent range.

10. Bettencourt, Samaniego, and Youn, "Professional Diversity."

11. Sen and Wasow, "Race as a 'Bundle of Sticks.'"

12. Bertrand and Mullainathan, "Are Emily and Greg More Employable?"

13. Ahern and Dittmar, "Changing of the Boards."

14. The primary explanatory variables here must include experience and age. If we were to compare cognitive repertoires of the women appointed to boards to those of the men in their cohorts, the germane differences could not be so large as to explain a 20 percent drop-off in performance. The cohort of successful midcareer businessmen and businesswomen in Norway attended similar schools, have similar work experiences, and for the most part share a common ethnicity. If one attempts to account for systematic differences in board members' attributes, gender effects remain, though they are less pronounced. The direct measurement of gender effects is subject to challenge because it assumes separability of effects. That assumption runs counter to the timber-framed house model, which argues that the contributions of a woman CEO cannot be decomposed into a woman component and a CEO component.

15. Ahern and Dittmar, "Changing of the Boards."

16. Matsa and Miller, "Female Style in Corporate Leadership?" A recent study that chooses a different start date from all of the other papers finds little to no effect of gender. That study explains the negative finding as driven by a small number of firms that were reliant on government contracts, and those firms had greater gender equity prior to the law's passage. Those firms performed well during the period of the study, a downturn, because of their government support. Eckbo, Nygaard, and Thorburn, "Gender-Balancing." Those firms were coded as performing better yet not increasing in diversity. I mention this study not because I find it more compelling but because it reveals a subtlety of interpreting regression coefficients. The regression shows the effect of adding women to a board. The data include firms that already had substantial female representation. Those firms performed better than average. When you fit a regression line, those firms will be data points with no added women and strong performance. Those data will cause the regression line to slope downward. In other words, successful firms with women already on boards increase the negative coefficient for adding women to boards that do not have them.

17. Ahern and Dittmar, "Changing of the Boards"; Matsa and Miller, "Female Style in Corporate Leadership?"

18. If disruption was a contributing factor, we might expect smaller performance dips for companies with more experienced boards. Ahern and Dittmar, "Changing of the Boards." We might also expect the opposite. The

data do not support that hypothesis. If disruption hindered monitoring, it did so uniformly.

19. Open Science Collaboration, "Estimating the Reproducibility." Findings from experiments involving people fail to replicate because what was true for one set of subjects at one point in time may not be true for another subject pool. People behave idiosyncratically and also conform. The behaviors of a few could steer an entire population to take an action. Physical scientists have fewer challenges with replicability. A measurement of the tensile strength of copper does not depend on the attitude of the copper that day.

20. Woolley et al., "Evidence for a Collective Intelligence Factor."

21. Jackson and Joshi, "Work Team Diversity"; Mannix and Neale, "What Differences Make a Difference?"

22. Jackson and Joshi, "Work Team Diversity"; Williams and O'Reilly, "Demography and Diversity in Organizations"; Mannix and Neale, "What Differences Make a Difference?"

23. Lakhani and Jeppesen, "Getting Unusual Suspects"; Jeppesen and Lakhani, "Marginality and Problem-Solving Effectiveness."

24. Woolley et al., "Evidence for a Collective Intelligence Factor."

25. Woolley, Aggarwal, and Malone, "Collective Intelligence and Group Performance."

26. For surveys of the literature, in addition to Williams and O'Reilly, "Demography and Diversity in Organizations," see Jehn, Northcraft, and Neale, "Why Differences Make a Difference"; Jackson and Joshi, "Work Team Diversity"; and Van Knippenberg and Schippers, "Work Group Diversity."

27. One study of sixty-four teams that perform intelligence analysis spanning six agencies found that six attributes explained three-fourths of the variation in performance. Successful teams have stable membership, a well-defined objective, supportive context, productive norms of conduct, resources, strong support, and access to coaching. Hackman and O'Connor, "What Makes for a Great Analytic Team?" A second study of 120 international business teams finds that by having the right people on the team, they can explain more than half of performance variation. Wageman et al., *Senior Leadership Teams.* A more recent series of laboratory studies also shows that the most effective teams include individuals able to recognize the reactions and emotional responses of other group members. Woolley et al., "Evidence for a Collective Intelligence Factor."

28. Homan et al., "Bridging Faultlines by Valuing Diversity"; Thomas and Ely, "Making Differences Matter"; Swann et al., "Finding Value in Diversity."

29. I served as an adviser to one of the teams.

30. Cattell, *Abilities*.

31. Mellers et al., "Identifying and Cultivating Superforecasters." The elite teams of forecasters became even more accurate, whereas the individuals in the top 3–5 percent regressed to the mean.

32. Mannes, Soll, and Larrick, "Wisdom of Select Crowds."

33. University of Michigan alumni will recognize the section heading as the words of Bo Schembechler. The quotation from which it is excerpted reads as follows: "No man is more important than The Team. No coach is more important than The Team. The Team, The Team, The Team, and if we think that way, all of us, everything that you do, you take into consideration what effect does it have on my Team? Because you can go into professional football, you can go anywhere you want to play after you leave here. You will never play for a Team again. You'll play for a contract. You'll play for this. You'll play for that. You'll play for everything except the team, and think what a great thing it is to be a part of something that is, The Team." "Team Speech," transcript.

34. Steinbeck, *East of Eden*, 131.

35. Janssen and Renn, "History."

36. Shenk, *Powers of Two*.

37. Singh and Fleming, "Lone Inventors."

38. Uzzi et al., "Atypical Combinations and Scientific Impact."

39. Phillips, "How Diversity Makes Us Smarter."

40. Shi et al., "Impact of Boundary Spanning"; Freeman and Huang, "Collaborating with People like Me"; Tetlock and Gardner, *Superforecasting*.

41. National Research Council, *Enhancing the Effectiveness of Team Science*.

42. Wuchty, Jones, and Uzzi, "Increasing Dominance of Teams."

43. Patel and Sarkissian, "To Group or Not to Group?"

44. Wuchty, Jones, and Uzzi, "Increasing Dominance of Teams."

45. National Research Council, *Enhancing the Effectiveness of Team Science*. Science and engineering rely more on teams than social science. This may be because science and engineering research involve more problem solving and prediction. Many social science papers describe history, derive theories, or offer interpretations and reviews of existing literatures. These activities require a coherent narrative, a trait that advantages single authors.

46. Jones, Uzzi, and Wuchty, "Multi-university Research Teams."

47. Singh and Fleming, "Lone Inventors."

48. Removing self-citations (which stacks the deck against larger teams, as coauthors often write much of the related research) does not alter the

results. Teams still receive more citations in 159 of the scientific subfields and 51 of the social science categories.

49. Far fewer than one in a thousand papers earns one thousand citations. Fewer than 1 percent of social science papers earn one hundred citations.

50. Singh and Fleming, "Lone Inventors."

51. Patel and Sarkissian, "To Group or Not to Group?" A basis point equals one-hundredth of a percent. So, this translates into a 0.6 percent increase in risk-adjusted return. To put this in perspective, investing $1,000 in a fund that returns 5 percent annually yields $11,467 after fifty years. A fund returning 60 basis points higher, or 5.6 percent, would yield $15,247.

52. Kozlowski and Bell, "Work Groups and Teams," 4.

53. Adamic et al., "Individual Focus and Knowledge Contribution."

54. Jones, Uzzi, and Wuchty, "Multi-university Research Teams."

55. Freeman and Huang, "Collaborating with People like Me." They use the Herfindahl Index as a measure of diversity. See Page, *Diversity and Complexity*, for a summary of diversity measures.

56. Shi et al., "Impact of Boundary Spanning."

57. Uzzi et al., "Atypical Combinations and Scientific Impact."

58. If novelty and conventionality were equally likely, each bin would contain one-fourth of all papers. That is not the case. While the papers not classified as conventional are roughly evenly split between novel and not novel, almost 44 percent of the conventional papers are not novel. Fewer than 7 percent of all papers are conventional and novel.

59. Schilling and Green, "Recombinant Search."

60. Cummings et al., "Group Heterogeneity."

CHAPTER 6

1. McDonald's Corporation, "Our Ambition."

2. REI Co-op, "About REI."

3. I interpret the word *business* broadly to include research institutes, nonprofits, government agencies, and educational institutions. Efforts to alleviate poverty, cure cancer, and improve educational outcomes can gain as much from diversity as attempts to design driverless cars, safer airplanes, and user-friendly web-based platforms.

4. Cameron and Quinn, *Diagnosing and Changing Organizational Culture*.

5. See University of Wisconsin, "Mission Statement," and Goodyear Corporate, "Our Responsibilities."

6. Based on data taken from a widely reported analysis of LinkedIn. *Business Insider*, "20 Schools."

7. Woolley et al., "Evidence for a Collective Intelligence Factor."

8. Steele, *Whistling Vivaldi*; Carney et al., "Implicit Association Test (IAT)."

9. The intelligence community develops and maintains diversity in three ways. First, it casts a wide net to attract diverse employees. Second, it encourages those employees to develop deep, diverse repertories. The analysts working behind the walls at Fort Meade and Langley receive constant opportunities for training in new analytic tools and frameworks. Third, the community structures activities to build cognitive diversity. They constitute competing red and blue teams to assess vulnerabilities. The red teams attack. The blue teams defend. Each team develops distinct sets of skills and knowledge bases.

10. Quoted in Maheshwari, "Big Brands Ask Ad Agencies."

11. In 2007, Beaner's rebranded as Biggby's at a cost of over $1,000,000. By 2011, it was the fastest-growing coffee chain in the country.

12. Cohen, Gabriel, and Terrell, "Case for Diversity."

13. Sapienza, Zingales, and Maestripieri, "Gender Differences in Financial Risk Aversion."

14. The same logic applies to diversity of nationalities. The Bank of New York Mellon operates in over one hundred markets spread across thirty-five countries. Google has seventy offices in more than forty countries. The Ford Motor Company exports to more than one hundred countries. Caterpillar sells farm equipment in more than one hundred countries.

15. Thomas and Ely, "Making Differences Matter."

16. These data are all readily available from multiple sources. See Lewis and Cantor, *Our Compelling Interests*, for one overview.

17. Valantine and Collins, "National Institutes of Health."

18. These men were very fast. The world record they set at the Olympics lasted more than twenty years.

19. Shetterly, *Hidden Figures*.

20. In this section, I lean on the prescient article by Thomas and Ely ("Making Differences Matter"), who describe the discrimination and fairness paradigm and the access and legitimacy paradigm and introduce the idea that diversity can produce benefits in an integrative fashion. My construction of diversity bonuses as a third narrative expands and formalizes their ideas.

21. This is his word choice, which I repeat out of respect for his witty opinions and not out of sarcasm.

22. Evidence for that claim can be found in support for affirmative action in admissions. In the 1960s and 1970s, elite universities admitted minority students in larger numbers but did little to promote inclusion or produce bonuses. Because the students from underrepresented groups were

not integrated into the university community, they graduated at low rates. They also contributed less to their universities than they might have had the universities changed their cultures to be more inclusive. Sander and Taylor (*Mismatch*) argue that law schools continue to lack nuance in their admissions decisions. They also make a more disputed claim that this has proved disadvantageous to minority law students. The effort at inclusion produced insufficient bonuses. As a result, affirmative action policies soon lost public support. A 2013 Gallup poll found that Americans oppose affirmative action in college admission by more than two to one.

23. Personal correspondence from Sheen Levine, February 15, 2017.

24. Thomas and Ely, "Making Differences Matter"; Liff, "Two Routes to Managing Diversity."

25. Swann et al., "Finding Value in Diversity."

26. I thank Mark Wiseman for a fun interchange on horses and camels that resulted in this section of the book.

27. See again Thomas and Ely, "Making Differences Matter." Mark Nivet refers to Diversity 1.0 as about numbers: discrimination and composition. Diversity 2.0 emphasized changing processes so that everyone could succeed individually. What he calls Diversity 3.0 links to mission. It seeks to identify and achieve diversity bonuses. See American Academy of Family Physicians, "Diversity 3.0."

28. Thomas and Ely, "Making Differences Matter."

29. Microsoft Corporation, "Mission Culture."

30. Groysberg and Connolly, "BlackRock."

31. Patel and Sarkissian, "To Group or Not to Group?"; Lutton and Davis, *Morningstar Research Report*.

32. Fink, "Annual Letter to CEOs."

CHAPTER 7

1. Dover, Major, and Kaiser, "Diversity Policies Rarely Make Companies Fairer"; Dobbin, Schrage, and Kalev, "Rage against the Iron Cage."

2. Gurin, Nagda, and Zuniga, *Dialogue across Difference*.

3. To see why requires thinking like a statistician. Imagine a process that produces potential employees. The cognitive repertoires of the potential employees can be thought of as coming from a distribution. Increasing the number of people considered increases the expected best employee. It also increases the maximum expected diversity between any two, three, or four people. Thinking in extremes helps see the logic. If there exist only two potential hires, neither may be very good and the two might not be diverse. From a pool of a million potential hires, there should exist some fantastic individuals and the potential for amazing, diverse teams.

4. Taylor and Binder, "Washington Talk."

5. African Americans, in particular, have suffered from multiple forms of institutional discrimination. For example, African Americans did not share equally in New Deal programs or in the postwar GI Bill. Katznelson, *When Affirmative Action Was White*. These surely contributed to today's economic and educational disparities. See also Roithmayr, "Reproducing Racism."

6. Moss-Racusin et al., "Science Faculty's Subtle Gender Biases"; Bertrand and Mullainathan, "Are Emily and Greg More Employable?" In considering the extent of discrimination by race in the workplace, we can distinguish between discriminatory actions and behaviors in hiring and promoting and differences in educational attainment. Differences in attainment in turn are partly the result of residential and social segregation. Discrimination results from a constellation of mutually reinforcing situations, policies, and behaviors. Therefore, we cannot end discrimination by reducing bias. O'Flaherty, *Economics of Race*. A more unified, multifront approach will be required. We see broader efforts by governments, foundations, universities, and some businesses. We see governments pushing for equality of resources in education and foundations coordinating on rebuilding communities. In Detroit, the Ford Foundation ($125 million), the Kresge Foundation ($100 million), the W. K. Kellogg Foundation ($40 million), the John S. and James L. Knight Foundation ($30 million), and the William Davidson Foundation ($25 million) participated in a grand bargain to salvage the pensions of city workers. We see universities devoting substantial resources to developing racially diverse student bodies and faculties and, as part of the anchor institutions movement, to building strong integrated communities.

7. Ross and Malveaux, *Reinventing Diversity*; Carney et al., "Implicit Association Test (IAT)"; Greenwald, Banaji, and Nosek, "Statistically Small Effects."

8. Danielle Allen, "Toward a Connected Society."

9. Fryer and Jackson, "Categorical Model of Cognition."

10. Moss-Racusin et al., "Science Faculty's Subtle Gender Biases"; Bertrand and Mullainathan, "Are Emily and Greg More Employable?"

11. Ayers, Banaji, and Jolls, "Race Effects on eBay."

12. The National Football League's Rooney Rule requires interviewing at least one minority for each head coaching vacancy.

13. My cousin Terry Page earned those second three degrees and went on to a faculty position at Johns Hopkins Medical School.

14. Scott, *Radical Candor*.

15. Bock, *Work Rules!*

16. Cameron and Quinn, *Diagnosing and Changing Organizational Culture*.

17. The company profile states "Recognized in 2015 as Canada's Outstanding CEO of the Year, Mr. Cope has earned a reputation as an innovative communications strategist and builder of high-performance teams." BCE, "Executive Team: George Cope."

18. See Friedman, "How to Get a Job at Google."

19. Woolley et al., "Evidence for a Collective Intelligence Factor"; Woolley, Aggarwal, and Malone, "Collective Intelligence and Group Performance."

20. Uzzi et al., "Atypical Combinations and Scientific Impact."

COMMENTARY

1. Phillips, Liljenquist, and Neale, "Is the Pain Worth the Gain?"; Sommers, "On Racial Diversity."

2. Apfelbaum, Phillips, and Richeson, "Rethinking the Baseline."

3. Phillips, Kim-Jun, and Shim, "Value of Diversity in Organizations," 255.

4. See, for example, Phillips et al., "Diverse Groups and Information Sharing"; Gruenfeld et al., "Group Composition and Decision Making"; and Stasser, Stewart, and Wittenbaum, "Expert Roles and Information Exchange."

5. Phillips, Kim-Jun, and Shim, "Value of Diversity in Organizations," 255.

6. See, for example, Vernon L. Allen and Wilder, "Group Categorization," and Tajfel and Turner, "Integrative Theory of Intergroup Conflict."

7. Williams and O'Reilly, "Demography and Diversity in Organizations."

8. Phillips, "Effects of Categorically Based Expectations."

9. For research on groupthink, see Janis, *Groupthink*, and Turner and Pratkanis, "Twenty-Five Years of Groupthink Theory."

10. See Sommers, "On Racial Diversity"; Phillips, Liljenquist, and Neale, "Is the Pain Worth the Gain?"; and Antonio et al., "Effects of Racial Diversity."

11. Phillips, "Effects of Categorically Based Expectations"; Phillips and Loyd, "When Surface and Deep-Level Diversity Collide."

12. Phillips and Loyd, "When Surface and Deep-Level Diversity Collide."

13. Ibid.

14. Sommers, "On Racial Diversity."

15. Antonio et al., "Effects of Racial Diversity."

16. Loyd et al., "Social Category Diversity Promotes Pre-meeting Elaboration."

17. See, for example, Vernon L. Allen and Wilder, "Categorization, Beliefs Similarity"; Vernon L. Allen and Wilder, "Group Categorization"; Heider, *Psychology of Interpersonal Relations*; and Holtz and Miller, "Assumed Similarity and Opinion Certainty."

18. Phillips, "Effects of Categorically Based Expectations."

19. Phillips, Liljenquist, and Neale, "Is the Pain Worth the Gain?"

20. Ibid.; Phillips, "Effects of Categorically Based Expectations"; Phillips et al., "Diverse Groups and Information Sharing"; Phillips and Loyd, "When Surface and Deep-Level Diversity Collide."

21. Phillips, Liljenquist, and Neale, "Is the Pain Worth the Gain?"

22. Williams and O'Reilly, "Demography and Diversity in Organizations."

23. Phillips, "Effects of Categorically Based Expectations."

24. Ibid.

25. Ibid.; Loyd et al., "Social Category Diversity Promotes Pre-meeting Elaboration"; Antonio et al., "Effects of Racial Diversity."

26. Phillips, "How Diversity Makes Us Smarter."

27. Rosette, Leonardelli, and Phillips, "White Standard."

APPENDIX

1. Page, *Difference.*

2. Ibid.

BIBLIOGRAPHY

Acemoglu, Daron, and James A. Robinson. *Why Nations Fail: The Origins of Power, Prosperity, and Poverty*. Cambridge, MA: Harvard University Press, 2012.

Adamic, Lada A., Xiao Wei, Jiang Yang, Sean Gerrish, Kevin K. Nam, and Gavin S. Clarkson. "Individual Focus and Knowledge Contribution." *First Monday* 15, no. 3 (2010). http://firstmonday.org/ojs/index.php/fm/article/view/2841/2475.

Ahern, Kenneth R., and Amy K. Dittmar. "The Changing of the Boards: The Impact on Firm Valuation of Mandated Female Board Representation." *Quarterly Journal of Economics* 127, no. 1 (2012): 137–197.

Ahuja, Gautam, and Curba Morris Lampert. "Entrepreneurship in the Large Corporation: A Longitudinal Study of How Established Firms Create Breakthrough Inventions." *Strategic Management Journal* 22, no. 6–7 (2001): 521–543.

Allen, Danielle. "Toward a Connected Society." In *Our Compelling Interests: The Value of Diversity for Democracy and a Prosperous Society*, edited by Earl Lewis and Nancy Cantor, 71–105. Princeton, NJ: Princeton University Press, 2016.

Allen, Vernon L., and David A. Wilder. "Categorization, Beliefs Similarity, and Intergroup Discrimination." *Journal of Personality and Social Psychology* 32 (1975): 971–977.

———. "Group Categorization and Attribution of Belief Similarity." *Small Group Behavior* 10 (1979): 73–80.

American Academy of Family Physicians. "Diversity 3.0: At the Core of Excellence." May 6, 2016. http://www.aafp.org/news/inside-aafp/20160506nccl-nivetplenary.html.

Anderson, Elizabeth. *The Imperative of Integration*. Princeton, NJ: Princeton University Press, 2010.

Antonio, A. L., M. J. Chang, K. Hakuta, D. A. Kenny, S. Levin, and J. F. Milem. "Effects of Racial Diversity on Complex Thinking in College Students." *Psychological Science* 15, no. 8 (2004): 507–510.

Apfelbaum, Evan P., Katherine W. Phillips, and Jennifer A. Richeson. "Rethinking the Baseline in Diversity Research: Should We Be Explaining the Effects of Homogeneity?" *Perspectives on Psychological Science* 9 (2014): 235–244.

Appiah, Kwame A. "The Uncompleted Argument: Du Bois and the Illusion of Race." *Critical Inquiry* 12, no. 1 (1985): 21–37.

Argote, Linda, and Dennis Epple. "Learning Curves in Manufacturing." *Science* 247, no. 4945 (1990): 920–924.

Arthur, W. Brian. *The Nature of Technology: What It Is and How It Evolves.* New York: Simon and Schuster, 2009.

Autor, David H., Frank Levy, and Richard J. Murnane. "The Skill Content of Recent Technological Change: An Empirical Exploration." *Quarterly Journal of Economics* 118, no. 4 (2003): 1279–1333.

Autor, David H., and Brendan Price. "The Changing Task Composition of the US Labor Market: An Update of Autor, Levy, and Murnane (2003)." Unpublished working paper, MIT, Cambridge, MA, 2013. https://eco nomics.mit.edu/files/9758.

Ayers, Ian, Mahzarin R. Banaji, and Christine Jolls. "Race Effects on eBay." *Rand Journal of Economics* 46, no. 4 (2015): 891–917.

Ban, Thomas A. "The Role of Serendipity in Drug Discovery." *Dialogues in Clinical Neuroscience* 8, no. 3 (2006): 335–344.

BCE. "Executive Team: George Cope." Accessed April 10, 2017. http:// www.bce.ca/aboutbce/executiveteams/cope.

Bendor, Jonathan, and Scott E. Page. "Optimal Team Composition for Tool Based Problem Solving." Unpublished manuscript, 2017.

Bertrand, Marianne, and Sendhil Mullainathan. "Are Emily and Greg More Employable than Lakisha and Jamal? A Field Experiment on Labor Market Discrimination." *American Economic Review* 94, no. 4 (2004): 991–1013.

Bessen, James. *Learning by Doing: The Real Connection between Innovation, Wages, and Wealth.* New Haven, CT: Yale University Press, 2015.

Bettencourt, Luís, Horacio Samaniego, and Hyejin Youn. "Professional Diversity and the Productivity of Cities." *Scientific Reports* 4, no. 5393 (2014). https://www.nature.com/articles/srep05393.

Bock, Laszlo. *Work Rules! Insights from Inside Google That Will Transform How You Live and Lead.* New York: Twelve, 2015.

Boulding, Kenneth E. *Economics as a Science.* New York: McGraw-Hill, 1970.

Bourke, Juliet. *Which Two Heads Are Better than One? How Diverse Teams Create Breakthrough Ideas and Make Smarter Decisions.* Sydney: Australian Institute of Company Directors, 2016.

Breiman, Leo. "Random Forests." *Machine Learning* 45, no. 1 (2001): 5–32.

Brown, G., J. Wyatt, R. Harris, and X. Yao. "Diversity Creation Methods: A Survey and Categorisation." *Information Fusion* 6, no. 1 (2005): 5–20.

Buchanan, Kyle. "The Stars Who Were Almost Cast in the Year's Biggest Movies." *Vulture*, October 2, 2013. http://www.vulture.com/2013/10/stars-almost-cast-in-the-years-biggest-movies.html.

Business Insider. "The 20 Schools with the Most Alumni at Google." September 4, 2015. http://www.businessinsider.com/schools-with-the-most-alumni-at-google-2015-10.

Cameron, Kim, and Robert Quinn. *Diagnosing and Changing Organizational Culture.* Reading, MA: Addison-Wesley-Longman, 1999.

Campbell, Donald. "Blind Variation and Selective Retention in Creative Thought as in Other Knowledge Processes." *Psychological Review* 67 (1960): 380–400.

Carnevale, Anthony, Tamara Jayasundera, and Artem Gulish. *America's Divided Recovery: College Haves and Have-Nots.* Washington, DC: Georgetown University Center on Education and the Workforce, 2016.

Carnevale, Anthony, and Nicole Smith. "The Economic Value of Diversity." In *Our Compelling Interests: The Value of Diversity for Democracy and a Prosperous Society*, edited by Earl Lewis and Nancy Cantor, 106–157. Princeton, NJ: Princeton University Press, 2016.

Carney, Dana R., Brian A. Nosek, Anthony G. Greenwald, and Mahzarin R. Banaji. "The Implicit Association Test (IAT)." In *Encyclopedia of Social Psychology*, edited by R. F. Baumeister and K. D. Vohs, 463–464. Thousand Oaks, CA: Sage, 2007.

Cattell, R. B. *Abilities: Their Structure, Growth, and Action.* New York: Houghton Mifflin, 1971.

Chivian, Eric, and Aaron Bernstein. "The Role of Traditional Medicine in Drug Discovery." *OUPblog*, November 24, 2008. https://blog.oup.com/2008/11/drug_discovery/.

CIA. *Diversity and Inclusion at the CIA.* Washington, DC: Central Intelligence Agency Office of Public Affairs, 2014. https://www.cia.gov/library/publications/resources/diversity-inclusion-at-the-cia/Diversity_And_Inclusion.pdf.

Clarke, Kevin A., and David M. Primo. *A Model Discipline: Political Science and the Logic of Representations.* Oxford: Oxford University Press, 2012.

Cohen, J. J., B. A. Gabriel, and C. Terrell. "The Case for Diversity in the Health Care Workforce." *Health Affairs* 21, no. 5 (2002): 90–102.

Cole, Elizabeth R. "Intersectionality and Research in Psychology." *American Psychologist* 64 (2009): 170–180.

Consumer Finance Protection Bureau. *Using Publicly Available Information to Proxy for Unidentified Race and Ethnicity.* White paper. Washington, DC: Consumer Finance Protection Bureau, 2014.

Corey, Elizabeth. "A More Moderate Diversity." *National Affairs* 31 (2017): 115–128.

Cox, Daniel, Juhem Navarro-Rivera, and Robert P. Jones. "Race, Religion, and Political Affiliation of Americans? Core Social Networks." Public Religion Research Institute, August 3, 2016. http://www.prri.org /research/poll-race-religion-politics-americans-social-networks/.

Crenshaw, Kimberle. "Demarginalizing the Intersection of Race and Sex: A Black Feminist Critique of Antidiscrimination Doctrine, Feminist Theory and Antiracist Politics." *University of Chicago Legal Forum* 140 (1989): 139–167.

Cummings, Jonathon N., Reza Zadeh, Sarah Kiesler, and Aruna Balakrishnan. "Group Heterogeneity Increases the Risks of Large Group Size: A Longitudinal Study of Productivity in Research Groups." *Psychological Science* 24, no. 6 (2013): 880–890.

Dawes, Robyn. "The Robust Beauty of Improper Linear Models in Decision Making." *American Psychologist* 34 (1979): 571–582.

Dawson, Julia, Richard Kersley, and Stefano Natella. *The CS Gender 3000: The Reward for Change*. Zurich: Credit Suisse Research Institute, 2016.

De Bono, Edward. *Six Thinking Hats*. New York: Little, Brown, 1985.

Dezsö, Christian, and David Gaddis Ross. "Does Female Representation in Top Management Improve Firm Performance? A Panel Data Investigation." *Strategic Management Journal* 33 (2012): 1072–1089.

Dietterich, T. G. "Ensemble Methods in Machine Learning." In *First International Workshop on Multiple Classifier Systems*, edited by J. Kittler and F. Roli, 1–15. New York: Springer Verlag, 2000.

Dobbin, Frank, Daniel Schrage, and Alexandra Kalev. "Rage against the Iron Cage: The Varied Effects of Bureaucratic Personnel Reforms on Diversity." *American Sociological Review* 80, no. 5 (2015): 1014–1044.

Dover, Tessa L., Brenda Major, and Cheryl R. Kaiser. "Diversity Policies Rarely Make Companies Fairer, and They Feel Threatening to White Men." *Harvard Business Review*, January 4, 2016.

Dvorkin, Maximilano. "Jobs Involving Routine Tasks Are Not Growing." *On the Economy* (blog), Federal Reserve Bank of St. Louis, January 4, 2016. https://www.stlouisfed.org/on-the-economy/2016/january/jobs -involving-routine-tasks-arent-growing.

Eckbo, B. Espen, Knut Nygaard, and Karin S. Thorburn. "Does Gender-Balancing the Board Reduce Firm Value?" University of Rochester Working Paper, Rochester, NY, 2016.

Economist. "Diversity Fatigue." Schumpeter, February 11, 2016. http:// www.economist.com/news/business/21692865-making-most-workplace -diversity-requires-hard-work-well-good-intentions-diversity.

Ellison, Ralph. *Invisible Man*. 1952. New York: Vintage, 1980.

Fink, Larry. "Annual Letter to CEOs: I Write on Behalf of Our Clients . . ." BlackRock website, January 24, 2017. https://www.blackrock.com/cor porate/en-us/investor-relations/larry-fink-ceo-letter.

Fleming, Lee. "Recombinant Uncertainty in Technological Search." *Management Science* 47, no. 1 (2001): 117–132.

Florida, Richard, and Gary Gates. "Technology and Tolerance: The Importance of Diversity to High-Technology Growth." In *The City as an Entertainment Machine*, ed. Terry Nichols Clark, 157–178. Lanham, MD: Lexington Books, 2011.

Flynn, James R. "Massive IQ Gains in 14 Nations: What IQ Tests Really Measure." *Psychological Bulletin* 101 (1987): 171–191.

———. *What Is Intelligence? Beyond the Flynn Effect*. Cambridge: Cambridge University Press, 2009.

Freeman, Richard, and Wei Huang. "Collaborating with People like Me: Ethnic Co-authorship within the U.S." In "US High-Skilled Immigration in the Global Economy," special issue, *Journal of Labor Economics* 33, no. 1 (2015): 289–318.

Frey, William H. "The 'Diversity Explosion' Is America's Twenty-First-Century Baby Boom." In *Our Compelling Interests: The Value of Diversity for Democracy and a Prosperous Society*, edited by Earl Lewis and Nancy Cantor, 16–35. Princeton, NJ: Princeton University Press, 2016.

Friedman, Thomas L. "How to Get a Job at Google." *New York Times*, February 22, 2014.

———. *The World Is Flat: A Brief History of the Twenty-First Century*. New York: Farrar, Straus and Giroux, 2005.

Fryer, Roland, and Matthew Jackson. "A Categorical Model of Cognition and Biased Decision-Making." *Contributions in Theoretical Economics* 8, no. 1 (2008): 1–42.

Gardipee, F. M., D. A. Strobel, F. W. Allendorf, G. Luikart, M. Hebblewhite, and R. Clow. "Development of Fecal DNA Sampling Methods to Assess Genetic Population Structure of Greater Yellowstone Bison." Master's thesis, University of Montana, Missoula, 2007.

Gardner, Howard. *Frames of Mind: The Theory of Multiple Intelligences*. New York: Basic Books, 1983.

———. *Intelligence Reframed: Multiple Intelligences for the 21st Century*. New York: Basic Books, 1999.

Gawande, Atul. *The Checklist Manifesto: How to Get Things Right*. New York: Metropolitan Books, 2009.

Gender Summit North America. *Diversity Fueling Excellence in Research and Innovation: A Roadmap for Action for North America*. Arlington,

VA: National Science Foundation, Office of International and Integrative Activities, 2013.

Gillespie, Daniel T. "Exact Stochastic Simulation of Coupled Chemical Reactions." *Journal of Physical Chemistry* 81, no. 25 (1977): 2340–2361.

Glaeser, Edward. *Triumph of the City: How Our Greatest Invention Makes Us Richer, Smarter, Greener, Healthier, and Happier.* New York: Penguin Books, 2012.

Goldstein, Daniel G., R. Preston McAfee, and Siddharth Suri. "The Wisdom of Smaller, Smarter Crowds." *Proceedings of the 15th ACM Conference on Economics and Computation,* Palo Alto, CA, 2014: 471–488.

Goodwin, Doris Kearns. *Team of Rivals: The Political Genius of Abraham Lincoln.* New York: Simon and Schuster, 2006.

Goodyear Corporate. "Our Responsibilities." Accessed May 2, 2017. http://www.goodyear.eu/corporate_emea/our-responsibilities/.

Gordon, Robert J. *The Rise and Fall of American Growth: The U.S. Standard of Living since the Civil War.* Princeton, NJ: Princeton University Press, 2016.

Greenwald, A. G., M. R. Banaji, and B. A. Nosek. "Statistically Small Effects of the Implicit Association Test Can Have Societally Large Effects." *Journal of Personality and Social Psychology* 108, no. 4 (2015): 553–561.

Groysberg, Boris, and Katherine Connolly. "BlackRock: Diversity as a Driver for Success." *Harvard Business Review* Case Study 415-047, February 2015.

Gruenfeld, D. H., E. A. Mannix, K. Y. Williams, and M. A. Neale. "Group Composition and Decision Making: How Member Familiarity and Information Distribution Affect Process and Performance." *Organizational Behavior and Human Decision Processes* 67 (1996): 1–15.

Guilford, Joy P. *The Nature of Human Intelligence.* New York: McGraw-Hill, 1967.

Gurin, Patricia, Jeffrey Lehman, and Earl Lewis. *Defending Diversity: Affirmative Action at the University of Michigan.* Ann Arbor: University of Michigan Press, 2004.

Gurin, Patricia, Biren (Ratnesh) A. Nagda, and Ximena Zuniga. *Dialogue across Difference: Practice, Theory, and Research on Intergroup Dialogue.* New York: Russell Sage Foundation, 2013.

Hackman, J. Richard, and Michael O'Connor. *What Makes for a Great Analytic Team? Individual versus Team Approaches to Intelligence Analysis.* Washington, DC: Intelligence Science Board, Office of the Director of Central Intelligence, 2004.

Hall, Edward T. *Beyond Culture.* New York: Anchor Books, 1976.

Harris, David R., and Jeremiah Joseph Sim. "Who Is Multiracial? Assessing the Complexity of Lived Race." *American Sociological Review* 67, no. 4 (2002): 614–627.

Heath, Chip, and Dan Heath. *Made to Stick: Why Some Ideas Survive and Others Die.* New York: Random House, 2007.

Heider, Fritz. *The Psychology of Interpersonal Relations.* New York: Wiley, 1958.

Hewlett, Sylvia Ann, Melinda Marshall, and Laura Sherbin. "How Diversity Can Drive Innovation." *Harvard Business Review*, December 2013.

Hollister, Michael. "21 Different Interpretations of the White Whale." American Literature, 2014. http://amerlit.com/documents/documents.php ?document=TwentyOneDifferentInterpretationsOfTheWhiteWhale.

Holtz, Rolf, and Norman Miller. "Assumed Similarity and Opinion Certainty." *Journal of Personality and Social Psychology* 48 (1985): 890–898.

Homan, A. C., D. van Knippenberg, G. A. Kleef, and C.K.W. de Dreu. "Bridging Faultlines by Valuing Diversity: Diversity Beliefs, Information Elaboration, and Performance in Diverse Work Groups." *Journal of Applied Psychology* 92, no. 5 (2007): 1189–1199.

Hong, Lu, and Scott E. Page. "Groups of Diverse Problem Solvers Can Outperform Groups of High-Ability Problem Solvers." *Proceedings of the National Academy of Sciences* 101, no. 46 (2004): 16385–16389.

———. "Problem Solving by Heterogeneous Agents." *Journal of Economic Theory* 97 (2001): 123–163.

Hunt, Vivian, Dennis Layton, and Sara Prince. "Why Diversity Matters." McKinsey & Company website, January 2015. http://www.mckinsey .com/business-functions/organization/our-insights/why-diversity-matters.

Hutchins, Edwin. *Cognition in the Wild.* Cambridge, MA: MIT Press, 1995.

Jackson, Susan E., and Aparna Joshi. "Work Team Diversity." In *APA Handbook of Industrial and Organizational Psychology*, edited by S. Zedeck, 1:651–686. Washington, DC: American Psychological Association, 2011.

James, Michael. "Race." In *The Stanford Encyclopedia of Philosophy*, edited by E. N. Zalta. Published May 28, 2008, substantive revision February 17, 2016. http://plato.stanford.edu/entries/race/.

James, William. *Pragmatism.* 1907. Edited by Bruce Kuklick. Indianapolis: Hackett, 1981.

Janis, I. L. *Groupthink: Psychological Studies of Policy Decisions and Fiascoes.* Boston: Houghton Mifflin, 1982.

Janssen, Michel, and Jurgen Renn. "History: Einstein Was No Lone Genius." *Nature* 527 (2015): 298–300.

Jehn, Karen A., Gregrory B. Northcraft, and Margaret A. Neale. "Why Differences Make a Difference: A Field Study of Diversity, Conflict, and

Performance in Workgroups." *Administrative Science Quarterly* 44 (1999): 741–763.

Jeppesen, Lars Bo, and Karim R. Lakhani. "Marginality and Problem-Solving Effectiveness in Broadcast Search." *Organization Science* 21 (2010): 1016–1033.

Johansson, Franz. *The Medici Effect: Breakthrough Insights at the Intersection of Ideas, Concepts, and Cultures.* Boston: Harvard Business School Press, 2004.

Johnson, Steven. *Where Good Ideas Come From: The Natural History of Innovation.* New York: Riverhead Books, 2010.

Jones, Benjamin F., Brian Uzzi, and Stefan Wuchty. "Multi-university Research Teams: Shifting Impact, Geography and Social Stratification in Science." *Science* 322, no. 5905 (2008): 1259–1262.

Jurvetson, Steve. "Braniac Steve Jurvetson on DFJ, Elon Musk and the Growing Divide between Rich and Poor." Interview by Connie Loizos. *TechCrunch*, September 28, 2015. https://techcrunch.com/2015/09/28/brainiac-steve-juvertson-on-dfj-elon-musk-and-the-growing-divide-between-rich-and-poor/.

Kahneman, Daniel. *Thinking Fast and Slow.* New York: Farrar, Straus and Giroux, 2011.

Kaplan, Sarah, and Keyvan Vakilim. "The Double-Edged Sword of Recombination in Breakthrough Innovation." *Strategic Management Journal* 36, no. 10 (2015): 1435–1457.

Kaplan, Steven, and Josh Lerner. "It Ain't Broke: The Past, Present, and Future of Venture Capital." *Journal of Applied Corporate Finance* 22 (2010): 1–12.

Katznelson, Ira. *When Affirmative Action Was White: An Untold History of Racial Inequality in Twentieth-Century America.* New York: W. W. Norton, 2005.

Kaufman, Gil. "Watch David Bowie Call Out MTV for Not Playing Black Artists in 1983." *MTV News*, January 11, 2016. http://www.mtv.com/news/2726379.

Kim, Rebecca Y. *God's New Whiz Kids: Korean American Evangelicals on Campus.* New York: New York University Press, 2006.

King, Molly, Shelly J. Correll, Jennifer Jacquet, Carl T. Bergstrom, and Jevin D. West. "Men Set Their Own Cites High: Gender and Self Citation across Fields and over Time." Unpublished manuscript, submitted June 30, 2016. https://arxiv.org/abs/1607.00376.

Kleinberg, Jon, Jens Ludwig, Sendhil Mullainathan, and Ziad Obermeyer. "Prediction Policy Problems." *American Economic Review: Papers and Proceedings* 105, no. 5 (2015): 491–495.

Kleinberg, Jon, and Maithra Raghu. "Team Performance with Test Scores." Working paper, Cornell University School of Information, Ithaca, NY, 2015.

Knight, Jack, and James Johnson. *The Priority of Democracy: Political Consequences of Pragmatism*. Princeton, NJ: Princeton University Press, 2014.

Knox, Grahame. *Lost at Sea: A Team-Building Game*. Insight: Resources for Christian Youth Ministry and Leadership, 2014. http://insight .typepad.co.uk/lost_at_sea.pdf.

Kopf, Dan. "How Many People Take Credit for Writing a Hit Song?" *Priceonomics*, October 30, 2015. https://priceonomics.com/how-many -people-take-credit-for-writing-a-hit-song/.

Kozlowski, Steve W. J., and Bradford S. Bell. "Work Groups and Teams in Organizations." ILR School, Cornell University, 2001. http://digital commons.ilr.cornell.edu/cgi/viewcontent.cgi?article=1396&context =articles.

Lakhani, Karim R., and Lars Bo Jeppesen. "Getting Unusual Suspects to Solve R&D Puzzles." *Harvard Business Review* 85, no. 5 (2007). http:// www.hbs.edu/faculty/Pages/item.aspx?num=24440.

Leung, Angela K.-Y., William W. Maddux, Adam D. Galinsky, and Chi-Yue Chiu. "Multicultural Experience Enhances Creativity: The When and How." *American Psychologist* 63 (2008): 169–181.

Levine, Sheen, Evan P. Apfelbaum, Mark Bernard, Valerie L. Bartelt, Edward J. Zajac, and David Stark. "Ethnic Diversity Deflates Price Bubbles." *Proceedings of the National Academy of Sciences* 111, no. 52 (2014): 18524–18529.

Lewis, Earl, and Nancy Cantor, eds. *Our Compelling Interests: The Value of Diversity for Democracy and a Prosperous Society*. Princeton, NJ: Princeton University Press, 2016.

Liff, Sonia. "Two Routes to Managing Diversity: Individual Differences or Social Group Characteristics." *Employee Relations* 19, no. 1 (1997): 11–26.

Liu, Yong, and Xin Yao. "Ensemble Learning via Negative Correlation." *Neural Networks* 12, no. 10 (1999): 1399–1404.

Loyd, Denise L., Cynthia S. Wang, Katherine W. Phillips, and Robert Lount. "Social Category Diversity Promotes Pre-meeting Elaboration: The Role of Relationship Focus." *Organization Science* 24 (2013): 757–772.

Lutton, Laura, and Erin Davis. *Morningstar Research Report: Fund Managers by Gender*. Chicago: Morningstar, 2015.

Maheshwari, Sapna. "Big Brands Ask Ad Agencies for Action on Diversity Hiring." *New York Times*, October 1, 2016.

Mannes, A. E., J. B. Soll, and R. P. Larrick. "The Wisdom of Select Crowds." *Journal of Personality and Social Psychology* 107 (2014): 276–299.

Mannix, Elizabeth A., and Margaret A. Neale. "What Differences Make a Difference? The Promise and Reality of Diverse Teams in Organizations." *Psychological Science in the Public Interest* 6 (2005): 31–55.

Manski, Charles. "Interpreting the Predictions of Prediction Markets." *Economic Letters* 91, no. 3 (2006): 425–429

Marcolino, Leandro S., Albert X. Jiang, and Milind Tambe. "Multi-agent Team Formation: Diversity Beats Strength?" *Proceedings of the 23rd International Joint Conference on Artificial Intelligence*, 2013: 279–285.

Martin, Emily. "The Egg and the Sperm: How Science Has Constructed a Romance Based on Stereotypical Male-Female Roles." *Signs* 16 (1991): 485–501.

Matsa, David A., and Amalia R. Miller. "A Female Style in Corporate Leadership? Evidence from Quotas." *American Economic Journal: Applied Economics* 5 (2013): 136–169.

Mauboussin, Michael. *The Success Equation: Untangling Skill and Luck in Business, Sports, and Investing.* Boston: Harvard Business Review Press, 2012.

Mauboussin, Michael, Daniel Callahan, and Darius Majd. *Organizational Structure and Investment Results.* Zurich: Credit Suisse Global Financial Strategies, July 8, 2016.

McDonald's Corporation. "Our Ambition." Accessed May 1, 2017. http://corporate.mcdonalds.com/mcd/our_company/our-ambition.html.

McLeod, Poppy, Sharon Lobel, and Taylor H. Cox Jr. "Ethnic Diversity and Creativity in Small Groups." *Small Group Research* 27, no. 2 (1996): 248–264.

McNamara, Robert. "Abe Lincoln and His Ax: Reality behind the Legend." *ThoughtCo*, updated January 1, 2017. http://history1800s.about.com/od/abrahamlincoln/ss/Abe-Lincoln-and-His-Ax.htm.

Medin, D. L., and A. Ortony. "Psychological Essentialism." In *Similarity and Analogical Reasoning*, edited by S. Vosniadou and A. Ortony, 179–195. Cambridge: Cambridge University Press, 1989.

Mellers, B., E. Stone, T. Murray, A. Minster, N. Rohrbaugh, M. Bishop, E. Chen, et al. "Identifying and Cultivating Superforecasters as a Method of Improving Probabilistic Predictions." *Perspectives on Psychological Science* 10, no. 3 (2015): 267–281.

Microsoft Corporation. "Mission Culture." Microsoft Careers. Accessed April 7, 2017. https://careers.microsoft.com/mission-culture.

Mill, John Stuart. *Principles of Political Economy.* 1848. New York: Augustus M. Kelley, 1987.

Mokyr, Joel. *The Gifts of Athena: Historical Origins of the Knowledge Economy.* Princeton, NJ: Princeton University Press, 2002.

Moss-Racusin, Corrinne A., John F. Dovidio, Victoria L. Brescoll, Mark Graham, and Jo Handelsman. "Science Faculty's Subtle Gender Biases Favor Male Students." *Proceedings of the National Academy of Sciences* 109, no. 41 (2012): 16474–16479.

National Research Council. *Enhancing the Effectiveness of Team Science.* Edited by Nancy J. Cooke and Margaret L. Hilton. Washington, DC: National Academies Press, 2015.

———. *The Mathematical Sciences in 2025.* Washington, DC: National Academies Press, 2015.

Nisbett, Richard E. *The Geography of Thought: How Asians and Westerners Think Differently . . . and Why.* New York: Free Press, 2003.

O'Flaherty, Brendan. *The Economics of Race in the United States.* Cambridge, MA: Harvard University Press, 2015.

Open Science Collaboration. "Estimating the Reproducibility of Psychological Science." *Science* 349, no. 6251 (2015). http://science.sciencemag.org/content/349/6251/aac4716.

Padgett, John, and Walter Powell. *The Emergence of Organizations and Markets.* Princeton, NJ: Princeton University Press, 2012.

Page, Scott E. *The Difference: How the Power of Diversity Creates Better Group, Teams, Schools, and Societies.* Princeton, NJ: Princeton University Press, 2007.

———. *Diversity and Complexity.* Princeton, NJ: Princeton University Press, 2010.

———. *Model Thinking.* New York: Basic Books, forthcoming.

———. "Not Half Bad: A Modest Criterion for Inclusion." In *Complexity and Evolution: A New Synthesis for Economics,* edited by D. S. Wilson and A. Kirman, 319–327. Strungmann Forum Reports 19, edited by J. Lupp. Cambridge, MA: MIT Press, 2016.

Patel, Saurin, and Sergei Sarkissian. "To Group or Not to Group? Evidence from Mutual Fund Databases." *Journal of Financial and Quantitative Analysis,* forthcoming.

Pattillo, Mary. *Black Picket Fences: Privilege and Peril among the Black Middle Class.* Chicago: University of Chicago Press, 1999.

Phillips, Katherine W. "The Effects of Categorically Based Expectations on Minority Influence: The Importance of Congruence." *Personality and Social Psychology Bulletin* 29 (2003): 3–13.

———. "How Diversity Makes Us Smarter." *Scientific American.* October 1, 2015.

Phillips, Katherine W., S. Y. Kim-Jun, and S. Shim. "The Value of Diversity in Organizations: A Social Psychological Perspective." In *Social Psychology and Organizations*, edited by R. van Dick and K. Murnighan, 253–272. New York: Routledge, 2010.

Phillips, Katherine W., K. A. Liljenquist, and M. A. Neale. "Is the Pain Worth the Gain? The Advantages and Liabilities of Agreeing with Socially Distinct Newcomers." *Personality and Social Psychology Bulletin* 35 (2009): 336–350.

Phillips, Katherine W., and D. L. Loyd. "When Surface and Deep-Level Diversity Collide: The Effects on Dissenting Group Members." *Organizational Behavior and Human Decision Processes* 99 (2006): 143–160.

Phillips, Katherine W., E. Mannix, M. Neale, and D. Gruenfeld. "Diverse Groups and Information Sharing: The Effects of Congruent Ties." *Journal of Experimental Social Psychology* 40 (2004): 498–510.

Pollack, Eileen. *The Only Woman in the Room: Why Science Is Still a Boys' Club*. Boston: Beacon, 2015.

Reagans, Ray, and Bill McEvily. "Network Structure and Knowledge Transfer: The Effects of Cohesion and Range." *Administrative Science Quarterly* 48 (2003): 240–267.

REI Co-op. "About REI." Accessed May 1, 2017. https://www.rei.com/about-rei.html.

Reilly, Maureen C., Sunita Vohra, Valeria E. Rac, Michael Dunn, Karla Ferrelli, Alex Kiss, Michael Vincer, and John Wimmer. "Randomized Trial of Occlusive Wrap for Heat Loss Prevention in Preterm Infants." *Journal of Pediatrics* 166, no. 2 (2015): 262–268.

Rheingold, Howard. *Smart Mobs: The Next Social Revolution*. New York: Basic Books, 2002.

Roithmayr, Daria. *Reproducing Racism: How Everyday Choices Lock in White Advantage*. New York: New York University Press, 2014.

Romer, Christina D., and David H. Romer. "The FOMC versus the Staff: Where Can Monetary Policymakers Add Value?" *American Economic Review: Papers and Proceedings* 98, no. 2 (2008): 230–235.

Rosette, Ashley S., Geoffrey J. Leonardelli, and Katherine W. Phillips. "The White Standard: Racial Bias in Leader Categorization." *Journal of Applied Psychology* 93 (2008): 758–777.

Ross, Howard J., and Julianne Malveaux. *Reinventing Diversity: Transforming Organizational Community to Strengthen People, Purpose, and Performance*. Lanham, MD: Rowman and Littlefield, 2013.

Sadoway, Donald. "PhD Should Be PSD (Problem Solving Degree)." *Big Think*, 2016. http://bigthink.com/big-think-tv/phd-should-be-psd-problem-solving-degree.

Sander, Richard, and Stuart Taylor Jr. *Mismatch: How Affirmative Action Hurts Students It's Intended to Help, and Why Universities Won't Admit It*. New York: Basic Books, 2012.

Sapienza, Paola, Luigi Zingales, and Dario Maestripieri. "Gender Differences in Financial Risk Aversion and Career Choices Are Affected by Testosterone." *Proceedings of the National Academy of Sciences* 106, no. 36 (2009): 15268–15273.

Satopää, Ville, Shane T. Jensen, Robin Pemantle, and Lyle H. Ungar. "Partial Information Framework: Model-Based Aggregation of Estimates from Diverse Information Sources." arXiv preprint, 2015. arXiv: 1505.06472.

Schilling, Melissa A., and Ehud Green. "Recombinant Search and Breakthrough Idea Generation: An Analysis of High Impact Papers in the Social Sciences." *Research Policy* 40, no. 10 (2011): 1321–1331.

Scott, Kim. *Radical Candor: Be a Kick-Ass Boss without Losing Your Humanity*. New York: St. Martin's, 2017.

Sen, Maya, and Omar Wasow. "Race as a 'Bundle of Sticks': Designs That Estimate Effects of Seemingly Immutable Characteristics." *Annual Review of Political Science* 19 (2015): 499–522.

Shenk, Joshua Wolf. *Powers of Two: Finding the Essence of Innovation in Creative Pairs*. New York: Houghton, Mifflin, Harcourt, 2014.

Shetterly, Margot Lee. *Hidden Figures: The American Dream and the Untold Story of the Black Women Mathematicians Who Helped Win the Space Race*. New York: William Morrow, 2016.

Shi, Xiaolin, Lada A. Adamic, Belle L. Tseng, and Gavin S. Clarkson. "The Impact of Boundary Spanning Scholarly Publications and Patents." *PLOS ONE* 4, no. 8 (2009): e6547.

Simon, Herbert. *Administrative Behavior*. 3rd ed. New York: Free Press, 1976.

Simonton, Dean K. *Origins of Genius: Darwinian Perspectives on Creativity*. New York: Oxford University Press, 1999.

Singh, Jasjit, and Lee Fleming. "Lone Inventors as Sources of Breakthroughs: Myth or Reality?" *Management Science* 56, no. 1 (2010): 41–56.

Sobel, Dava. *Longitude: The True Story of a Lone Genius Who Solved the Greatest Scientific Problem of His Time*. New York: Walker, 2007.

Sommers, S. "On Racial Diversity and Group Decision-Making: Identifying Multiple Effects of Racial Diversity on Jury Deliberations." *Journal of Personality and Social Psychology* 90 (2006): 597–612.

Sparber, Dan. "Racial Diversity and Aggregate Productivity in US Industries: 1980–2000." *Southern Economic Journal* 75, no. 3 (2009): 829–856.

Stasser, Garold, Dennis Stewart, and Gwen M. Wittenbaum. "Expert Roles and Information Exchange during Discussion: The Importance of Knowing Who Knows What." *Journal of Experimental Social Psychology* 31 (1995): 244–265.

Steele, Claude. *Whistling Vivaldi: How Stereotypes Affect Us and What We Can Do*. New York: W. W. Norton, 2011.

Steinbeck, John. *East of Eden*. New York: Putnam Penguin, 1952.

Sternberg, R. J., and L. A. O'Hara. "Creativity and Intelligence." In *Handbook of Creativity,* edited by R. J. Sternberg, 251–272. Cambridge: Cambridge University Press, 1999.

Stulp, Gert, Louise Barrett, Felix C. Tropf, and Melinda Mills. "Does Natural Selection Favour Taller Stature among the Tallest People on Earth?" *Proceedings of the Royal Society B* 282, no. 1806 (2015): 21–28.

Sugrue, Thomas J. "Less Separate, Still Unequal: Diversity and Equality in 'Post-Civil Rights' America." In *Our Compelling Interests: The Value of Diversity for Democracy and a Prosperous Society*, edited by Earl Lewis and Nancy Cantor, 39–70. Princeton, NJ: Princeton University Press, 2016.

Suroweicki, James. *The Wisdom of Crowds*. New York: Anchor, 2006.

Swann, William B., Jr., Jeffrey T. Polzer, Daniel Conor Seyle, and Sei Jin Ko. "Finding Value in Diversity: Verification of Personal and Social Self-Views in Diverse Groups." *Academy of Management Review* 29, no. 1 (2004): 9–27.

Sweeney, Latanya. "Discrimination in Online Ad Delivery." *Communications of the Association of Computing Machinery* 56, no. 5 (2013): 44–54.

Tajfel, Henri, and John C. Turner. "An Integrative Theory of Intergroup Conflict." *Social Psychology of Intergroup Relations* 33, no. 47 (1979): 33–47.

Taylor, Stuart, Jr., and David Binder. "Washington Talk: Briefing; Marshall on Racism." *New York Times*, August 11, 1988.

"The Team Speech." YouTube video, 1:23, speech given by Bo Schembechler, 1983. Posted by Fritz Seyferth, February 26, 2013. https://www.youtube.com/watch?v=UrvwWfIeHu0.

Tegmark, Mark. "Is 'Theory of Everything' Merely the Ultimate Ensemble Theory?" *Annals of Physics* 270 (1998): 1–51.

Tetlock, Phillip. *Expert Political Judgment: How Good Is It? How Can We Know?* Princeton, NJ: Princeton University Press, 2005.

Tetlock, Phillip, and Dan Gardner. *Superforecasting: The Art and Science of Prediction*. New York: Crown Books, 2015.

Thomas, David A., and Robin J. Ely. "Making Differences Matter: A New Paradigm for Managing Diversity." *Harvard Business Review*, September 1996.

Triandis, Harry C., Eleanor Hall, and Robert Ewen. "Member Heterogeneity and Dyadic Creativity." *Human Relations* 18, no. 1 (1965): 33–55.

Tully, John C., George H. Gilmer, and Mary Shugard. "Molecular Dynamics of Surface Diffusion: The Motion of Adatoms and Clusters." *Journal of Chemical Physics* 71 (1979): 1630–1642.

Turner, M. E., and A. R. Pratkanis. "Twenty-Five Years of Groupthink Theory and Research: Lessons from the Evaluation of a Theory." *Organizational Behavior and Human Decision Processes* 73 (1998): 105–115.

University of Wisconsin. "Mission Statement." Revised statement, adopted June 10, 1988. Accessed May 2, 2017. http://www.wisc.edu/about/mission/.

US Government. *A Tradecraft Primer: Structured Analytic Techniques for Improving Intelligence Analysis.* Washington, DC: US Government, 2009.

Uzzi, Brian, Satyam Mukherjee, Michael Stringer, and Ben Jones. "Atypical Combinations and Scientific Impact." *Science* 342, no. 6157 (2013): 468–471.

Valantine, Hannah A., and Francis Collins. "National Institutes of Health Addresses the Science of Diversity." *Proceedings of the National Academy of Science* 112, no. 40 (2015): 12240–12242.

Van Buskirk, Eliot. "How the Netflix Prize Was Won." *WIRED*, September 22, 2009.

Vance, J. D. *Hillbilly Elegy: A Memoir of a Family and Culture in Crisis.* New York: HarperCollins, 2016.

Van Knippenberg, Daan, and Michaela C. Schippers. "Work Group Diversity." *Annual Review of Psychology* 58 (2007): 515–541.

Vélez, William Yslas, James Maxwell, and Colleen Rose. "Report on the 2013–2014 New Doctoral Recipients." *Notices of the American Mathematical Society* 62, no. 6 (2015): 771–781.

Von Hippel, Eric. *The Sources of Innovation.* Oxford: Oxford University Press, 1988.

Wageman, Ruth, Deborah A. Nunes, James A. Burruss, and J. Richard Hackman. *Senior Leadership Teams: What It Takes to Make Them Great.* Boston: Harvard Business School Press, 2008.

Waldron, Jeremy. "The Wisdom of the Multitude: Some Reflections on Book 3, Chapter 11 of Aristotle's Politics." *Political Theory* 23, no. 4 (1995): 563–584.

Weitzman, Martin L. "Optimal Search for the Best Alternative." *Econometrica* 77 (1979): 641–654.

———. "Recombinant Growth." *Quarterly Journal of Economics* 2 (1998): 331–361.

Williams, Katherine Y., and C. A. O'Reilly. "Demography and Diversity in Organizations: A Review of 40 Years of Research." In *Research in Organizational Behavior*, edited by B. M. Staw and R. Sutton, 20:77–140. Greenwich, CT: JAI, 1998.

Wood, Andrew, Tonu Esko, Jian Yang, Sailaja Vedantam, Tune H. Pers, Stefan Gustafsson, Audrey Y. Chu, et al. "Defining the Role of Common

Variation in the Genomic and Biological Architecture of Adult Human Height." *Nature Genetics* 46, no. 11 (2014): 1173–1186.

Woolley, Anita W., Ishani Aggarwal, and Thomas M. Malone. "Collective Intelligence and Group Performance." *Current Directions in Psychological Science* 24, no. 6 (2015): 420–424.

Woolley, Anita W., Christopher F. Chabris, Alexander Pentland, N. Hashmi, and Thomas M. Malone. "Evidence for a Collective Intelligence Factor in the Performance of Human Groups." *Science* 330, no. 6004 (2010): 686–688.

Wuchty, Stefan, Benjamin F. Jones, and Brian Uzzi. "The Increasing Dominance of Teams in Production of Knowledge." *Science* 316, no. 5827 (2007): 1036–1039.

Youn, Hyejin, José Lobo, Luís M. A. Bettencourt, and Debora Strumsky. "Invention as a Combinatorial Process: Evidence from U.S. Patents." *Journal of the Royal Society Interface* 12 (April 2015): 272.

Zimmer, Carl. "White? Black? A Murky Distinction Grows Still Murkier." *New York Times*, December 14, 2014.

INDEX

OUR COMPELLING INTERESTS

External Advisory Board

Anthony Appiah, Professor of Philosophy and Law,
  New York University

Lawrence E. Bobo, W.E.B. Du Bois Professor of the Social Sciences,
  Harvard University

Sumi Cho, Professor of Law, DePaul University

Stephanie A. Fryberg, Associate Professor of American Indian Studies
  and Psychology, University of Washington

Thelma Golden, Director and Chief Curator, Studio Museum in
  Harlem

Patricia Y. Gurin, Nancy Cantor Distinguished University Professor
  Emerita of Psychology and Women's Studies, University of
  Michigan

Ira Katznelson, President and Ruggles Professor of Political Science
  and History, SSRC and Columbia University

Gary Orfield, Professor, Education, and Co-Director, Civil Rights
  Project/Proyecto Derechos Civiles, University of California at Los
  Angeles

Scott E. Page, Leonid Hurwicz Collegiate Professor, Complex Systems,
  Political Science, and Economics, University of Michigan

George J. Sanchez, Professor of American Studies and Ethnicity, and
  History, and Vice Dean for Diversity and Strategic Initiatives,
  University of Southern California

Claude M. Steele, Professor of Psychology, University of California,
  Berkeley

Susan P. Sturm, George M. Jaffin Professor of Law and Social Responsibility, Columbia University Law School

Thomas J. Sugrue, Professor of Social and Cultural Analysis and History, New York University

Beverly Daniel Tatum, President Emerita, Spelman College

Marta Tienda, Maurice P. During '22 Professor, Demographic Studies, and Professor, Sociology and Public Affairs, Princeton University

Sarah E. Turner, Chair, Department of Economics, University of Virginia

Internal Advisory Board

Saleem Badat, Program Director, The Andrew W. Mellon Foundation

Armando I. Bengochea, Program Officer, The Andrew W. Mellon Foundation

Nancy Cantor, Co-chair, Chancellor, Rutgers University-Newark

Makeba Morgan Hill, Deputy to the President and Chief Planner, The Andrew W. Mellon Foundation

Cristle Collins Judd, Senior Program Officer, The Andrew W. Mellon Foundation

Earl Lewis, Co-chair, President, The Andrew W. Mellon Foundation

Doreen N. Tinajero, Program Associate and Project Manager, The Andrw W.Mellon Foundation

Eugene M. Tobin, Senior Program Officer, The Andrew W. Mellon Foundation

Michele S. Warman, Vice President, General Counsel and Secretary, The Andrew W. Mellon Foundation

Laura Washington, Director of Communications, The Andrew W. Mellon Foundation

Mariët Westermann, Executive Vice President for Programs and Research, The Andrew W. Mellon Foundation